RONALD L. PARTIN

CLASSROOM TEACHER'S Survival Guide

Practical Strategies, Management Techniques, and Reproducibles for New and Experienced Teachers

THE CENTER FOR APPLIED
RESEARCH IN EDUCATION
West Nyack, New York 10994

Library of Congress Cataloging-in-Publication Data

Partin, Ronald L.
    Classroom teacher's survival guide : practical strategies, management
techniques, and reproducibles for new and experienced teachers /
Ronald L. Partin.
      p. cm.
    Includes bibliographical references.
    ISBN 0-13-084474-8
    1. Classroom management—Handbooks, manuals, etc. 2. Teaching—
Handbooks, manuals, etc. I. Title.
LB3013.P32 1995
371.1'024—dc20
                                        95-18036
                                          CIP

© 1999 *by* The Center for Applied Research in Education

Printed in the United States of America

10 9   (spiral)   10 9 8 7 6 5 4 3 2   (pbk)

ISBN 0-87628-909-X (spiral)   ISBN 0-13-084474-8 (pbk)

ATTENTION: CORPORATIONS AND SCHOOLS

The Center for Applied Research in Education books are available at quantity dis-
counts with bulk purchase for educational, business, or sales promotional use. For
information, please write to: Prentice Hall Career & Personal Development Special
Sales, 240 Frisch Court, Paramus, New Jersey 07652. Please supply: title of book, ISBN
number, quantity, how the book will be used, date needed.

**THE CENTER FOR APPLIED RESEARCH
IN EDUCATION**
West Nyack, NY 10994

On the World Wide Web at http://www.phdirect.com

About the Author

Ronald L. Partin holds a Ph.D. degree in educational psychology and counseling and has more than twenty-five years' experience as an educator, scholar, and counselor. He was a professor in the department of Educational Foundations and Inquiry, and Coordinator of the Guidance and Counseling Graduate Program at Bowling Green (Ohio) State University. As a counselor educator, he taught courses in counseling, educational consultation, group dynamics, and learning psychology. A former high school teacher and coach, Ron is in frequent demand as a speaker, trainer, and consultant. He uses his classroom experiences to teach and motivate, using his everyday examples and ready-to-implement techniques.

Ron is author of numerous journal articles in the areas of time management, goal setting, creative problem solving, stress management, and effective teaching skills. He is the co-author of *P.R.I.D.E.*, a training program on effective classroom management, which has been completed by over 40,000 teachers nationwide. Ron is the co-author of *The Social Studies Teacher's Survival Kit* and author of *The Social Studies Teacher's Book of Lists*, both published by The Center for Applied Research in Education. He is also the author of *The Prentice Hall Directory of Online Social Studies Resources* (Paramus, NJ: Prentice Hall, 1988).

Ron and his wife, Janet, are the parents of twin sons, both now in college. He has a broad range of interests, including woodworking, golf, basketball, genealogy, flower gardening, bluegrass music, and making stained-glass windows. His overwhelming passion continues to be teaching.

**Dedicated with much love and appreciation to my parents,
Troy and Marie Partin.**

About This Book

Each year 15,000 new teachers assume teaching positions in the elementary, middle, and high schools of America. Most are filled with enthusiasm—ready to enrich the minds of their students—only to be dismayed to find that not all of their students are on the edge of their seats ready to receive their inspired words of wisdom. Beginning teachers are often unprepared to cope with the overwhelming paperwork, flying spitballs, irate parents, machines that don't work, occasionally cantankerous administrators, and the unpredictable challenges of the real-world classroom.

Most survive; but the first year can be a most stressful, frustrating, and painful learning process. Some teachers do not survive their rookie season and 40 percent leave the profession within the first four years, disillusioned and prematurely burned out. While colleges of education strive to adequately prepare students for what lies ahead in their first classroom assignment, general education requirements, methods courses, and state-mandated courses fill the teacher-preparation curriculum, leaving the burden of reality-testing the textbook knowledge of classroom teaching to a single student-teaching experience. Most of the daily survival techniques are left to "on-the-job" experience. The cost of such "trial by fire" is high—impaired mental and physical health of the "defeated" teachers, lost learning opportunities for their students, and the lower organizational effectiveness and decreased morale of the school community.

The content for *Classroom Teacher's Survival Guide* is derived from experienced teachers' depositories of "all the things I wish I had known when I started" or "things I had to learn the hard way." This survival guide provides a smorgasbord of strategies and tips for solving the main problems faced by teachers: organizing and managing the classroom, achieving a working relationship with students and maintaining classroom control, working with other adults in the school community (including parents), developing competence as an effective instructor, and coping with the daily stresses of teaching. Teachers can learn from the mistakes and successes of veteran educators. This treasury of survival skills is not intended as a simple cookbook, but rather provides a range of practical options to be adapted by teachers to fit their unique classroom situations. These ideas and strategies are to be tested and modified to fit the grade level and specific needs of the user.

Much research suggests that the teacher's success is determined by the events of the first few weeks of school. Hence, much of the book focuses upon strategies for beginning the school year. It also provides scores of practical tips, most gathered from successful classroom teachers or gleaned from research on outstanding teachers. The *Classroom Teacher's Survival Guide* provides a treasury of suggestions, tips, checksheets, reproducible transparency masters, posters, and activities. The ready-to-use forms, letters, overhead transparency masters, and posters will help beginning and experienced teachers save time while tapping the wealth of knowledge of successful educators.

Ronald L. Partin

Acknowledgments

The clip art in this book was selected from a variety of electronic sources, including: *DeskTop Art* by Dynamic Graphics, *Desk Gallery* by Zedcor Corporation, *Digit Art* from Image Club Graphics, *Metro ImageBase, Click Art* from T/Maker Company, *Image Club, Imagenes With Impact!, School Clip Art* from Quality Computers, and *Volk Clip Art* from Dynamic Graphics.

The greatest source of ideas from this book came from the hundreds of teachers who have participated in my workshops and classes over the past twenty years. Where known, the original sources are credited for any ideas used. The patient efforts of my graduate students—Lisa Fuller, Melissa Samolis, Nicki Quick, and Scott Bieniek—were most valuable. This project would have been much more difficult without the emotional support and encouragement of my wife Janet. The diligent efforts of Connie Kallback, Diane Turso, Tom Curtin, and the editorial and production staff at The Center for Applied Research in Education are most appreciated.

Contents

CHAPTER 6
Effective Use of School Time • 209

CHAPTER 7
Helpful Teaching Resources • 259

CHAPTER 1

Creating a Supportive Learning Environment

The First Day of School

The foundation for a successful school year is laid on the first day of school. Every thing you do the first day sets the tone for the rest of the year. Time spent planning and organizing the first day's activities is one of the most valuable investments you can make as a teacher. It is wise to develop a checklist of items to cover the first day. Your three primary objectives the first day of school are to "get acquainted," to establish your expectations, and to stimulate enthusiasm and interest in what you are teaching. The best advice for the first day is "Be prepared." You want to convey to your students that you are organized, in control, and know what you are doing.

ARRANGING SUCCESSFUL CLASSROOMS

Before the first day of school spend time in your classroom organizing it for the maximum efficiency. The physical arrangement of your classroom can influence the behavior and learning of your students. The placement of desks, bookshelves, pencil sharpeners, and cabinets can direct traffic flow, student interaction, noise level, attention, or disruption. The influence of the room arrangement is too important to be left to chance.

Plan the learning environment of your classroom before the beginning of the school year. Your goals for the class must guide your choices. Whether you wish to maximize group interaction with lots of small-group activities or lecture most of the time, the physical arrangement can help or hinder. Students get a pretty good picture of what their year is going to be like from the decor and arrangement of the classroom as they enter for the first time.

More than creating aesthetic appeal, each piece of furniture redefines a part of the classroom space, directing attention, pupil interaction, or traffic flow. It is easy to overlook the importance of even casual rearrangements within the classroom. Something as simple as installing a new pencil sharpener or a new bookshelf or an area rug can have a significant impact on the learning events of your classroom.

The environment as seen by you may be quite different from that perceived by your students, especially younger ones. When no one else is around, crouch down to the children's eye level and view your room as they see it. Waddle around the room to see how the furniture directs your attention and movement.

Draw your current classroom arrangement to scale on graph paper. Include all the furniture, windows, doors, bulletin boards, electrical plugs, cabinets, wastebasket, and pencil sharpener. Observe your class for a day, noting on your drawing the traffic patterns. Indicate any bottlenecks. Are there any areas that invite students to stop and talk? Does the present arrangement direct students through work centers or group activities? Are there dead spaces that no one ever enters? Be sure to place electrical equipment so students cannot trip over the cords.

Arrange any special areas in the room. Some teachers have reading areas, perhaps with stuffed furniture, a rug, or pillows. Have the necessary supplies and materials sorted and organized for any learning centers, art area, writing area, labs, etc.

Give special attention to minimizing unnecessary noise in your classroom. Where possible use soft, quiet, sound-absorbing materials: carpeting, rubber, sponge, cardboard, styrofoam.

STUDENTS' DESKS

The single most important decision influencing the physical classroom environment is the seating arrangement assigned to students. Ideally, the arrangement of students' desks should not be permanent, except for large lecture halls or laboratories. The purpose of the learning activity should dictate the most favorable seating pattern. Unless furniture is bolted to the floor, it can be moved during the day as the lesson dictates. The custodial staff's ease of cleaning should play only a minor role in such decisions.

If several seating arrangements are used regularly, teach your students how they should move from one to another as quickly and quietly as possible. You may want smaller children to help each other carry desks without dragging them across the floor.

Seating students in clusters or around a table facilitates group interaction. It enhances small-group discussions and cooperative learning, but it also invites chatting and socializing.

Whole-class discussion is facilitated with circular, semi-circular, or an open-ended rectangular seating arrangement. Traditional rows are probably least supportive of student-to-student interaction.

Traditional seating in rows has endured because it is very functional for many classroom purposes. Particularly early in the year, seating students in rows enables you to observe behavior more easily and minimizes distractions. Research has shown row seating produces higher levels of on-task behavior in elementary classrooms. The farther the distance between students, the less they distract each other. Independent seatwork, lecture, movies, and tests are activities that can be facilitated with row seating.

Performance classes, labs, and special activities, such as story time, might dictate atypical seating choices, or even no seats at all. The important thing is to monitor the effects of your seating pattern. Don't be afraid to experiment with different arrangements to achieve different results.

After a few weeks experiment with different seating arrangements. Simply changing the seating patterns, even which direction the seats face, will influence the dynamics of your group.

To minimize the tendency to look primarily at the students in the front and center of a classroom, make a conscious attempt to scan the back corners where the more disruptive students tend to cluster. It is often wise to move disruptive students to the front center as that is the natural region of most eye contact. Interestingly, some researchers have discovered that students' test scores are increased after moving them to the front center. However, avoid seating two troublesome students next to each other.

The direction students normally face in your chosen seating arrangement should be given careful consideration. As they will attend most to whatever is in their direct line of sight, try to arrange for students to face away from windows and doors to minimize distractions. Facing windows or bright lights creates excessive glare, causing eye strain.

➤ If you have several learning centers or areas in your room, separate noisy from quiet areas.

➤ Plan your seating so you can move freely among students when providing individual assistance. Avoid seating arrangements that hide some students behind bookshelves or cabinets. Avoid creating mazes that force students into long, winding traffic patterns to reach the pencil sharpener or wastebasket.

SEAT ASSIGNMENTS

You must decide before school begins whether to assign students to specific seats or to allow them to select their seats. Most teachers prefer to assign seats at first. It is best to announce that the initial seating assignments will only be temporary. After you have learned their names, established behavioral control, and taught students your desired procedures and routines, you might allow them to choose (or assign them) different seats. However, if you have several difficult students it is best to maintain control over the seating pattern, separating troublemakers from one another and keeping them where you can easily monitor their behavior. You need not single them out or draw attention to the fact that you are putting them where you want them. Whatever seating pattern you select, always be sensitive to the special needs of hearing- or visually-impaired students.

If you use printed seating charts, use a pencil to fill them in as they will change. Keep any seating charts current in case you are absent and a substitute must use them.

Another option is to tape or staple a clear transparency over the master seating chart. Names can be easily changed using an erasable marker on the transparency film.

KEEPING DESKS CLEAN

The desks of some students begin to resemble the proverbial attic, hiding assorted old papers, tattered books, pencil stubs, broken crayons, pens, and miscellaneous treasures. Teachers have resorted to a range of tactics for encouraging students to keep their desks tidy, from spot checks to formal inspections with checksheets. Some choose to ignore the mess and allow students to suffer the consequences.

One strategy adopted by many teachers is to institute a "desk fairy," a mythical creature who visits their desks after school. If the desk is orderly, the fairy leaves a special surprise such as a certificate, sticker, or ribbon.

THE TEACHER'S DESK

Not all teachers require a desk. If your room is crowded and you find you spend little time at your desk, consider removing it or replace it with a small table and a filing cabinet. Some prefer an old-fashioned writing desk. This makes it easier to monitor students. A high stool eases the burden on the feet.

If you do have a desk, the next choice is where to place it. It does not have to be at the front center of the classroom. If you do not usually sit at your desk during class, place it in a front corner, or even at the back of the classroom. It is best not to place it near the door. It is too easy for people to grab things off it as they are leaving the room. Also you are more likely to be interrupted or distracted as you work at it. Make sure your desk does not block the view of the chalkboard for any students.

Teachers have different perspectives on the ownership of their desks. Some prefer to define their desks as private territory, off limits to students. They may even arrange bookshelves and filing cabinets to create barriers from the intrusions of others. Other teachers have an "open desk" policy. Students are invited to help themselves to staplers, tape, and other materials. Of course, a locked drawer or closet might be reserved for private belongings or confidential records. Whichever practice you adopt, communicate your expectations to your students at the beginning of the year.

Basic Classroom Supplies

First-aid kit	Staples
Disposable tissues	Glue
Paper towels	Tape
Cleaning rags	Felt pens
Extension cord	Grade book
Paper	Desk calendar
Chalk	Dictionary
Eraser	Yardstick
Roladex	Hole punch
Note cards	Whistle
Paper clips	Rubber bands
File folders	Clock
Rulers	Teacher's manuals for texts
Thumb tacks	Attendance forms
Stapler	Tardy slips

THE ROOM ENVIRONMENT

Be creative in arranging your room. You need not be bound by the traditional configurations. Not everything need be arranged rectangularly. Filing cabinets or bookshelves do not have to be placed against the walls. Placed at right angles to the wall, they create study areas or redirect traffic.

Plan the traffic patterns you wish to create. Clear high traffic areas, such as the pencil sharpener, of obstructions. If a student's desk is placed immediately in front of the pencil sharpener, a disturbance is inevitable when the students use the sharpener. Avoid patterns that create congestion by funneling many students through a small path.

When working with small groups, place their chairs so that the students face away from the rest of the class. That prevents their being distracted by the rest of the class, and it allows you to monitor all students. If an aide is working with small groups, you may use a portable chalkboard to screen the small group activity from the rest of the class.

Keep the room tidy. Before a class is allowed to leave the room, have them pick up litter around their desks. A cluttered and dirty environment invites further abuse. Similarly, have any graffiti removed immediately. Research has shown that its presence serves as a stimulus for more graffiti. It may involve some additional effort at first but saves time and damage later. Avoid creating an impression that abuse of the room is acceptable.

Use posters, decorations, banners, signs, artifacts, and displays to create an inviting atmosphere. It is especially effective if you change them periodically to reflect the topic your class is studying.

Before school begins inspect your classroom to identify any broken, dirty, or unsightly clutter. Broken windows, hinges, desks, shades, or locks should be repaired or replaced. It may take time, but see your principal about how to get these things done. Don't give up easily if you encounter delays in getting these things done. It may be easier to do some smaller tasks yourself.

The physical arrangement of your classroom can minimize off-task behavior and invite learning. Make it a regular part of your preparation. Experiment with changing your room set-up, including the arrangement of students' desks. It pays dividends.

GREETING YOUR STUDENTS

The first day greet all students at the door with a smile and tell them where to sit. You might have a seating chart on the overhead with their names placed on their assigned seats. Some elementary teachers have name tents already at each student's desk. It is wise to direct them to begin work on a specific task as soon as they take their seats. It might be to complete a word puzzle, to fill in a personal information survey, or to scan the table of contents of their textbook. You are creating an expectation that learning begins as soon as your students enter the classroom, not necessarily when the bell rings.

The first day of school is likely the most important single day of the school year. Expectations are created; the foundation of routines and procedures are established; and first impressions are formed. You should be better organized and better prepared the first day than any other of the year. It will take a long time to recover from a bad start.

Do post your name and room number beside your door. That will help students avoid the embarrassment of discovering ten minutes into the class that they are in the wrong room.

The first 5-10 minutes of the first day's contact with your students is probably the most important segment of time the entire school year. Consider carefully what you want to accomplish these first few minutes and the most effective means of doing so. Choose your words carefully. Your goal is to create a warm yet businesslike atmosphere. You must convey that you know what you are doing, have confidence in yourself, and expect appropriate behavior and effort from your students.

Don't waste the most precious minutes of the year taking roll. That can wait. First, introduce yourself. Have your name printed on the board. Clearly and slowly pronounce it for your students and tell them how you expect to be addressed. If you have an aide in the room, introduce him or her. Spend a couple of minutes telling the class a little about yourself and your background. Share a bit of your life: family, hobbies, pets, interests, where you went to school, or experiences. If you are just beginning your teaching career, it is best not to emphasize your inexperience. Don't overdo it. A couple of minutes is sufficient. Some teachers allow students to ask them questions. Other teachers construct a biographical display or bulletin board. How much you choose to share about yourself and when are matters of personal comfort and judgment.

If you are particularly skilled in some aspect of what you will be teaching, you might exhibit your skill by demonstrating something they will be learning. Show them you are a pro; it helps establish respect and credibility.

During these first few minutes your students are sizing you up. Who are you? How will you treat them? What are the boundaries of what they can do in your classroom? It is wise to convey positive expectations and enthusiasm. You aren't going to get them very excited about your class if you don't seem too enthusiastic yourself. Whatever you say in your opening, put some energy into it. Also use your most poised, assertive body language. If possible, stand, scan the class with your eyes, and don't be afraid to smile.

GETTING TO KNOW YOUR STUDENTS

Time spent getting to know your students is one of the most valuable investments of your time. Establishing rapport helps build mutual respect and minimize classroom behavior problems. A deeper understanding of the needs, problems, and interests of your students will enable you to plan instruction that succeeds.

➤ Some teachers prefer to look at the cumulative folders of each of their students before school begins. This gives them a sense of the special talents and problems of their class. Of course, this is probably not feasible for high school teachers with 120 students.

➤ Allow some time the first day to get acquainted with your students. A fun icebreaker activity, particularly if it can relate to your subject area, can be helpful. One way to learn a bit more about your students is to call the class roll, but instead of replying "here," have them respond by naming their favorite hobby or sport. The next day you could have them answer with their favorite song or food.

➤ The first day may be the only time you actually call the roll. The main purposes are to clarify the pronunciation of students' names and to identify what they prefer to be called. One of the best ways you can show respect for your students and earn their respect and trust is to learn their names. This should be a prime objective for the first week of school. Any time you address a specific student the first week, make a special effort to use his or her name.

➤ It may help to have them make name tents or interesting name tags which they use each day. Be sure to pronounce their names correctly. Failure to do so communicates a lack of respect and interest. Take photographs of students the first week and attach their names and cut-outs of their faces on a master seating chart.

➤ If you have a printed roster the first day be sure it is accurate. Make any corrections, but do not write your class roster in the gradebook the first week. It will change. Indeed, no matter when you finally write your class roll into your gradebook, you can assume a new student will show up the next day!

➤ Do make a special effort to welcome students new to the school or area. Try to see that they get paired up with a returning student and included in some of the student groups during lunch and recess.

➤ Some kindergarten and first grade teachers send notes to their students inviting them to come to school in small groups a couple of days early. They might bring a favorite toy to share. This provides an opportunity for the teacher to get to know their students before school begins and the students get a chance to meet their teacher and a few of the other students in a safe, inviting environment.

➤ Many effective teachers use name tags or name tents to aid learning students' names. If you want to really impress your students, end the first day by having them remove their name tags or name tents, and then proceed around the room, identifying each student by name. You don't have to hit 100%; they will be impressed that you even tried. It doesn't take a great memory, just a focused, determined effort. If you accomplished little else that day, the year would be off to a good start. Knowing and using a student's name communicates that you regard that person as more than an anonymous face among a group of students. It has been suggested that a person's favorite word to hear is his or her own name.

➤ Attempt to connect a student's name with another person you know of the same name. For example, if you have a student named "Brett" and that is also your son's name, try to visualize the two playing together. If you don't personally know anyone by that name, associate that person with a famous person of the same name. Visualize a new student named "George" with a powdered wig like George Washington's. As you make a mental connection, consciously use that student's name every time you talk to or call on him/her for the next week. Stand by the door and greet each one by name to reinforce your name awareness.

CLARIFYING EXPECTATIONS

The establishment of your hopes, expectations, rules, and routines is an essential first-day goal. Explain, demonstrate, and allow time for students to practice the routines that will help get things done smoothly throughout the year. Clarify specific procedures for taking attendance, beginning work each day, turning in assignments, requesting help, going to the bathroom, and other reoccurring classroom routines. It is not essential to introduce every routine the first day, but certainly do focus on them as the need arises. (See Chapter 6 for suggestions on how these routines are managed by some teachers.)

In communicating your hopes for the class, you might say something like, "I don't expect you to be perfect. I do hope you will strive for excellence and work to improve. We all will make mistakes. The important thing is to learn from those mistakes."

TASKS TO ACCOMPLISH

There are several important tasks to accomplish during the first week, if not the first day.

➤ Explain the rules. As described elsewhere a few rules (ideally, not more than five) are preferable to a long list. Some teachers prefer to hold a class meeting, allowing students to provide input into the norms which should be enforced. Beyond giving them a channel of influence over their school lives, it also provides practice in the process of democracy.

➤ Discuss emergency procedures. Clarify and perhaps practice the drills for fire, tornadoes, or other emergencies. Be sure everyone knows which exits they are to use in the event of an evacuation.

➤ Distribute books and other materials. This provides a good opportunity to practice routines for distributing materials. Be sure to have students complete the necessary records for end-of-the-year collections of signed-out materials.

➤ Assign lockers or drawers. If combination locks are provided, be sure to keep a master list for those who forget their combination.

➤ Clarify what materials and supplies students will need for your class. What items will the students be expected to bring every day? Which will they need tomorrow? Are there any fees that will need to be collected? It is generally best to distribute a written list they can take home.

➤ Discuss your grading procedures. Many (but not all) students want to know, "What do I have to do to get an 'A' in this class?" or at least to pass it. Clarify what their academic responsibilities will be, what criteria you will be using to evaluate their performance, and how grades will be allotted. Clarity and fairness here can eliminate a lot of arguments and protestations at the end of the term. Many effective teachers distribute a handout detailing their class expectations and grading scheme.

➤ Explain the schedule your class will typically follow. At least the first day it is a good idea to have the day's activities listed on the board.

➤ In laboratory or shop classes and in elementary classrooms, a tour of the classroom will be helpful in orienting students to the various stations and features they will be using during the year.

ADDITIONAL SUGGESTIONS

Arrive early the first morning, allowing ample time to tend to any last-minute details. Be available to greet students as they enter the room. You cannot do that if you are in the office waiting for the copy machine. Also, if you are in the room when students arrive they are less likely to engage in mischief.

Expect the unexpected. The first day is always a bit hectic. Murphy's Law will rule; things *will* go wrong. Students will show up in the middle of the class because they have been sitting in the wrong class. There may not be enough textbooks, desks, or supplies. Strive to remain calm and flexible the first day. Remember, students are assessing your meddle the first day. If you are easily flustered, it will undermine your credibility and respect. A true professional can handle any situation, even when things don't go as planned. Be patient.

Overplan the first day. It is better to have too much to do than to have a class of students sitting idly or for you to aimlessly wing it.

Dress your best the first day. It is part of creating a professional image and establishing credibility. It also communicates that you value your students enough that you will make a special effort to look your best for them. We also tend to be more confident when we are well groomed.

Set your standards from the very beginning. Classroom management style is very much established the first day. Be fair yet firm in enforcing your classroom rules. Once a behavior is tolerated it is difficult to change it later.

Show you do have a sense of humor. Don't try to be a stand-up comedian, but allow yourself to laugh with, not at, your students. An amusing cartoon on the door or overhead helps create a warm, inviting atmosphere.

Don't hesitate to ask your principal or colleagues questions if you don't understand something. If you are new be sure to explore the building and meet some of your colleagues before the first day. Also read the policy manual.

First Day of School Checklist

BEFORE SCHOOL BEGINS

____ Become familiar with the building.

____ Name, grade level or subject and room number posted beside your door.

____ Name tags and markers available.

____ Your name written on the chalkboard.

____ Sufficient number of textbooks available (remember teacher's edition).

____ The day's class schedule written on the board.

____ Double check school schedule for the day (recess, lunch, class changes).

____ Class roster readily accessible.

____ All teaching materials ready for first day's lesson.

____ Know the school rules/policies.

____ First day's lesson plans complete.

____ Arrange desks in desired pattern.

____ Create an inviting atmosphere (bulletin boards, posters).

____ Set-up tape player and any music to be played.

____ Have "sponge" activities available.

OPENING DAY

____ Greet students at the door—smile!

____ Assign temporary seats.

____ Begin learning students' names (check pronunciation).

____ Take attendance.

____ Establish rules.

____ Get students started on learning.

____ Specify supplies and fees students must provide.

____ Make any assignments for the next class.

___ Begin training routines and procedures.

___ Show enthusiasm for your subject!

Creating an Inviting School Climate

For all too many students school has become something to avoid. It is viewed by many as a boring, depersonalized, irrelevant institution. Fortunately, it doesn't have to be that way. There are classrooms and schools, even in the most impoverished of environments, that remain inviting and nurturing. Schools that maintain a positive school climate are marked with a high degree of cohesiveness and high level of morale, among students as well as staff. There is research evidence that school climate is related to the level of academic achievement.

Interestingly, research of school drop-outs reveals that their self-esteem increased immediately upon dropping out of school. The students had been in an environment that daily communicated that they were "losers," incompetent, and "slower" than everyone else. When they stop going to school they suddenly escape those degrading messages and begin to accept themselves more. (Unfortunately, that gain in self-acceptance may later erode as they face the challenge of surviving in the economic world without a diploma.) Positive school climates occur when students believe they have a shared responsibility in developing and maintaining a warm and supportive environment.

➤ Always remember the adage, "Students do not care how much you know until they know how much you care." We only earn respect by showing respect; we gain trust by trusting. Develop a student-centered rather than subject-centered classroom.

➤ Schools are most likely to be successful when students experience a sense of ownership and belonging. Both are nurtured when students have some degree of choice and control in their daily experience. Involving students in classroom decisions, valuing student contributions, and respecting individual differences help meet these needs.

➤ Make a conscious effort to get to know the good things about your students. Publicly, as well as privately, acknowledge their achievements outside of your class.

➤ Treat all students fairly. While it is natural for teachers to enjoy teaching some students more than others, overt favoritism can create a divisive and resentful climate.

➤ Strive to be consistent in your enforcement of rules, grading, and treatment of students. While we all have our "good days" and "bad days," the inability to predict a teacher's expectations and responses is poisonous to an atmosphere of trust and respect.

➤ Take time to listen to your students. Not only does it convey your respect for them, but you may also receive feedback that might help you become a better teacher. Solicit their opinions about how they perceive your class. Occasionally invite them to complete open-ended questions anonymously, such as "The thing I enjoy most about this class is . . ." or "I would enjoy this class more if . . ."

➤ Communicate your expectations clearly, both for academic tasks as well as behavioral norms. Don't make students guess what you want.

➤ Invitational teachers communicate that they expect all students to succeed. Everyday, both verbally and nonverbally, inviting teachers genuinely communicate that each student is capable, unique, and valued.

➤ Provide opportunities for choice. The ability to have control over one's life is a basic human need. While many school tasks are not optional, there are ample opportunities to allow students a degree of freedom. For example, offering a choice of learning activities or homework assignments may not only give students a greater sense of freedom, but may actually enhance their learning as well.

➤ Treat students decently. Treat them as you would have wished to be treated as a student, not necessarily as you were treated.

➤ Consider holding periodic classroom meetings in which students can openly discuss their views on the class procedures and climate. Of course, to succeed you must convey to your students that you are genuinely interested in their views. The best way to communicate that is to listen non-judgmentally.

➤ Plan lessons that offer more instructional techniques than the talking head in front of the classroom. Teacher talk is still the dominant instructional mode in many of our schools. Education has become a very passive endeavor. Strive to actively involve students in meaningful learning activities. Construct lessons with ample student interaction, challenging content, and variety of instructional approaches.

➤ Pay attention to the physical environment of your classroom. The seating arrangement, wall decorations, bulletin boards, special reading areas, learning centers, and posters all contribute to the emotional tone of your classroom.

➤ Always try to convey an attitude of acceptance toward all students. This does not mean you must approve of all they do, but when you must condemn an unacceptable behavior do so without rejecting the child.

➤ Recognize, encourage, and reinforce positive behaviors and achievements. Especially express your appreciation for deeds that contribute to a positive class climate: cooperation, helpful behaviors, caring, and inclusion. Reward direction, not perfection. Small gains should be acknowledged.

➤ Pay attention to the students in the middle of the normal curve—those who neither lag nor excel. For the most part the academically "average" student is ignored in our classrooms. Recognize and encourage their small successes and progress.

➤ Don't be afraid to smile. A gentle smile conveys warmth, acceptance, and caring. Avoid the perpetual wide, toothy pseudo-smile. A genuine smile is conveyed with the eyes as well as the mouth. If smiling is not a natural behavior for you, practice in front of a mirror (privately, of course!).

➤ Avoid developing a highly competitive classroom climate. While some argue that competition prepares students for the "real world," there is a great deal of evidence that it is destructive and unnecessary. Even corporate America is teaching its employees to work in cooperative teams and strive for win-win solutions to conflict.

➤ Empathize with the students who are always at the bottom of the normal curve, in academic achievement, athletic ability, popularity, or physical development. Consider ways in which you might help make them feel included and valued. Emphasize growth over perfection or "being the best." No matter how hard they try, most students will never be the "top of the class."

➤ Always remain sensitive to the influence you have in the lives of your students. Your choice of words, disapproving nonverbals, harsh tonality, ignoring, or sarcasm can have long and profound effects upon your students' self-esteem.

➤ Strive to "catch the student being good." Too often we ignore students until they misbehave. They are reprimanded or punished. Acknowledging what they are doing right is more important than only giving criticism of what they do wrong.

➤ Never use sarcasm or ridicule when talking to students. It accomplishes nothing permanently positive. Once used it is hard to retract and erodes the teacher-student relationship. When reprimanding a student for misbehavior, condemn the behavior, not the person.

➤ Pay attention to multicultural and gender inclusiveness in all your teaching activities. Use examples and visuals that include persons of a variety of cultural and ethnic backgrounds and of both genders. Also, do not tolerate bigoted behavior in your classroom.

➤ Remain sensitive to the fact your students will come from a variety of religious backgrounds. Avoid imposing your religious views on your students. Holidays, especially religious ones such as Christmas or Hanukkah, may not hold the same meaning for some of your students. Respect their freedom of religion and avoid activities that clearly endorse one particular religion to the exclusion of others (unless you teach in a parochial school).

➤ Remember the adage, "Praise publicly, criticize privately." Even when offering reprimands or criticizing a student's behavior, do so in a style that leaves their dignity in tact. If at all possible, never cause a student to lose face in front of his or her peers. It achieves nothing positive in the long run.

➤ Aim to talk with each student every day, even if it is only a smile and greeting as they leave or enter the classroom. Attempt to get to know your students better during these mini-conversations. It helps build rapport as well as discover the frustrations, challenges, disappointments, and conflicts facing your students.

➤ Become an inveterate note writer. Keep a stack of note paper. Make a commitment to recognize good deeds performed by students, colleagues, custodians, secretaries, administrators, librarians, aides, parents, or volunteers. Five minutes each day spent sending a couple of thoughtful notes will pay dividends and contribute to making your school a more pleasant place.

➤ When a student is ill for any extended period of time, send a "Get Well Soon" message from the entire class. If feasible, let the group use their creative talents to create their own message, perhaps even a videotape.

➤ Make a special effort to make new students feel welcome. Moving to a new school can be a very stressful, awkward experience. Spend a few minutes getting to know a little about their background. Consider pairing the new person with a reliable student mentor who can teach your routines and procedures.

➤ Recognize birthdays and other special occasions. (Use the happy birthday message handout to make a poster or transparency. You only need fill in the student's name.) The first day of school have your students enter their birthdates on a personal information sheet. Transfer all their birthdates to your calendar. You might make birthday cards for each student. Computer software such as Print Shop makes that rather quick and inexpensive.

➤ In the primary grades you might want to designate a "Birthday Chair" and extend special privileges (e.g., first in line) to the honoree. Sing "Happy Birthday."

➤ Send birthday messages to the other adults in the building as well. Secretaries and custodial staff will be appreciative of being included.

➤ Find special occasions to celebrate: athletic or quiz bowl team victories, change of seasons, holidays, or individual student achievements. Let students decorate a bulletin board in recognition of the occasion.

➤ Develop the habit of saying "please" whenever you make a request of a student. Convey respect by responding with "thank you" whenever a student complies with a request, no matter how grudgingly he or she may do so. The appreciation is strengthened if you also use the student's name.

➤ Don't be afraid to make learning fun. Dress-up days, field trips, skits, songs, demonstrations, and learning games can break the predictable, dull, passive approach to instruction experienced by many students.

➤ Bring in a camera to take pictures of each student in your class the first week. Post the pictures along with their names on a bulletin board display. It will help you learn the names of your students. Take informal shots of various learning activities throughout the year. Put these onto a bulletin board display for 2-3 weeks, then let the students have the pictures.

➤ Develop a repertoire of anecdotes and amusing stories related to your academic content. Search for related cartoons that can be incorporated into lessons.

➤ Be creative in planning your teaching activities. Challenge yourself to invent new, more interesting ways to help your students learn. Learn from successful teachers through workshops, books, and magazines. Keep an idea notebook with you at all times to jot down interesting possibilities—anecdotes, examples, quotations, anything that might be of use in one of your classes. Part of being a professional is seeking continual improvement in your skills and curriculum.

➤ Convey your own enthusiasm for the topic you are teaching. It will be nearly impossible to get your students excited about a topic if you are unenthusiastic.

➤ Publicize your students' successes to the parents and the community. Use local newspaper articles, school assemblies, school and class newsletters, local television stations, parent-teacher associations, and open houses to showcase the accomplishments of your students. It has multiple beneficial effects for your students as well as the school.

Humor in the Classroom

Mary Pettibone Poole's observation that "He who laughs, lasts" is probably no where more true than in teaching. A moderate touch of humor can nurture an inviting class climate. Bob Hope has suggested that humor serves as a welcome mat between speakers and their audiences. It is a powerful tool that can break the ice and get the listener on your side. Humor recaptures students' attention and anchors their memory, improving achievement. One classic study found students to be more creative after listening to a humorous recording. Humor can defuse tense situations, combat resistance, and reduce stress in the classroom. It provides "comic relief" from the serious, sometimes tedious business of learning. Humor tends to make any experience more fun and brings a group closer together.

Laughter has been called internal jogging. It's good for the soul, the mind, and the body. As so capably demonstrated by John Kennedy and Abraham Lincoln, we can be quite serious about our subject, yet still infuse it with humor.

The cardinal rule in the use of humor in the classroom is that it must never be used to harm, humiliate, ridicule or otherwise make fun of students. Cruel, sarcastic humor is totally inappropriate and must not be tolerated. Likewise, humor that is sexual or involves ethnic or gender slurs is taboo. If you have a doubt as to whether an anecdote, quip, or joke is appropriate, don't use it in school. The safest target of humor is yourself. Make a self-disparaging remark about your handwriting or stick-figures drawn on the board.

Humor can be spontaneous or planned. Some people have a natural gift for finding humor in the everyday ironies and foibles in their world. Just in the normal course of daily classroom interactions, amusing predicaments will emerge on their own. A smile or chuckle on our part communicates that we are also human and can enjoy a good laugh, granting permission to our students to do the same. Good-natured kidding and puns can be forms of spontaneous humor. If you are not spontaneously witty, plan your humor by looking for cartoons, anecdotes, and quotations that you find amusing and can share with your students.

Your humorous quips or observations need not evoke knee-slapping, rip-snorting belly laughs. Lighthearted humor that brings a twinkle to the eye, a smile to the face, or a groan or chuckle serves its purpose. You're not running a comedy shop. You don't have to be hilarious to weave humor into your class presentations.

More tips on using humor in your classroom:

➤ Props, such as costumes, hats, masks, or unusual objects, can inject some levity into otherwise very serious subjects. Many teachers collect unusual pencils and pens. Accumulate inexpensive toys and puzzles with which students can spend a few minutes playing before class or during breaks.

➤ Use odd or funny noise makers to signal the class to be quiet and give you their attention.

➤ Some teachers convey their sense of humor through their dress and accessories. Colorful, funny ties, scarves, sweaters, socks, and watches are widely available.

➤ Successful teachers develop a repertoire of stories and anecdotes illustrating various aspects of the subjects they teach. Some of the tales may be naturally amusing or can be made so with a bit of exaggeration, animated gestures, or surprising twists. Begin by drawing upon funny things that have happened to you.

➤ Most people who believe they are not funny argue, "I can't tell a joke. I never remember the punch line." If so, then don't try to tell jokes in class (or if you do, overrehease it until it flows naturally). Jokes are probably overrated as a source of humor in the everyday classroom. It is the most difficult form to use successfully. Even if a teacher is a good joke teller, the technique should not be overused. If you do tell a joke, make sure it is pertinent to the topic you are teaching. At least if it bombs, you've made an academic point.

➤ If a joke bombs don't try to explain the punch line. Better to use a self-disparaging comment, "That's why I keep the day job" or "I told my writers that wouldn't work."

➤ In most classes you'll have at least one student who will be spontaneously, genuinely witty. Sometimes all you have to do is play "straight man" to the amateur comedian. Such a person often enjoys the attention, so care must be taken to not let it become disruptive or excessive.

➤ An easy source of humor is the comic section of the newspaper. Read it every day with an eye toward cartoons that illustrate some point related to your curriculum. Columns that frequently feature school and child-related topics include: *Peanuts, Funky Winkerbean, For Better or Worse, Dennis the Menace,* and *Bloom County*. Gary Larson's *Far Side* cartoons are rich with off-the-wall quips students love. His past cartoons are still available in books. Educational journals such as *Phi Delta Kappan* and the *Chronicle of Higher Education* include cartoons related to various aspects of education. Clip these and make them into transparencies. It helps to enlarge them and add color with markers. Post some cartoons on the door, use others on tests or handouts, or post some on the bulletin board. If you are going to reproduce a cartoon for instructional use, most cartoonists will freely grant you permission. Call the local newspaper for their addresses.

➤ Quotations and proverbs are another planned source of humor. You don't have to be funny, just recognize what is. Chances are if a quotation makes you laugh, it will also make your students laugh. Periodicals such as *Reader's Digest* are good sources for quotations. Invite students to be on the lookout for ones they find funny and relevant to your subject. You might even designate a section of a bulletin board where they might post humorous clippings. Specify they must make some point relevant to your course.

➤ Construct your own variation of David Letterman's "Top Ten Lists" or allow your students to brainstorm their own lists. Do remind them to stay within the bounds of good taste.

➤ When a lesson isn't going well, carry on a monologue with yourself in a stage whisper. Some teachers pick up a puppet, stuffed animal or other object and begin talking to it. Pull out a picture of the person you are studying and have a chat. Or talk to the class goldfish or hamster. You can ask it rhetorical questions and then answer them yourself.

➤ When several unexpected events disrupt your class, react with humor rather than stress. "Well, it went better in rehearsal."

➤ Personification, treating objects as though they were people, can be funny. Give your chalkboard eraser a name. Talk to it. They will chuckle. They may lock you up, but they will chuckle.

➤ Suddenly shifting to an accent for emphasis gets attention. Or have students try doing a routine task in a different accent than normally expected (such as reading Shakespeare or Poe in an exaggerated southern drawl or Bronx accent).

➤ Intentionally slaughtering a foreign phrase ("Mercy bow cup" for "merci, beaucoup") can be amusing. Of course, the students need to be familiar with the phrase to recognize what you've done. It isn't essential that everyone catch it and don't pause to wait for a laugh.

➤ Insert a touch of humor into your tests, perhaps by using the name of your principal (in a tasteful way), a local celebrity, a rival school, or alluding to a current school event.

➤ Find a humorous poem or song to celebrate a special occasion or holiday. Teach it to the class.

➤ Check bookstores and educational supply catalogs for humorous posters. Draw your own if you are artistic.

➤ A humorous song related to the topic being studied can grab students' attention and inject a touch of levity. This can be a good way to open a challenging or controversial subject.

➤ Cultivate "inside jokes" within your class. Some funny things just happen, without planning. They can become part of the class lore, which can be referred to from time to time throughout the year.

➤ Create a comedy file. Save in a folder or a notebook items that might be used later in your class. Include news items, cartoons, anecdotes, jokes, and quotations. As your file expands you might categorize your items by topic.

➤ Discover your own humor style. Rather than forcing some brand of humor that is unnatural, experiment and rely on the kinds of humor that you already enjoy and use.

➤ Observe your students to see what works. Listen to them talking among themselves to discover what they think is funny.

➤ Become a student of humor. Read the daily comics, watch funny movies, read humorous books, go to comedy clubs, watch the good (though rare) situation comedies on television.

➤ One last piece of advice: Don't try too hard. With experience you'll discover what kind of humor works and how much helps but does not hinder.

"Laughter is the shortest distance between two people."
    —VICTOR BORGE

FOR MORE INFORMATION

Cornett, C.E. (1986). *Learning Through Laughter: Humor in the Classroom.* Bloomington, IN: Phi Delta Kappa Educational Foundation.

Hill, D.J. (1988). *Humor in the Classroom: A Handbook for Teachers (and Other Entertainers!).* Springfield, IL: Charles C. Thomas.

Hill, D.J. (1993). *School Days, Fun Days: Creative Ways to Teach Humor Skills in the Classroom.* Springfield, IL: Charles C. Thomas.

Kelley, W.E. (1985). *Laughter and Learning: Humor in the Classroom.* Portland, ME: J. Weston Walch.

Klein, A. (1989). *The Healing Power of Humor.* Los Angeles: Jeremy Tarcher, Inc.

Levine, C.A. (1984). *Silly School Riddles and Other Classroom Crack-ups.* Niles, IL: A. Whitman.

Loomans, D. and Kolberg, K. (1993). *The Laughing Classroom: Everyone's Guide to Teaching with Humor and Play.* Tiburon, CA: J. Kramer, Inc.

Metcalf, F. (1988). *The Penguin Dictionary of Modern Humorous Quotations.* New York: Viking Penguin, Inc.

Perret, G. (1984). *How to Hold your Audience with Humor: A Guide to More Effective Speaking.* Cincinnati, OH: Writer's Digest Books.

Stopsky, F. (1992). *Humor in the Classroom: A New Approach to Critical Thinking.* Lowell, MA: Discovery Enterprises.

CATALOGS OF HUMOR-RELATED RESOURCES:

Funny Side Up
425 Stump Rd.
North Wales, PA 19454

HUMOResources
The Humor Project, Saratoga Institute
110 Spring St.
Saratoga Springs, NY 12866

The Lighter Side
P.O. Box 25600
Bradenton, FL 34206

What on Earth
2451 Enterprise East Pkwy.
Twinsburg, OH 44087

Whole Mirth Catalog
Allen Klein Publisher
1034 Page St.
San Francisco, CA 94117

"My way of joking is telling the truth. That is the funniest joke in the world."
—GEORGE BERNARD SHAW

"True humor springs not more from the head than from the heart; it is not contempt; its essence is love. "
—THOMAS CARLYLE

Seeking Student Feedback

Developing an inviting classroom is facilitated by listening to the views of your students. The following open-ended statements can be used to stimulate feedback on how your students see the day-to-day operation of the classroom. Students can occasionally anonymously write their responses to one or more of these sentence stems. They can also be used to stimulate discussion during class meetings.

➤ I like this class because...
➤ I would like this class better if ...
➤ In this class I wish we spent more time...
➤ I like it when the teacher...
➤ The most interesting part of this class is...
➤ I feel special when the teacher...
➤ One thing I feel proud about in our school is...
➤ I would like our class to improve...
➤ When I enter our classroom I usually feel...
➤ When I leave our classroom I usually feel...
➤ I am most bored when...
➤ My favorite part of school is...
➤ I feel left out when...
➤ My favorite activity in class is...
➤ This class is most fun when...
➤ I feel challenged when...
➤ I don't like it when other students...
➤ I think I could learn better if...
➤ One thing I would like to achieve in this class is...
➤ I would like to have more choice in...
➤ I believe our teacher wants us to...
➤ I think the teacher most values me when...
➤ Everyday, I look forward to...
➤ I become discouraged when...
➤ I feel special when the teacher...
➤ One thing in our class I would like to see changed is...
➤ I wish we spent less time...
➤ The best teachers seem to...
➤ When I must be corrected by the teacher, I would prefer...

Rules

The research on effective teachers suggests they are in control of their classrooms, but not obsessed with the idea of control. A necessary (though not sufficient) first step in establishing standards of acceptable behavior in a classroom is to set some norms or rules of conduct.

➤ Some teachers prefer to involve students in the rule-setting process the first day of class. The class meeting as advocated by William Glasser can be an effective device for involving students and gaining their commitment to the rules they set.

➤ Most effective teachers establish a few, positively stated rules. Sample rules established in classes of successful teachers include:

  ➤ Keep your hands to yourself.
  ➤ Ask permission before using others' things.
  ➤ Bring your materials and books to class.
  ➤ Only one person should talk at a time.
  ➤ Always be on time.
  ➤ Complete and turn in all assignments.
  ➤ Respect the rights of others.

➤ The maximum of enforceable rules seems to be around five to seven. Many classrooms function very well with only three or four rules.

➤ It is important to establish your own set of rules, based upon your needs and experience, your students' maturity, and the school climate.

➤ Don't try to cover every possible unacceptable behavior; you aren't writing a penal code. On the other hand don't be so vague that no one really knows what the rule means ("Be respectful.").

➤ Motivation to comply with rules seems highest when they are stated positively. When possible, convey what you do want to happen rather than trying to list all the possible unacceptable behaviors.

➤ It is essential the first day not to let behaviors slide that are clear violations. It becomes very difficult to enforce a higher standard later once a lower standard of behavior has been previously tolerated. It is easier to start out a bit firm and ease up later.

➤ Early in the year hold a class discussion on students' rights in your classroom. Solicit ideas from your students as to what is a "right" and which ought to be accorded all students. Examples might include: the right to make mistakes or the right to express one's opinion. Also focus the discussion on the responsibilities that must accompany any right (e.g., the responsibility to learn from our mistakes).

➤ Construct (or let a volunteer student) a poster listing the class rules. Display it prominently where students can easily be reminded of the rules. It is imperative that every student knows your rules.

➤ It does little good to establish rules if you have no plan for enforcing them. Your plan should in some fashion provide encouragement and reinforcement for students complying with the rules as well as some penalty or consequence for those who choose to violate the class rules.

➤ If you find it necessary to add a new rule, you certainly can add one later in the year. Dr. Harry Wong, expert on classroom management, suggests replacing an old rule with the new one. The old one can become an "unwritten" rule or expectation.

➤ Of course, there are school or district rules beyond those established for your classroom (e.g., restrictions on drug use, weapons in the school, attendance policies). You are responsible for knowing and enforcing these. If you don't, ask for a copy of the teacher or student handbook. Post these rules and assure that all students know them. You can be held legally liable if you fail to enforce them.

➤ There is no substitute for consistently and fairly enforcing your class rules. Doing so assures some predictability in the students' learning environment.

➤ Allow students to role-play scenarios in which rules might be violated. Present several hypothetical situations for small groups or volunteers to role play. Encourage them to resolve the dilemma by practicing a behavior that does not break the rules. They learn by seeing others model appropriate responses and also by practicing responsible behaviors. Examples might include:

  ➤ Sandy asks to copy your homework to hand in as hers.

  ➤ Lynn trips and accidentally pushes you from behind.

  ➤ Pat slips on a wet spot and falls while returning from the pencil sharpener. Other students begin to laugh at him and call him "names."

  ➤ Shoving breaks out between two students over who was first in line.

  ➤ The student seated behind you pokes you with a pencil.

➤ The classroom routines and procedures you establish at the beginning of the year convey your standards and expectations. They help you get things done in an orderly manner. Such informal rules or expectations complement your formal rules.

Hot Tips for Managing Classroom Behavior

The ability to manage students' behaviors is the number one concern of beginning teachers, and is near the top for most experienced teachers. Indeed, the ability to develop harmonious, mutually respectful relationships with students is one of the best predictors of who will survive in the teaching profession. The inability to effectively manage students' behavior accounts for more teacher dismissals than any other cause, including lack of knowledge of subject matter. Here are some tips on effective classroom management gleaned from research and observations of effective teachers.

➤ Invest in relationship building from the beginning, accumulating a "psychological bank account" with your students. Remember the adage, "They don't care how much you know until they know how much you care." This does not mean trying to be their "buddy." It does mean treating each student with dignity and respect. Show interest in their lives as you chat before and after class. Sure, it takes time, but much of the success of outstanding teachers, such as Jaime Escalante, the celebrated real-life model for the film, *Stand and Deliver*, can be understood in terms of the caring relationship they developed with their students. It is a case of "You can pay me now or pay me later." You'll either spend time building a mutually respectful relationship or you'll spend it later in a classroom power struggle. If you've made regular deposits to the "psychological bank account" you can make withdrawals later when you ask students to comply with your demands. They'll also be more likely to forgive your mistakes than to capitalize on them.

➤ Expect to be tested by some students to determine the boundaries of acceptable behavior and your competency to respond. While such tests are usually minor infractions (whispering, note passing, etc.), they do constitute a challenge to your classroom control. It is essential to react immediately, calmly, and appropriately to these infractions, but it is vital not to overreact.

➤ Preserve your classroom momentum at all costs. "Momentum" means every student is on-task, the lesson is rolling along smoothly. Most discipline problems do not occur during periods of momentum, but rather during those periods of chaos—when something has broken the momentum of the lesson. These classroom interruptions may sometimes be beyond our direct control: announcements over the P.A., a knock at the door, a fire engine passing the building, or the custodian riding by the window on a power mower. However, sometimes teachers may unwittingly break their own momentum—because they didn't have the necessary audio-visual equipment ready, by hunting for misplaced items in the middle of the lesson, or by stopping to reprimand an offending student. Note what happens when momentum is lost: the class goes from 95 or 100% on-task behavior to 0% on-task. Now the teacher faces the challenge of regathering everyone's attention and getting all students back on task. Pay special attention to effecting smooth, orderly transitions from one activity to another.

➤ It may sound cliché, but the best way to prevent classroom misbehavior is to deliver interesting, fast-paced, organized learning experiences, particularly ones that actively engage students in the lesson. A dull lesson is an invitation to misbehave. Much student acting out is simply a reaction to boredom. While the best, well-prepared teachers occasionally have behavioral infractions in their classroom, they are less frequent and less severe. Additionally, it is less difficult to recapture students' attention and get them back on task.

➤ Be sure your rules and expectations are clear. Some teachers haven't given much thought to what they do want, but only to what they don't want. Such negative focusing is inefficient. Don't assume students will correctly guess what you expect of them. Also develop high expectations of your students, of their academic performance, as well as classroom conduct. Students will not always meet your expectations, but seldom will they exceed them.

➤ It is also better to have a few, rather than many rules. Remember you have to enforce them. You have a right to be in control of your classroom, but do not become obsessed with control. Rules should also be conspicuously displayed in the room.

➤ Avoid causing students to lose face in front of their peers. Avoid needless public confrontations. You will almost always lose in the long run; kids can, and do, get even. Whenever possible, reprimand privately; avoid giving your perpetrator an audience.

➤ Keep your eyes moving. Eye contact is your most powerful tool in maintaining classroom control. Probably 80% of potential classroom misbehaviors can be "nipped in the bud" through timely, direct eye contact. Keep your eyes moving to scan the entire room at least once every minute or less. You actually don't have direct eye contact with every single student every minute, but rather focus upon clusters of four or five students at a time. Hold that gaze for four or five seconds and then move on to another group. Remember that most teachers have less eye contact with students sitting in the furthest corners of the room, and that is exactly where most troublemakers choose to sit!

➤ Continually monitor what is happening in your classroom. Some researchers refer to this as "having eyes in back of your head." Always know what's going on in your classroom. Avoid standing or sitting with your back to the class. For example, when working in a small group sit so you are facing the rest of the class. It is also difficult to monitor all of the class if you are sitting at your desk in front of the room. It is generally better to pace around the room during whole-class instruction. Effective teachers seem to develop a sixth sense in anticipating potential problems and appropriately intervening to nip them in the bud.

➤ Practice the principle of "escalation." This means don't go after a fly with a baseball bat; if you have a small problem use a small tool. If your initial strategy doesn't work, you can always escalate to a more potent strategy. You can always go up, but you can never effectively go down to a lower level strategy if a more confrontational one does not work. Direct eye contact might be the lowest level of challenge. If the student does not correct his or her behavior then escalate, perhaps by moving into his or her body space, standing near his or her desk. All of this can occur while you are still teaching the rest of the class, without directing everyone's attention toward the transgressing student. You've not broken your own momentum.

➤ Use the power of silence. Follow your behavioral directives with a pause while maintaining direct eye contact. Silence is power; use it constructively. After each behavioral directive it is a good idea to pause and take two slow, deep breaths. Not only does it give time for compliance, but the breathing also helps you to remain calm. You don't want to convey either fear or hostility. If you must escalate to the next level of confrontation, pause again for two deep breaths. Say no more than absolutely necessary. Avoid haranguing or degrading the student. You'll only fuel resentment and create sympathy for the offender among the rest of the class. You don't need to get drawn into a power struggle.

➤ Don't overreact. When you lose your composure in front of the class, they, not you, are in control of your behavior. Some students will test you to discover your "hot buttons," which behaviors cause you to lose control. Also, remember that most of the things students do in our classrooms to annoy us are not evil, dastardly deeds. They are simply inappropriate; they are not acceptable in that situation. Of course, if a student's misbehavior is potentially harmful to others or destructive of property, then we must employ the necessary strategy to deter that behavior. This might mean getting immediate help from other adults. When you correct a student's behavior, don't dwell excessively. Nagging will only alienate the student.

➤ Develop selective hearing. Learn to ignore some minor infractions, particularly when you suspect that student's motive is to bait you into a confrontation. Of course, potentially harmful or disruptive outbursts must be handled. Even things that are ignored during class can be dealt with after class. This also is a way to buy time if you're not sure what to do about a behavior.

➤ Divide and conquer. If you have two or three people who sit next to each other and frequently collude to disrupt the classroom, rearrange the classroom seating arrangement to separate the offenders. Sometimes this can be done subtly without revealing your true intent. For example, in forming groups you can count off so that the perpetrators are in different groups. As you assign groups to different areas of the room, you can assure that the troublesome ones are seated as far apart as possible.

➤ Never argue with a student in front of the class. Decline to argue the issue now, but offer to discuss it privately with the student later. Public arguments inevitably lead to one of you losing face in front of the class. Either way, you lose! Students who lose face in front of their peers do get even.

➤ Quiet reprimands are much more effective than loud ones. Indeed, some research suggests that loud reprimands are actually more disruptive. Avoid shouting at students! It reveals your loss of control. However, your tonality and nonverbals must be congruent. If your body language is too nonassertive, students will receive a mixed message that you aren't really serious.

➤ When you do discuss a student's misbehavior, make it clear that you find the behavior, not the student, unacceptable. Remain firm, yet compassionate. If possible, praise what they do well, but encourage improvement in their erroneous ways.

➤ Understand the school's student behavior code. What disciplinary measures are to be taken for serious infractions (e.g., fighting, drugs, alcohol, truancy)? What is the procedure for reporting such problems? Is in-school suspension or detention used? If so, how? How are parents involved in correcting misbehavior?

➤ Reinforce positive behaviors. A great many students go through school generally being ignored, as long as they don't "step out of line." They may not be the greatest students, but they don't usually create trouble. They may receive little of the teacher's time or attention. Find ways to show recognition and appreciation of their gains, even when small. Reward appropriate behavior, don't ignore it. "Catch the student being good." This involves a different kind of attitude, a new, more positive outlook on the world.

➤ Use praise effectively. While verbal praise can be effective in encouraging positive behaviors, it is often used ineffectively. To be most constructive, praise should be specific rather than general. Rather than "good job," offer specific information on what you liked about the student's work: "Excellent paragraph transitions" or "Your use of color in this picture was very unique." Also, be aware that public praise does not work for everyone. It may backfire when used with some adolescents; they'll be ribbed by their peers ("Aw, teacher's pet!"). However, private encouragement still might be influential with such students.

➤ Use group contracting to reward good performance, both behavioral and academic. This can be done informally (e.g., "As soon as we all have put away the art supplies, we'll go out for recess.") or in a more structured, formal contract. It allows the group to earn a group reward, which might be free time to play an educational game, no homework for a night, a field trip, or special treat.

➤ When you use rewards, they must be varied to be effective. The same reward used over and over quickly satiates, losing its value to motivate. Variety and novelty are powerful reinforcers.

➤ Early in the year develop classroom routines. Carefully explain how students are to handle the details of daily classroom activities: taking attendance, procedures for making up missed work, distributing and collecting materials, going to the bathroom, leaving for lunch, etc.

➤ Be cautious of touching students when they are very angry. It can stimulate a violent response in some students.

➤ Be aware of concealment activities occasionally employed by students (for example, covering their mouths when whispering, hiding behind their desks, standing books on edge to hide other reading material). Moving about the classroom discourages such strategies.

➤ Avoid branding a student a "failure" because of one mistake. Help your students recognize that we all make mistakes, but we also have a responsibility to learn from our mistakes.

➤ Avoid punishing the whole class for the misbehavior of one student. It is simply unfair and will be perceived as so by the innocent students. It will only turn the whole class (and probably their parents) against you.

➤ Try to find acceptable means for students to receive the attention and approval they often seek through misbehavior. Provide an opportunity for them to earn the spotlight through appropriate behavior.

➤ Always have a couple of "sponge activities" (e.g., small group brainstorm, word puzzle, review game) available which you can use when the unexpected happens (the projector bulb burns out, a visitor comes to the door, or a student becomes ill in class) or when some students complete seatwork or tests ahead of others.

➤ Don't be too quick to send students to the principal's office or to call their parents. If done too frequently it suggests that you have a problem with classroom management. Involve others only for serious or persistent misbehavior.

➤ Don't send students out into the hallway as a punishment. Aside from potential liability problems, for many students the hall is a pretty exciting place to be, especially if the class is boring.

➤ For persistent, serious problems with a student, use the private teacher-student conference. Explain in non-blameful language exactly what behaviors you find inappropriate and why. Avoid verbally attacking the student and do listen to his or her view. Push them for a plan for correcting their behavior in the future and to make a commitment to follow through with that plan.

➤ If you feel overwhelmed by a student's challenging behavior don't be afraid to consult other professionals: your principal, experienced teachers, school psychologist, or counselor. They have likely confronted the same problems. Ask several persons for a variety of opinions. Allow yourself to learn from their mistakes and successes. A secondary benefit is that they will probably be flattered that you came to them for advice.

➤ There are a number of excellent nationally marketed programs on effective classroom management: Performance Learning Systems' *P.R.I.D.E.* course; Lee Canter's *Assertive Discipline*; Curwin & Mendler's *Discipline with Dignity*; Linda Albert's *Cooperative Discipline*, or Bob Wubbolding's *Managing the Disruptive Classroom*. If you are having difficulty in managing student behavior, find one of these courses being offered locally, often for graduate credit. Ask colleagues if they have taken any of these courses and their evaluation of its effectiveness.

HELPFUL RESOURCES

Burke, J.C. (1992). *Decreasing Classroom Behavior Problems: Practical Guidelines for Teachers*. San Diego, CA: Singular Pub. Group.

Canter, L. & Canter, M. (1992). *Assertive Discipline: Positive Behavior Management for Today's Classroom*. Santa Monica, CA: Lee Canter and Associates.

Eakin, S. (Ed.). (1994). *A Comprehensive Guide to Implementing Curwin & Mendler's Discipline with Dignity; Prevention Action Resolution*. Bloomington, IN: National Educational Service.

Epanchin, Betty C., Townsend, B., & Stoddard, K. (1994). *Constructive Classroom Management: Strategies for Creating Positive Learning Environments*. Pacific Grove, CA: Brooks/Cole Pub. Co.

Froyen, L.A. (1993). *Classroom Management: The Reflective Teacher-Leader*. New York: Maxwell Macmillan International.

Glasser, W. (1993). *The Quality School Teacher*. New York : Harper Perennial.

Hoppenstedt, E.M. (1991). *A Teacher's Guide to Classroom Management*. Springfield, IL : Charles C. Thomas.

Kounin, J.S. (1983). *Discipline and Group Management in Classrooms*. Huntington, NY: R.E. Krieger Pub. Co.

Martin, J. & Sugarman, J. (1993). *Models of Classroom Management: Principles, Applications and Critical Perspectives*. Calgary, Alberta, Canada: Detselig Enterprises.

Mendler, A.N. (1992). *What Do I Do When—?: How to Achieve Discipline with Dignity in the Classroom*. Bloomington, IN: National Educational Service.

Spaulding, C.L. (1992). *Motivation in the Classroom*. New York: McGraw-Hill.

Potential Classroom Rewards

TANGIBLE (PHYSICAL) REINFORCERS

popcorn	trinkets
pretzels	T-shirts
fruit	bumper stickers
pizza	pencils
cookies	notebooks
lemonade	books
posters	scented crayons
stickers	plaques
cassette tapes	trophies
food coupons	

ACTIVITY REINFORCERS

choose seats	parties
breaks, recess	make videos
lunch with teacher/principal	preferred seating
reserved parking space	work with younger students
teacher tell personal story	assemblies
be first in line	take pictures
hold class outdoors	dress-up days
feed the class pet	sharpen pencils
reserved seat at sports events	use learning center
hall passes	independent study activity
parties	
display work	"no homework" pass
picnics	work in "quiet" corner
do artwork	learn magic tricks
field trips	extra locker space
teacher read a story	computer time
early dismissal	

HELP THE TEACHER

construct bulletin boards	take attendance
pass out materials	take pictures or movies
collect papers	free time to _____
dust erasers	play games
tutor other students	play sports

cook	think
photocopy materials	draw
help with experiments	do puzzles
work in office	watch TV
arrange furniture	watch movies/videos
construct bulletin boards	attend concerts
clean classroom	sing
no homework pass	use the computer
independent study	listen to records
make videos	talk with friends
preferred seating	do homework
run audiovisual equipment	go to library
be on safety patrol	play musical instrument
floor hockey in gym	exercise
dress-up days	

RENTAL PRIVILEGES AS POTENTIAL REINFORCERS

games	sports equipment
magic markers	musical instruments
hand puppets	paints
typewriter	calculator
chalk	baseball mitts
video camera	weights
funny hats	punching bag
tape recorders	sports equipment
football	books
computer software	blocks
computer	scented markers
video cameras	videos
frisbee	jump rope
computer games	magazines
colored pencils	playground equipment
audiotapes	

SOCIAL REINFORCERS

grades	honor rolls
smiles, nods, hugs	stickers
certificates of merit	approval
winks, eye contact	athletic letters

peer approval

encouragement

positive comments on papers

standing ovations, applause

positive nonverbal gestures

compliments

acceptance in honor societies

drawings on papers, smiling faces

offices

pats on the back

drum rolls

awards

check marks

mysterious "warm fuzzy" notes

principal's signature on good papers

being asked opinions, advice

RECOGNITION BY

name mentioned in assembly

letter to parents

phone call to parents

name in paper

"student of the week"

work displayed

photograph in paper

trophies, stars

photograph on bulletin board

INTRINSIC (INTERNAL) REINFORCERS

fun

meeting goals

learning (for the sake of learning)

self-sufficiency

philosophical humor

relaxation, tranquility, serenity

meaningfulness

novelty, surprises

self-satisfaction

success

enjoyment of beauty

improvement

openness

having options, alternatives

playfulness

self-awareness

constructive feedback

achievement

CREATIVE SELF-EXPRESSION

arts/crafts	cooking
painting	poetry
gardening	music
athletics	dance

Corporal Punishment

The practice of whipping, flogging, paddling, thumping, birching, whacking, caning and otherwise inflicting physical pain upon students is embedded in the history of American education. Writings of the Puritans frequently refer to the use of the rod to "beat the devil out of" misbehaving students. The use of corporal punishment is seldom discussed dispassionately; it evokes heated arguments from both its proponents and opponents.

In *Reading, Writing and the Hickory Stick,* a thorough examination of the use of corporal punishment in schools, Irwin Hyman reviewed studies documenting the following practices:

➤ Corporal punishment occurs more frequently at the primary and intermediate levels.

➤ Boys are paddled much more frequently than girls.

➤ Minority and poor white children receive corporal punishment four to five times more frequently than middle- and upper-class white children.

➤ Corporal punishment is used least in schools in the Northeast.

➤ It is a myth that corporal punishment is used as a last resort. Studies suggest corporal punishment is frequently the first punishment for minor and nonviolent misbehaviors.

➤ There is evidence that corporal punishment is one of the causes of school vandalism.

➤ Corporal punishment is forbidden in the schools of Europe, Japan, Israel, Ireland, Russia, China, Turkey, Iceland, Puerto Rico, twenty-seven states, and many metropolitan area schools in America. The United States, Canada, parts of Australia, and South Africa remain the only industrialized nations tolerating corporal punishment in their schools.

➤ Teachers who frequently paddle tend to be authoritarian, dogmatic, relatively inexperienced, impulsive, and neurotic as compared to their peers.

➤ Generally, teachers who do not paddle were rarely, if ever, spanked or paddled as children. This modeling effect has been repeatedly demonstrated. The more teachers were hit as children, the more they tend to hit their students.

➤ Schools with high rates of corporal punishment also have high rates of suspensions and are generally more punitive in all discipline responses than schools with low rates of corporal punishment.

Some states now restrict the use of corporal punishment, mandating that a witness be present, paddliing not be done in front of other students, and in some locations only after parental consent has been granted. Some areas continue to permit spanking by the hand but prohibit the use of paddles or other objects. Many organizations, including the National Education Association, American Civil Liberties Union, the American Academy of Pediatrics, the National Committee on the Prevention of Child Abuse, Association of Childhood Education International, American Medical Association, Children's Defense Fund, National Association of Social Workers, and the Parent Teacher Association have lobbied to restrict or ban the use of corporal punishment in schools. The majority of states do now ban the use of corporal punishment. Others restrict its use. Although reliance upon corporal punishment has declined, over one million instances of corporal punishment still occur each year in the United States.

The arguments that paddling develops character or reforms errant behavior simply are not supported by any objective examination of the data. Indeed, there is evidence that corporal punishment is counterproductive.

THE CASE AGAINST CORPORAL PUNISHMENT

➤ Corporal punishment does not extinguish undesirable behaviors. It merely temporarily suppresses them.

➤ Physical punishment models aggression and violence as appropriate means of getting what you want.

➤ All child abuse begins as punishment. There is a relationship between how severely and frequently a child experienced physical punishment and the propensity toward violence later in their lives. Researchers estimate between 20,000 and 150,000 children each year require medical treatment as a result of corporal punishment received at school. Circulatory and nervous system problems, paralysis, broken bones, knocked-out teeth, brain damage, and Post-traumatic Stress Disorder have all been documented in instances of school-administered corporal punishment.

➤ There is an unfairness inherent in who gets punished. Paddling is not distributed equally, even for similar offenses. Race, gender and socio-economic level influence whether a particular student will experience corporal punishment.

➤ Paddling in schools can lead to stress reactions, such as school phobias, nightmares, loss of appetite, bed-wetting, and nervousness.

➤ Punishing situations tend to be avoided. Schools that rely heavily upon corporal punishment also experience higher rates of absenteeism, truancy, and dropping out.

➤ Paddling poisons the teacher-student relationship. It breeds mistrust. Fear is not the equivalent of respect.

➤ In instances where paddling was banned, the amount of student misbehavior did not increase. Indeed, in at least one instance, vandalism actually decreased.

➤ There is increased risk today of being sued or charged with child abuse when paddling students.

Despite overwhelming evidence that corporal punishment has detrimental effects upon students, as well as teachers, and virtually no evidence that it has any long-term benefits the practice has its supporters, including some administrators, parents and teachers. The long-term effects cannot be justified by any short-term gains the teacher may reap from this sadistic behavior. Yet, teaching remains the sole profession that is permitted to beat its clients. The beating of criminals or animals is forbidden, yet many states still legally sanction the paddling of students.

There is substantial evidence that corporal punishment is not essential to the maintenance of decorum and obedience in today's schools. See the earlier section "Hot Tips for Managing Classroom Behavior" for alternatives to the use of corporal punishment.

> *"A teacher does best armed only with knowledge. Corporal punishment is a cruel and obsolete weapon. The battle for children's minds should not be waged on their behinds."*
>
> —**U.S.A. TODAY** EDITORIAL, AUGUST 22, 1990

FOR ADDITIONAL READING

Bauer, G.B., Dubanoski, R., Yamauchi, L.A., & Honbo, K.A.M. (1990). Corporal Punishment and the Schools. *Education and Urban Society, 22* (3), 285-299.

Buechler, M., McCarthy, M.M., & Dayton, J. (1989). *The Debate Over Corporal Punishment.* Policy Memo Series No. 5. Bloomington, IN: Consortium on Educational Policy Studies.

Greven, P.J. (1991). *Spare the Child: The Religious Roots of Punishment and the Psychological Impact of Physical Abuse.* New York: Knopf.

Hyman, I.A. (1986). *Reading, Writing and the Hickory Stick: The Appalling Story of Physical and Psychological Abuse in American Schools.* New York: Free Press.

Hyman, R.T. & Rathbone, C.H. (1993). *Corporal Punishment in Schools: Reading the Law.* Topeka, KS: National Organization on Legal Problems of Education.

Maurer, A. (1986). *1001 Alternatives to Corporal Punishment: Volume Two.* Berkeley, CA: End Violence Against the Next Generation, Inc.

Maurer, A. (1981). *Paddles Away: A Psychological Study of Physical Punishment in Schools.* Palo Alto, CA: R & E Research Associates.

The Teacher as a Skilled Helper

It is not uncommon for students to turn to teachers for help in times of stress, disappointment, frustration, and loss. Almost daily every teacher has the opportunity to respond to the emotional turmoil of at least one student. In the course of a year it is very likely some students in your class may experience the death or disability of a family member or classmate, the divorce of their parents, unemployed parents, the loss of pets, moving to new schools, academic failure, or rejection by classmates or sweethearts.

There are some high-yield, low-risk listening skills that all compassionate teachers should have in their repertoire. They are high-yield skills because if they are done well, these basic counseling tools have the potential to make a large difference in the lives of students. They are labeled low-risk because as long as teachers stick to these skills and don't venture off into freelance, amateur psychotherapy, no harm is likely to occur. No one has ever been hurt by being listened to and a great many people have been helped.

The skills described here the basic attending skills learned by every beginning counselor. They are often termed "active listening" skills. Passive listening is the kind of listening that occurs when students are staring at you during a lecture. Maybe they even occasionally nod their heads to signal they are still awake, but you have no idea whether they are actually hearing a word you have said. Passive listening is one-way. Active listening, on the other hand, is a two-way process; it involves a true dialogue. What one person is saying is clearly and directly related to what the other has said. The listener must actively prove that he or she has heard the speaker.

Become a good listener and the world will beat a path to your door. Truly good listeners are all too rare; they stand out. Effective listeners have mastered the fine art of inviting people to talk about themselves, and the listener seems genuinely interested. Listening is one of the most precious gifts you can give to your students. You may be the only adult in their lives who truly takes time to listen.

Becoming a skilled helper does not mean having to sit down with a student and become involved in a long tearful conversation. Everyday in every classroom, students are struggling with emotional pain and conflict. One compassionate moment of listening can let the child know he or she has been heard, that you care. It may indeed take less than ten seconds. And that brief encounter may be remembered by that student for the rest of his or her life.

WHAT GOOD LISTENING IS NOT

Good listening is not advice giving. Indeed it is tempting to give advice to others, especially when the solutions to their problems are so obvious to us. Take a moment to recall the last time someone freely offered you advice, especially if it was unsolicited. Chances are it fell on deaf ears; we tend to reject unsolicited advice, no matter what the source. Though it may not be the intent of the giver, advice subtly communicates, "I can run your life better than you can." Not a message most people are eager to hear.

Even if the student asks for advice, giving it is not necessarily the best thing to do. There is an old Chinese proverb, "Give me a fish and I eat for a day; teach me to fish and I eat forever." We should be more interested in teaching people how to fish, not in giving fish away. It is far more important to equip our students with the skills needed to face and solve life's challenges than to ease their short-term discomfort. When we prematurely give advice, we rob students of a valuable learning experience. Further, we, not the student, have assumed responsibility for the problem. Embedded in the use of active listening is the assumption that students can work out the solutions to their problems given support and time. (Of course, advice-giving is appropriate if you are in the role of an academic advisor. We are referring here to discussion of students' personal, not academic problems.)

REFLECTION OF FEELINGS

Reflection of feelings is a powerful counseling tool, used by almost every counselor. It appears on the surface to be a simple skill. Do not be deceived—it is very difficult to do well and genuinely. The aim is to practice reflections of feeling until they become reflexive, so the next time you are sitting with a person in pain you automatically respond with such a response.

The basic structure of a reflection of feeling is "You feel ___ " filling in the blank with a feeling word that accurately reflects the feeling the student is experiencing at that moment. After you have mastered the technique, experiment with putting it into your own phrasing, such as "You seem...," "It sounds like you are...," or "You are ...." The key ingredient is that the feeling word *must* be included in your observation. Later you might also add the source of the perceived feeling, "You feel ____ about (or because) _____.

Reflection of feeling is one of several perception checking devices. They are used to verify what we think we have heard. They develop a crucial helping condition called "empathy." Empathy (not sympathy) is the ability to communicate to other persons that you are trying to understand what it is like to be them. That is why "I know how you feel" is an inadequate response. Maybe you know, maybe you don't. Only when you test your hypothesis with a reflection of feeling ("You seem pretty discouraged.") do you really prove that you heard what the student has said. You are striving for a deeper level of understanding.

The beauty of a reflection of feeling is that you potentially gain either way. If you are accurate in your perception, the student will almost always respond "Yes..." and then will elaborate. They will almost never stop at yes, unless you have raised your tonality at the end of your observation, making your statement into a closed-ended question. If you are off in your observation the student will almost always reply, "Well, no, it's not so much (discouraged) as it is ...."), giving you more accurate feedback. Either way you gain.

Reflections of feeling are always offered tentatively. The intent is to check out what you perceive their feelings to be. The fact is you can never know with absolute certainty what another human being is feeling. You can project how you would feel; you can guess how they feel, but you can never know with 100% certainty. Take the risk of checking out your perceptions.

As a skilled helper it is important to listen more to the feelings a student expresses than the surface content. People, including students, seldom say all they mean and seldom mean all they say. It is critical to learn to listen between the lines. Sometimes a student may mean exactly the opposite of what he or she really says (e.g., "I don't need your help!"). By listening to the students' feelings we help them move to a deeper level of understanding than if we focus only on the content, which tends to stay at an intellectual level. Persons who listen empathically by using reflections of feeling are perceived as being more caring by students.

Listening to students' feelings prevents them from bottling up their emotions and ultimately erupting in aggressive and destructive acts. Good active listening helps defuse stress and tension.

There are very practical reasons for using reflections of feeling in working with your students. In a classic set of research studies by David Aspy and Flo Roebuck, reported in their book *Kids Don't Learn from Teachers They Don't Like*, students of teachers using such active listening skills scored higher on academic achievement tests, attendance, and measures of self-esteem. Good listening *does* make a difference.

OTHER TIPS FOR BECOMING A BETTER LISTENER

➤ To be a successful listener you must be genuinely interested in what the student has to say. If you don't have time at the moment, offer to talk with the student later.

➤ In a counseling role listen non-judgmentally, achieving what Carl Rogers termed "unconditional positive regard." By the time students come to their teachers with a problem, they have probably had advice and lectures from others. They often just need someone who cares who will listen for a few minutes. Nothing nips trust like critical judgment and negative labeling. Beware of conveying disapproval through your tonality, leading questions, or nonverbal responses.

➤ The next time you have a student sitting knee-to-knee in front of you with tears streaming down his or her cheeks, resist the urge to give advice or sugar-coated reassurance. Just take time to listen, compassionately. Follow the adage, "Talk a little less; listen a little more."

➤ Become comfortable with silence in a counseling relationship. These pauses can create valuable reflection time for students.

➤ Use a variety of listening skills. Paraphrasing is restating a student's comment in your own words. It tends not to include the reference to feelings which are included in reflections of feeling. Good clarifiying questions, used sparingly, can be most helpful in encouraging students to examine the causes and possible solutions to their problems.

➤ Be sure your nonverbal messages are congruent with your verbal ones. Although there are some cultural exceptions, for most students offer direct eye contact while the student is talking. It helps establish trust and communicates interest. Leaning forward is also interpreted as an expression of concern and interest.

➤ Brief responses such as "Mm-hm" or "I see" or "Go on" are useful in communicating that you are still with the speaker. Occasional head nods also encourage the student to continue.

➤ Avoid finishing the statements of others. Besides being rude, it also communicates impatience and a lack of interest. More important, it's lazy listening. Sometimes, you will just be wrong in your interpretation. It's also generally best not to interrupt the speakers unless they begin to ramble. Then you might inject a clarifying phrase or question.

➤ Invest in rapport building with your students by listening to them when they don't have serious problems. Acknowledge and validate their positive feelings, as well as the negative ones (e.g., "You're really excited about making the team" or "You must be very proud of your award").

➤ Study outstanding listeners in your daily life and in the public media. Larry King and Barbara Walters are good models to observe. Note their nonverbal posture and the quality of their open-ended questions.

➤ Reflective listening is also a valuable technique to employ with angry students or adults. You are not getting into the blame game. You are neither saying, "You're wrong!" nor are you saying, "I'm wrong." By listening to their feelings (for example, "You're pretty upset with the way your child has been treated") you are simply communicating that you are listening to them at the deepest level. It is like verbal judo. Instead of meeting force with force, you are letting their anger dissipate into the wind. Once the angry person has vented his or her feelings and you refuse to get caught up in a shouting match, the person will begin to calm down.

➤ Avoid the "Have you tried _____ ?" trap. Most students will respond with "I tried that" or "It won't work because...." They will wait for you to suggest one more solution so they can chop it down. It creates a no-win game.

COMMENTS THAT DO MORE HARM THAN GOOD

What you'd better do is _____.

What's wrong with you?

I wish you didn't feel that way.

Others have problems worse than yours.

Don't worry; everything is going to turn out just fine.

Here's what I'd do if I were you: _____.

Why do you feel that way?

Everyone feels that way.

Why don't you _____?

➤ "Why" questions tend to put a student on the defensive, asking them to justify their actions or feelings. It is preferable to ask "what" and "how" questions.

➤ Feelings are neither good nor bad. They just exist. What counts is how we handle those emotions. Don't say, "I wish you didn't feel that way." Now the student may feel guilty about the emotions he or she is experiencing. Accept and help the students explore the feelings they are experiencing.

➤ A particularly helpful question is "What would you like to have happen?" It encourages the student to focus upon a goal.

➤ Be cautious of projecting your own issues onto the student. If racial or sexual harassment is an issue in your life, don't assume your students are wrestling with the same issues.

➤ It is often helpful to help students explore the potential long- and short-term consequences of their anticipated actions in resolving a problem.

➤ Respect the confidentiality of things students tell you. Of course, you must report instances of suspected child abuse or threatened harm to another or themselves, but don't gossip with other faculty about things students tell you in private.

➤ Do be aware of when a student needs professional help. Offer to go to the school psychologist's or counselor's office with the student to make an appointment. Do communicate that you are concerned but that the student needs someone else with specific training in counseling to help with the problem. A classroom teacher will seldom have the time or the training to engage in long-term, in-depth counseling relationships with students.

➤ Pay attention to what is *not* said. Are any obvious pieces of information or concerns not mentioned? That does not mean you must force the issue, but do make a mental note of what is being avoided.

➤ Conclude a helping session with a summary of the main points discussed and any action the student might be planning to deal with the issue. Try to end on a hopeful, encouraging note.

➤ One of the most valuable things you can give a student is hope, an expectation that things can and will eventually get better. Some students come from deplorable home environments. You have limited power to change the world the student returns to at the end of the day, but knowing that someone genuinely cares can make a tremendous difference.

➤ Keep a phone list of various support services, both within the school system and the greater community, to whom you might choose to refer parents. It is much easier if you have the information readily at your grasp rather than having to hunt it and then get back to the parent later.

➤ The kinds of information you might want to accumulate could include:

Sources of children's health services

Emergeny food, housing, clothing assistance

Sources of scholarship funds

Counseling services for individuals and families

Tutoring programs

Counseling services

Child protective services

Teachers do become significant persons in the lives of many of their students. If you were to list the ten most significant persons in your life, chances are there would be at least one teacher on that list. Do you think that teacher realizes how important he or she was in your life? Probably not. It is indeed a joy when former students return years later to let us know how dramatically we shaped their lives, but it is all too rare. Yet, it is a certainty we must accept on faith. You never know how much impact you are having. Teachers plant seeds and do everything they can to nurture them. Sadly we aren't always around for the harvest.

"Talking is sharing, but listening is caring."
—ANONYMOUS

"Take my advice, don't give advice."
—MARK TWAIN

"The first duty of love is to listen."
—PAUL TILLICH

"Education is the ability to listen to almost anything without losing your temper or your self-confidence."
—ROBERT FROST

BARRIERS TO EFFECTIVE COMMUNICATION

➤ Advice giving
➤ Overuse of closed-ended questions
➤ Criticizing and labeling
➤ Becoming distracted
➤ Daydreaming

➤ Sugar-coated reassurance
➤ Preaching or moralizing
➤ Interrupting
➤ Fixing other people's problems
➤ Listening only to content; not hearing feelings
➤ Not attending to nonverbal cues
➤ Finishing another person's sentences
➤ Prejudging the speaker
➤ Jumping to conclusions
➤ Talking, not listening
➤ Leading questions
➤ Interpreting, diagnosing
➤ Incongruent body language

Sample Letter of Welcome to Students - Before School Starts

August, 25, 199_

Greetings,

In less than two weeks school will begin. As you probably know by now, I will be your fifth grade teacher. This is my sixth year of teaching at Einstein Elementary School. I love teaching and very much enjoy the students at Einstein. I always look forward to meeting my new class each year.

I hope you have had an enjoyable summer and look forward to hearing about what you did. My family spent a week camping in a national forest. I'll be showing some of the slides in our geography class this year.

School begins at 8:00 A.M. Tuesday, September 3. You should come directly to Room 78. I do expect all students to be on time every day. I think most students find my classes to be fun, although we also work hard. We do a lot of cooperative work in groups. Most nights you can expect to have 30-45 minutes of homework.

I have enclosed a list of supplies you will need. The only ones you definitely need the first day are the pen, spiral note pad, and glue. The rest of the items you should have by Monday, September 9. If you or your parents have any questions I can be reached at home at 646-3371. It will be easiest to reach me between 5 and 9 in the evenings.

Best wishes for a most successful year!

Sincerely,

Mr. Green

Getting to Know You

Please complete the following sentences. There are no right or wrong answers.

1. During the summers I most enjoy _____

_____

2. I wish I could _____

_____

3. What I like to do most is _____

_____

4. The thing I enjoy best about school is _____

_____

5. I am happiest when _____

_____

6. My favorite television program is _____

_____

7. I learn best when _____

_____

8. My favorite sports are _____

_____

9. One thing I do well is _____

_____

10. One thing I would like to do better is _____

_____

11. I dislike school when _____

_____

12. When I grow up I hope to be _____

_____

Get Acquainted BINGO

Directions: Find a person who fulfills each of these categories. Collect their signatures in the appropriate boxes. Write your favorite activity, sport, or hobby in the middle box. Try to get as many different signatures as you can.

Enjoys Fishing	Is an only child	Has seen the Grand Canyon	Has ridden a horse	Likes to cook
Has been on television	Owns red shoes	Has lived on a farm	Owns a cat	Has ridden a subway
Visited Canada	Has written a poem	Your favorite activity	Loves the beach	Is wearing blue socks
Has a 1990 coin on them	Has been in a play	Has been to a college	Reads	Knits
Keeps a diary or journal	Likes broccoli	Loves to dance	Plays a musical instrument	Is left handed

1995 by The Center for Applied Research in Education

HAPPY BIRTHDAY!

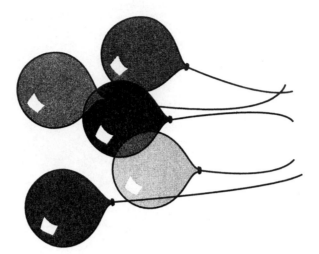

WOW!

I'm excited for you.

Keep up the good work!

Hurray!

Bravo!

Well Done!

EXCELLENT!!

Fantastic!

Super!

We're very proud of your
accomplishment of

Best wishes for continued success.

Date

Teacher

45

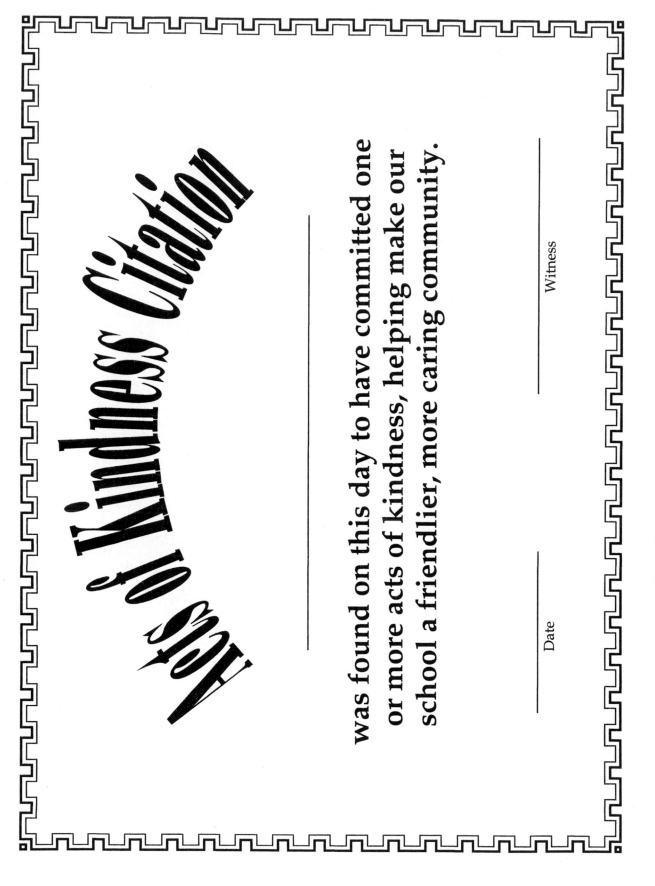

Acts of Kindness Citation

_____

was found on this day to have committed one or more acts of kindness, helping make our school a friendlier, more caring community.

_____
Witness

_____
Date

© 1995 by The Center for Applied Research in Education

46

Student Personal Record

Name _____

Street Address _____

City _____

State _____ ZIP _____ Home Phone _____

Parent or guardian(s)' name _____

Brothers' and Sisters' names and ages: _____

_____

_____

Your favorite sports, hobbies, activities: _____

_____

_____

_____

_____

_____

_____

_____

_____

_____

_____

_____

Outstanding Student of the Week

awarded to

for a high level of effort and performance.

Date

Teacher

48

You're on target!

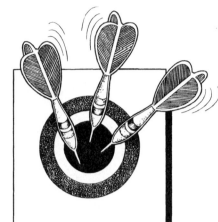

Presented to _____
for outstanding progress in

_____ .

_____

Date   _____

Congratulations to _____

for _____

_____

49

Welcome back!

The mind is not a vessel to be filled but a fire to be ignited.

- Plutarch

Problem Behavior Checklist

Indicate the frequency with which each of the following behaviors occurs in your classroom:

	Frequently	Occasionally	Rarely	Never
Hitting, fighting	___	___	___	___
Shouting, loud talking	___	___	___	___
Calling out	___	___	___	___
Students talking with each other in class	___	___	___	___
Stealing	___	___	___	___
Cheating on tests, quizzes, homework	___	___	___	___
Tardiness to class	___	___	___	___
Namecalling	___	___	___	___
Use of obscenities	___	___	___	___
Handing in assignments late	___	___	___	___
Not bringing necessary materials to class	___	___	___	___
Not completing homework	___	___	___	___
Leaving room without permission	___	___	___	___
Wearing hats in the classroom	___	___	___	___
Students out of their seats without permission	___	___	___	___
Classroom vandalism	___	___	___	___
Chewing gum in class	___	___	___	___
Bullying others	___	___	___	___
Weapons at school	___	___	___	___
Violations of school dress code	___	___	___	___
Non-compliance with teacher's requests	___	___	___	___
Rude comments to others	___	___	___	___
Littering	___	___	___	___
Whining	___	___	___	___
Tattling	___	___	___	___
Abuse of books, equipment	___	___	___	___
Incessant talking	___	___	___	___
Truancy	___	___	___	___
Non-participation, apathy	___	___	___	___
Sexual harassment of other students	___	___	___	___
Doing work for other classes in your class	___	___	___	___
Playing dumb	___	___	___	___
Excessive messiness	___	___	___	___
Teasing other students	___	___	___	___
Other (_____)	___	___	___	___

© 1995 by The Center for Applied Research in Education

Documented Interventions

Student's name _____

Parents' names _____

Parent's daytime phone(s) _____

Teacher _____ Subject/grade _____

Intervention	Date	Comments
Discuss problem with student	_____	_____
Clarify rules	_____	_____
Change seats	_____	_____
Telephone parents/guardian	_____	_____
Parent conference	_____	_____
Peer tutoring	_____	_____
Extra help after school	_____	_____
Adapt assignments	_____	_____
Refer to counselor	_____	_____
Student contract	_____	_____
Time out	_____	_____
Home/school daily or weekly notes	_____	_____
Individual conference with student	_____	_____
Refer to principal	_____	_____
Refer to counselor	_____	_____
Refer to school psychologist	_____	_____
Refer to specialist _____	_____	_____
Conference with parent and student	_____	_____
Home visit	_____	_____
Team conference	_____	_____

Notes:

Proficiency Notice

Date _____

To: _____

From: _____

I am most pleased to report that the performance of _____ in my class has been noteworthy and deserving of recognition. In particular, I wanted to bring to your attention the following success:

_____

_____

_____

I hope we can both encourage this progress to continue. Please feel free to contact me if you have any questions or concerns.

Special Achievement Award

to recognize

for a job well done!

_____ Date

_____ Teacher

Thanks for your help!

It really is appreciated.

_____

_____

_____

_____

Certificate of Appreciation

Presented to

in recognition and gratitude for

Certificate

of Completion

Let it be known that

_____

has satisfactorily completed

_____

Certificate of Outstanding Performance

Let it be known to all that on this _____ day of _____ 19___ that

_____

is hereby recognized for outstanding achievement in

_____

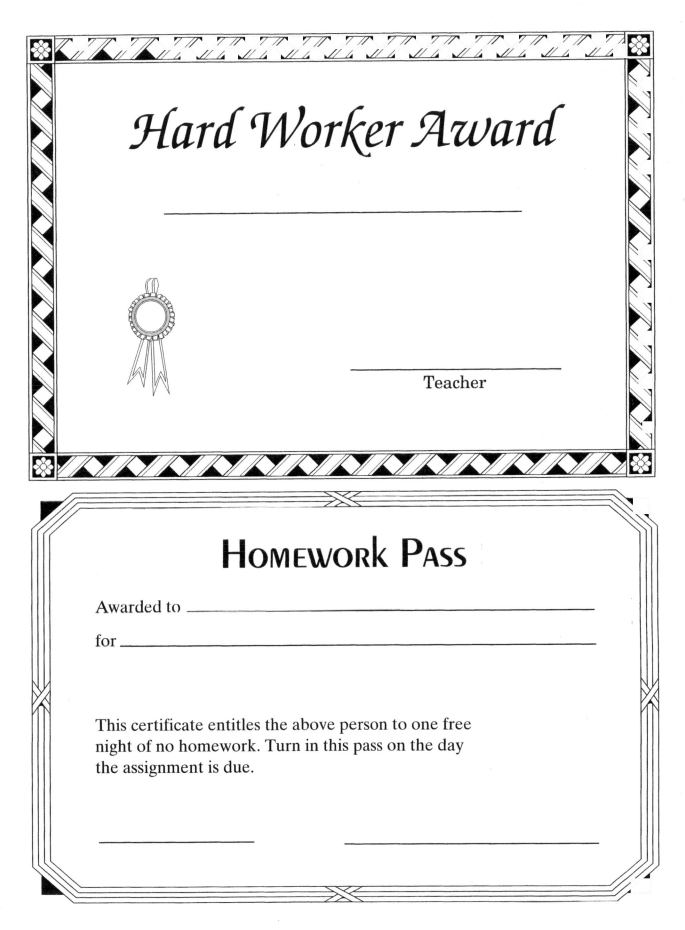

Hard Worker Award

_____

_____
Teacher

HOMEWORK PASS

Awarded to _____

for _____

This certificate entitles the above person to one free night of no homework. Turn in this pass on the day the assignment is due.

_____   _____

Much Better!

You're on the right track now!
Keep up the good work.

_____

Student Contract

It is hereby agreed that if _____ has fulfilled the
following condition(s):_____
_____

by the date of _____ he/she is entitled to the following
consequence: _____

Signed: _____   _____
            Teacher   Student

CHAPTER 2

Creating Successful Lessons

Lesson Plans

The aim of any lesson is change—purposeful change. Each day you walk into a class-room you should know exactly what you expect to accomplish and how you are going to do it. Generally, too little time is spent on instructional planning. A list of assignments or textbook pages to cover is not a plan. A lesson plan is simply a sequential guide to how you plan to accomplish your instructional objectives or goals. Can you imagine a builder trying to construct a house without a blueprint? Lesson plans tell you what you will be doing and what your students will be doing. Lesson plans also help identify the resources, including time, needed to accomplish these activities. While you may not always be able to stick to your plan, you'll be more likely to intentionally affect your students' learning if you start with a plan. Some courses will require more detailed plans than others. At least early in your teaching career, clearly written plans are essential for success. There is no one right format for these plans. Develop a format that works for you. It should be simple, yet complete.

➤ First make a general plan for the year. It will necessarily be vague and deal with general concepts, topics, and skills. These are usually drawn from any written program of study the school is obligated to follow. Monthly plans begin to add more detail. Weekly plans should be quite specific in both objectives and instructional strategies.

➤ Try to plan at least a week in advance. The first time you must unexpectedly be absent you (and your substitute) will appreciate it.

➤ Make a master lesson plan form filling in all the details and activities that will remain the same each week. Place these in a large loose-leaf notebook. In each class's notebook also keep any additional information needed for that class, such as rosters, form letters, phone numbers, etc.

➤ The first step in every lesson is to focus upon the goal(s) you hope to accomplish. These should be stated in terms of how the students should be different after encountering your instruction. You are planning to effect an intentional change in the students' knowledge, skills, or attitudes. Be specific. Also be reasonable in what you can realistically accomplish in a week or a day. It is better to teach less, well than give superficial coverage to much that is quickly forgotten.

➤ Don't over-rely upon knowledge-level objectives. Within one year students for-get 80% of what they learn, most of that being facts they were required to mem-orize. Skills and attitude changes tend to have a much more permanent effect.

➤ In each subject notebook keep all the lesson plans, handout masters, tests, quizzes, and lists of audio-visual requirements for one subject. It will save you much time next year.

➤ Some teachers prefer to develop and store their lesson plans on the computer. This makes revision much simpler. Of course, a paper copy will be needed for classroom use in most instances.

➤ First schedule the blocks of time your students have to be out of the room. Then schedule the topics and content you are responsible for teaching. Effective teach-ers cover the curriculum, but teach more than the written course of study. Embellish and enrich the established curriculum with your interests, talents, and creativity.

➤ In planning any lesson develop the body of the instruction first, including specifics on what you will do and what the students will do. Then give special attention to developing a powerful and interesting opening and ending. These are often overlooked in planning, yet the most likely parts to be remembered by students. Be sure to list any equipment, supplies, and preparations that will need to be arranged before the class.

➤ Where possible schedule challenging and new content early in the day. Generally, student attention and concentration wane in the afternoon. Ideally, save the less mentally challenging, more energizing activities for afternoon.

➤ Likewise, schedule the most demanding content on Monday, Tuesday, and Wednesday. Student productivity and enthusiasm diminish after Wednesday. Friday shouldn't be discarded, but save it for more active learning experiences and fun review opportunities. Simulations, field trips, films, guest speakers, and other special activities can keep students motivated at the end of the week.

➤ Always have several "sponge" activities available for students to work on if they complete an assignment or test early. These should have an educational purpose yet be interesting, lest they will be perceived as punishments.

➤ After you teach each lesson, note on your lesson plan sheet which parts of the lesson went well and which need to be improved. Don't rely on your memory to make those changes next year.

➤ Use colored folders to arrange each day's lesson plans and student papers. Use a different color for each class. Use the same color to identify any materials for that class.

➤ Some teachers choose to put their lesson plans on note cards, a single idea or activity on each card. That makes it easier to reshuffle the order or add and delete items in the future. (**Tip:** Punch holes in all your cards and put them on a large ring. If you drop them they don't become scattered.)

➤ Use checklists to help organize your lessons. For example, if you use a simulation game, develop a checklist to record any items you'll need or tasks to include.

➤ Some items, such as ordering films or arranging speakers, must be done well in advance. Ideally, you'll save time by ordering all films for the semester at one time. While it may be difficult the first year or two to do such long-term planning, it will become easier.

➤ Try to have materials for the next day's lesson ready before you leave school. Even if you have to stay after school to copy handouts or prepare other materials, it will prove less stressful than racing in the next morning to complete your preparation. Even early morning preparation periods can't always be counted on to be free to handle those last-minute tasks. A hallmark of any professional is being prepared.

➤ Develop a card file or loose-leaf notebook to collect teaching ideas. These might include copies of ideas you find in professional magazines. At least once a month scan through your file to see if you can incorporate any of the activities into your upcoming lessons.

➤ If you see another teacher or presenter use a successful technique or strategy brainstorm ways you might adapt the idea for one of your lessons.

➤ Visit teachers who teach the grade above or below yours to discover how your lessons fit into the larger picture.

➤ Save a few moments at the end of each day to reflect on your day's lessons. What went well? What clearly needs to be improved? Any ideas on how to make your lesson more effective the next time? Jot down these ideas on your lesson plan and file in your notebook.

Beginning a Class

Students are most likely to remember the first and last things you do in a lesson. Indeed, many believe the first three minutes of a class are the most important. An effective opening can serve several valuable purposes. It can focus students' attention on what they are about to learn. An effective opening can also arouse students' curiosity and interest in the lesson. It helps motivate them to become involved in the lesson. The beginning sets the tone for the rest of the lesson. It creates psychological readiness to engage in learning. The opening of the lesson stimulates your students' emotions, such as puzzlement, curiosity, tension, empathy, wonderment, excitement, amusement, pride, skepticism, or fascination. Remember that students of all ages approach any lesson with the question, "What's in it for me?" If your opening addresses that question, you will have a motivated learner.

➤ Learning begins before the bell rings. Use posters, door signs, music, transparencies, and other techniques to engage the students' minds, capture their attention, and arouse anticipation before the class officially begins. Many teachers have music playing as students enter to set the appropriate mood. Attention getters, such as trivia and interesting facts related to the day's topic, might be suspended from the ceiling, hung upside down, or otherwise interestingly displayed to grab students' attention.

➤ Be sure you have everyone's attention before you begin. Don't try to talk over the group noise. Convey enthusiasm for the lesson. It can be contagious. If you don't sound very interested in what you are teaching, it is improbable your students will be. Be especially cognizant of maintaining eye contact with your students during the opening. Scan the entire class to include everyone.

➤ The opening must be connected to the main lesson. Your students must be able to see that the opening is relevant to the rest of the lesson.

Avoid beginning the class with routine, procedural tasks (taking attendance, collecting homework, general announcements, etc.). Remember, your students most remember the first and last things that happen in the class. Later, while students are working individually or in small groups, you can unobtrusively take attendance. Get your lessons off to a good start; give them punch.

It is essential to get your students actively involved within the first two minutes of the lesson. There are many way this might be accomplished, and it need not take a big chunk of time; a three- or four-second response actively draws their attention to the lesson. Here are several strategies successfully used by effective teachers to engage their students in the lesson:

➤ Begin with a personal anecdote. A personal illustration that ties to the topic makes it more personal and interesting. Remember, it must be relevant to the lesson you are teaching.

➤ Pose a challenging question. Give careful thought to your opening questions. You may have students respond by jotting down their answer, volunteering to share it aloud, or simply answering silently to themselves. It is often helpful to ask a question to which everyone is likely to raise their hands (e.g., "How many are ready for a vacation?").

➤ Present a startling statistic or fact about some aspect of the lesson.

➤ Open the class with an unusual, surprising behavior or event.

➤ Present an interesting, relevant problem.

➤ Start with a funny story. It can be a true incident or a fictional tale. It is even better if it is something that really happened to you. Don't try for jokes. Most important, the story must pertain to the day's topic.

➤ Use a true/false quiz reflecting major issues or research related to the topic. Before you give students the right answers, devise ways for them to share their "guesses" as to the correct answer. You might tabulate their responses on the board, or move their bodies to different spots on a "live" continuum to indicate how sure they are of each answer.

➤ Display interesting visuals: a cartoon, poster, or quotation. In groups or as a whole class, you might have them discuss their reaction to the visual.

➤ Use a prop—an unusual piece of equipment, artifact, collection, toy, or creature. Use a gimmick to grab your students' attention. Walk into class with a portable telephone. Carry on a conversation over the phone in which you introduce the day's topic. Add humor or a personal anecdote. Use your imagination.

➤ Use drama to let students introduce the issue or problem that will be the focus of the day's lesson.

➤ Experiment with using costumes or hats related to the topic being introduced. Pull off a shirt to reveal a tee-shirt depicting a quotation or graphic related to the lesson.

➤ Make a promise ("By the end of this lesson you will be able to...").

➤ Draw analogies between what has been learned previously and the new skills or content being learned in the current lesson.

➤ Use a magic trick. There are many good books suggesting simple tricks you can easily master. Or visit a magic shop looking for gimmicks or tricks that might fit into one of your lessons. Your banter during the trick is what ties it into your lesson. Don't let it just hang by itself.

➤ On a large sheet of newsprint or butcher paper, ask groups to draw three large circles at least a foot in diameter. Label them "What I know about..." (the topic being studied). Give the groups five to ten minutes to brainstorm and record any thing they know about the topic under consideration. They should then label the second circle, "What I hope to learn about..." (the same topic). Give them five minutes to list in that circle any questions they hope to have answered about the topic. The students then post all their sheets on the wall. At the end of the lesson direct the groups to retrieve their sheets and to label the third circle, "What I learned about..." (name of the topic studied). Give the groups ten minutes to list everything new they learned about the subject.

➤ *Memory Dump Activity.* Pair students and give them the following directions: "Tell your partner everything you know about..." (the new topic). (Allow 90 seconds.) Have students switch and repeat the process. (Allow another 90 seconds.) Switch and continue for 60 seconds. Switch and repeat for 60 seconds. Switch and continue for 30 seconds more. Switch a last time for 30 seconds. (*Idea adapted from Cerylle Moffett, ASCD consultant.*)

➤ It is a sound practice to frequently build in some form of review of the previous lesson at the beginning of a lesson. However, to be effective strive to make the review segment interesting and active. Mind-maps, analogies, brainstorming, role playing, or a cooperative learning activity will generally be more effective than just telling the students what was studied previously.

➤ To maximize their impact, vary your openings. Strive to be creative and occasionally use the element of surprise. If your openings become the best part of the lesson, you have much less problem with tardiness!

Action Verbs for Writing Instructional Objectives

Effective teachers know what they are trying to accomplish in each lesson. Their instruction has a purpose or clearly focused object. That objective may be for students to master a new skill, to change a behavior, attitude, value, or to memorize a fact. Some research suggests that as much as 80% of what students learn in school is forgotten within one year. Most of what is lost are facts—those pieces of data learned solely through rote memory. Most likely to be retained are the skills, attitudes, and values learned in the classroom.

Objectives that remain at the "knowledge level" include verbs such as "memorize," "list," "name," or "know." While a degree of factual information must be retained to allow higher level thinking, most educators recognize the value of teaching higher level critical thinking. You are seeking to answer the question, "What will my students be able to do as a result of my instruction?" Action verbs assure that you are focusing upon *doing,* not merely knowing. Here are some verbs that will help you construct objectives at a higher level:

advise	debate	improve	propose
analyze	decide	initiate	provide
appraise	deliver	inspect	rate
arrange	demonstrate	instruct	recommend
assemble	design	interpret	report
assign	determine	investigate	represent
assist	develop	locate	research
build	devise	maintain	resolve
calculate	direct	manage	review
collaborate	discuss	measure	revise
collect	draw	negotiate	schedule
compare	establish	obtain	secure
compile	estimate	operate	select
compute	explain	organize	show
conduct	evaluate	participate	solve
consolidate	execute	perform	submit
construct	exercise	place	teach
contrast	formulate	plan	train
coordinate	furnish	prepare	transcribe
criticize	implement	process	verify

Hot Tips for Maintaining Interest

It is absurd to expect all students to be constantly on the edge of their seats, mesmerized by masterful instruction. Students do bring outside agendas into the classroom. Divorces, deaths, infatuations, conflicts, and the normal growing pains can distract even the most conscientious students. While you cannot control these outside events, you do have a significant effect upon the learning of most students. Some teachers have greater skill at teaching lessons that hold students' attention and that result in higher achievement than other teachers. Probably all teachers have a few lessons that always excite and interest students. Those successful attention-holding lessons likely adhere to most of the following principles. Here are some ideas that may help you gain and maintain learner interest:

> ➤ Learning begins before class starts. Challenge yourself to devise creative ways to capture students' attention and engage their minds the moment they enter

the room. Every day plan to have something available related to the day's topic to arouse curiosity and stimulate thinking before the bell rings. **Examples:** a quotation on the board or overhead, a word puzzle for individuals or groups to complete, a couple of thought questions, a startling statistic, a related cartoon.

➤ Get the class actively involved in the first three minutes of the lesson. This might be through raising their hands in response to a question related to the day's lesson (e.g., "How many have ever visited a dairy farm?"), participating in a small group brainstorm, or writing a response. Strive to create an atmosphere of active involvement, not passive listening, early in the class period.

➤ Plan carefully and fully. Lessons that are run smoothly keep students' attention and minimize interruptions. This has little to do with charisma. Lessons run smoothly because they are carefully planned and organized. Time is invested up front to assure that materials are ready, the teacher knows what to do next, and the unexpected is anticipated. This helps create a businesslike, task-oriented atmosphere.

➤ Clarify the specific objective(s) for each lesson. The single most important question you can ask yourself each day is, "What do I want my students to learn from this class?" Unfortunately, some teachers have no clearer notion of where they are headed than "to make it through the textbook" or "to make it to the Civil War by Christmas."

➤ Share your objectives with your students. Let them know what they should get out of this lesson. Of course, you cannot tell them if you don't know yourself. With purposes clear and instruction systematic, students will more readily master that lesson.

➤ Divide learning tasks into smaller sub-skills. Present those sub-skills in logical and manageable lessons. Sequence your lessons so that you aren't trying to teach skills for which students have not yet mastered necessary prerequisites. Otherwise, both you and your students will be frustrated.

➤ Design lessons that encourage students to contribute their views and knowledge. Many have special talents or experiences they might enjoy sharing and from which other students can learn.

➤ Make a conscious effort to connect your lesson to students' lives beyond school. Incorporate their interests as illustrations. Provide opportunities for them to apply what they are learning to their daily lives and problems they face.

➤ Employ visual aids—transparencies, pictures, slides, props, demonstrations, and posters. Overall, the visual is the most powerful learning modality. Maximum learning is likely to occur when the instruction is both auditory and visual, and where possible also kinesthetic (involving doing things and motor movement).

➤ Keep moving while you talk. An easy way to lose any group's interest is to become the stationary "talking head" in front of the room. Talking while seated is also more likely to lead to a monotone speaking voice. An additional benefit of moving while teaching is that you are better able to monitor the class, nipping in the bud potentially disruptive misbehavior.

➤ Generally, it is best not to start each class with housekeeping chores. The reason is that students most remember the first and last thing you do in a class period. Don't waste this valuable learning time on mundane distracting content.

➤ Build a "breath of fresh air" or energizing activity into your lesson about every eight to ten minutes. It doesn't have to be long, but something that changes the pace and regathers the students' attention. Examples include a humorous cartoon, a prop, personal illustration, sharing a response in pairs or small groups, a role-play, demonstration, visualization. Anything that actively engages their brains is likely to be helpful in refocusing attention. Provide opportunities for active involvement through exercises and activities that break up long formal presentations. When asked, most students prefer lessons in which they act out parts, build things, interview people, or carry out projects. Least favored are those classes in which they are only allowed to listen.

➤ Variety is the spice of life and the secret to successful lessons! Effective teachers don't use the same teaching techniques day after day. They employ an assortment of instructional strategies. Most ineffective teachers do tend to use the same few techniques for every lesson—usually lecture and worksheets.

➤ Strive to develop the broadest range of teaching approaches, and employ that variety. Experiment with simulations, role playing, video taping, and cooperative learning. Students generally are more excited about working in groups.

➤ Involve students in real-life activities that have a practical useable product. The Foxfire project has been a remarkably successful project in which students interviewed their Appalachian neighbors and relatives and produced and sold books they wrote and published. Other classes have developed handbooks for teenage consumers, constructed solar walls, or set up community car pools. Hands-on activities by far are most successful in arousing student interest.

➤ The element of surprise works wonders in building student enthusiasm and motivation. Some teachers dress up in costumes, have surprise guest speakers, or use drama to capture students' attention. (For example, students are much more excited about reading Shakespeare when they act it out using an exaggerated Southern drawl—or Bostonian accent if they are from the South!). Occasionally, do the unexpected! Allow suspense to build in anticipation as the class unfolds. Questions, storytelling, and props are especially effective in creating intrigue.

It is by surprises that experience teaches all she designs to teach us.
—COLLECTED PAPERS OF CHARLES SANDERS PIERCE, VOL. V.

➤ Use anecdotes. Personal illustrations of events from your life experiences and those of your students make academic content come alive. It is essential that such stories pertain to the topic being studied. Irrelevant "war stories" add nothing to the lesson.

➤ Try to relate new content to things the students already know. As much as possible, encourage the students to make those connections themselves. Personalize as much of your content as possible.

➤ Minimize criticism and offer praise when appropriate. If students are too frequently criticized, they quickly learn to avoid volunteering their answers or opinions. There is no quicker way to squelch creativity or participation than to criticize the first couple of contributors. Use praise judiciously. Praise specific behaviors, not general characteristics. Be aware that for many adolescents, public praise can backfire. Their peers may taunt them for being the teacher's pet.

➤ Become aware of your voice level and patterns of speaking. Tape record a couple of classes and listen for your tonality, verbal tics (e.g., um, er, so). Or solicit feedback from a speech and hearing specialist as to the pitch of your voice.

➤ Vary your speech pattern. Use pauses or stage whispers for emphasis. Always remember to talk to the students at the furthest corner of the room. If students must strain to hear you, it will be hard to hold their attention.

➤ Make your presentations clear. Use vocabulary appropriate to the intellectual level of your students. Speak at a pace they can understand. If you tend toward a monotone voice, work on developing more animated speech. Periodically record or videotape your lessons. Seeing or hearing yourself as your students do may reveal areas of needed improvement.

➤ Remain flexible in your teaching. Read your audience and adjust accordingly. Furrowed brows and frowns will tell you some students did not grasp a point. Squirming, fidgeting, or daydreaming may cue you to pick up the pace or change your approach. Good planning must remain flexible. There is little sense in plowing ahead with a lesson plan that isn't working.

➤ Use your sense of humor. Do not try to become a stand-up comic, but don't be afraid to laugh or add humorous remarks to your presentation. The guiding principle relative to using humor in the classroom is that it should be relevant to the topic under discussion. Avoid the temptation to entertain with jokes that don't have an educational point. Interesting lessons make learning fun, and a natural response to fun activities is the occasional laugh. You need not strive for a belly laugh, but when a humorous incident or anecdote presents itself, use it to your advantage.

➤ Incorporate students' names in your presentations. For most people, their name really is their favorite sound.

➤ Use appropriate analogies, especially humorous ones.

➤ Use props whenever possible. Student interest is piqued when they enter the room and see a jar of beans, a model airplane, guitar, telephone, or parrot sitting on the teacher's desk. Almost any lesson can benefit from the inclusion of one or more props. If what you need is not immediately available, try using "invisible props." Describe the needed item in detail, using gestures as though you were actually holding it in your hand.

➤ A special form of prop is the collection. Campaign buttons, artifacts, insects, leaves, rocks, tools, costumes, or postcards are among items that interest students and enrich their knowledge of the academic subject. You can develop your own collections or invite parents and other community members to share theirs. It is best if they can bring their collection and talk briefly about it. Ask students questions about the items in a collection to encourage them to think about its value, purpose, and meaning.

Give me a lever long enough
And a prop strong enough,
I can single handed move the world.
                    —ARCHIMEDES

➤ Use music. Many effective teachers successfully incorporate music into their classes. Music playing as students enter the classroom begins to set the mood for the day's class. You can let students take turns bringing their favorite tapes to play before class or during breaks or recess. Soft music, played quietly in the background during individual seatwork can be pleasant and inviting. The beat of baroque compositions seems to work best for this.

➤ Music related to the topic (e.g., The Civil War, Ireland, China, the Roaring Twenties) can bring the topic to life and enrich the students' understanding of the subject. Use sound effects recordings for emphasis of important points. Some teachers even write new lyrics for familiar tunes. The new song conveys a message related to the day's lesson or an upcoming school event. It is fairly easy to devise your own composition using a rap beat. Either you can sing it or get a group of students or even the whole class to perform. Try reading the day's assignments to a rap beat!

➤ Take timely breaks. Continually monitor the nonverbals of your students. When nodding heads and drooping eyelids suggest you are losing their attention, insert a 30 second stretch break. It can be something as subtle as standing up as soon as they have figured out an answer or turning their chairs to face a different direction. Of course, you don't want to create chaos or disrupt the flow of your lesson. It works best if your "mini-break" can tie into your lesson.

➤ Avoid becoming too involved with one student during class discussions. The rest of the class may assume they are not a part of the discussion and turn their attention elsewhere. While being sensitive to individuals, teach to the whole class. Maintain control of the discussion. If one student is monopolizing the interaction, ask questions of others to get them involved.

➤ Assume the role of a character (an old woman, Superman, George Washington, a Civil War soldier). Embellish your character with props or a costume. (Garage sales and thrift shops are good sources for inexpensive costumes.) You might teach part of the lesson as your "character" for a few minutes or the whole period. Or alternate between two characters, debating with yourself. Consider acting out a real historical role in the actual setting as part of your vacation. Dress in authentic costumes and have someone videotape or take slides as you re-enact some historical event or journey. These can be edited and used in class (or all-school assemblies).

➤ Use quotations to make an emphatic point. Sometimes the impact of this technique can be enhanced if a brief quotation is read aloud to the class directly from the original source rather than merely from your notes.

➤ Build in brief, one- to three-minute pauses for reflection or writing. Give them a question to consider. For variety you may have all students stand and share their responses with someone else.

➤ End each lesson answering the "So what?" question. Encourage your students to consider why this content is important. Help them connect their new learnings with previous knowledge and with their personal lives, wherever possible.

➤ If a lesson falls flat, refine it or discard it. Why intentionally bore your students. Learning isn't happening. Spend your time on something that is working.

➤ Most importantly, remember that it is unlikely you will get students enthusiastic about a topic or activity if you are not enthusiastic about it. Conversely, if you believe what you are teaching is interesting, fun, or useful, that view might become contagious.

Cardinal Rules for Effective Visuals

Good visuals have the potential to enhance attention and retention. Most learners perform better when they receive information through more than one learning modality. Slides, transparencies, flip charts, and posters all can be used to effectively embellish any presentation.

Any material you repeatedly write on the chalkboard each time you teach a lesson is a good candidate for a permanent visual, such as an overhead transparency or slide. Pre-prepared visuals can also be much easier to read, more eye-catching, and faster than hand printing on the board or newsprint.

Have you ever heard a teacher or presenter say, "I know you can't read this, but..." as he placed a transparency on the overhead project? Some feel that should be grounds for instant dismissal, or worse. Visuals that can't be read are as useless as a parachute that doesn't open! Some simple rules will make your visuals more effective. These same principles generally apply to both overhead transparencies and slides.

➤ To construct visuals that will be readable, remember the number 6: no more than 6 lines on a visual and no more than 6 words on a line. Another way of gauging whether your overhead transparency is readable is to place it on the floor at your feet as you stand. If you can't read it, the print is too small.

➤ With the near universal availability of computers and laser printers, there really is no excuse for poorly constructed visuals. However, resist the temptation to clutter up your visuals with too many cute graphics and all the fonts at your disposal. No more than two font styles should be used on any one visual, and sans serif fonts (such as Geneva, Avant-Garde, or Helvetica) tend to be more readable. Use at least a size 24, and preferably a 36 font. Always avoid typewriter print in constructing transparencies. Print them by hand if necessary. If you still doubt whether your transparencies can be read, put one on the projector and view it from the last row of your classroom.

➤ It is better to put long lists on several transparencies or slides than to cram too much on one. It is more effective to use progressive exposure where each successive visual reveals one more line of information. This can be accomplished with several slides or with a transparency covered with a sheet of paper and gradually pulled down to reveal the next line.

➤ Tape four pennies along one long edge of a sheet of paper to make a mask to place over transparencies and pull down, gradually revealing one line at a time. The pennies keep the paper from slipping off as you get to the bottom of the transparency.

➤ Whenever possible use graphs and charts instead of tables for your visuals. Tables are more difficult to read and understand.

➤ Try something other than just black on white overhead transparencies. Use variety; experiment with color. Thermofax machines that run black and white transparencies can also produce transparencies with color backgrounds. If none are available, use Vis-a-Vis markers to add some color. White on dark colored backgrounds produces very readable transparencies.

➤ When you are done talking about a transparency, turn off the projector. Don't just remove the transparency, leaving a blinding and distracting white screen. An alternative is to hinge a 5 × 8 card with tape on top of the projector lens. Simply flip the card down to block the light when you are done with a transparency.

➤ Square the projector in front of the screen to minimize the keystone image. Because the distance from the projector image is further from the top of the screen than the bottom, the image will always appear wider at the top than at the bottom. This can be cured by using a screen that tilts forward about 7 degrees. If your screen is bolted flat to the wall, you'll have to live with it.

➤ Don't read your transparencies aloud. It's insulting to your audience.

➤ In preparing overhead transparencies or slides, use a horizontal format rather than vertical. Since most screens are horizontal rectangles, your visual will fit more neatly on the screen. When you project onto the screen try to use the upper 3/4's of the screen. The bottom quarter tends to be difficult for some participants in the back to see.

➤ Use colored, erasable, water-soluble pens to highlight transparencies during presentations.

➤ Arrange your transparencies in the order they will be used and place them near the projector.

➤ After placing a transparency on the projector step away so you do not block the view of any students.

➤ Use frames on your transparencies. You can make your own out of scrap cardboard. Many presenters use the transparency frames as cue cards, writing key words in large print. A quick glance as you place the transparency on the projector reminds you of points to emphasize.

➤ When using flip charts or newsprint, experiment with using a variety of dark colors. Print large and legibly. Notes to yourself can be penciled lightly on the newsprint beforehand. Tape sheets to the wall when they are completed.

➤ Another option widely used in businesses is the storyboard. A 4 × 4 sheet of corkboard (or regular blank bulletin board), push pins, felt-tip markers, and 4 × 6 index cards are all the materials needed. As the group brainstorms ideas they are pinned into clusters or under specific headings on the board. Storyboards can be adapted to a variety of uses in the classroom.

Review Techniques

Successful teachers allow ample time for reviewing new concepts and skills and integrating them into the students' prior knowledge. The purpose of review is to clarify, reinforce, and set the stage for new content. The challenge is to make review interesting. Here are some options that may help.

➤ Have each student draw three large balloons (or box cars, apples, or diamonds) on a sheet of paper. They are asked to write the three most important (or interesting) things they learned about the day's topic in the balloons. After a couple of minutes invite them to share their ideas in pairs. Finally, you can solicit ideas from the total group, providing three separate opportunities to review some aspect of the day's content.

➤ In the middle of a lesson you can stop and ask each student to jot down one idea from the lesson he or she most wants to remember. Allow a minute for reflection, then solicit ideas from various members of the class.

➤ Post on the walls several sheets of newsprint, each listing a major idea or concept studied during the previous lesson. At the signal, students are to move from one sheet to another, adding one fact or idea they know about each topic.

➤ Another fun way to stimulate reviews is for one student to draw on the board or newsprint a picture representing an idea related to the previous lesson. The rest of the students attempt to guess the word or topic in a *Pictionary* or *Win, Lose or Draw* format.

➤ One of the most powerful techniques for organizing ideas and concepts is the mind map. The mind map is also a most useful note-taking device. Every student should have this tool in their repertoire. It can also be used in a variety of ways to stimulate reflection and review.

The mind map begins by writing the key word or general topic (e.g., Presidents) in a circle in the middle of a sheet of blank paper. The sub-topics (e.g., The White House, elections, First Ladies, political parties, assassinations) are written on spokes

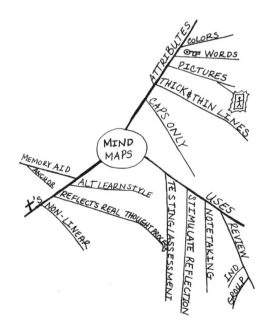

drawn out from the circle. A good way to generate the sub-topics is to ask students to brainstorm the main chapters they would include if they were going to write a book on the selected topic. Ideas and facts associated with the sub-topics are drawn on shorter lines branching from the spokes containing the sub-topics. Encourage students to use symbols or small pictures whenever possible. Using different colored markers or pens for the sub-topics also helps stimulate creative thought.

After individual students have developed their mind maps of the topic, ask them to join another person and combine their two separate mind maps into one. After several minutes redirect each pair to join another pair and again combine their mind maps into one. An option is to finally have all the students then gather around one large sheet of newsprint (or tape four regular sheets of newsprint together to form a gigantic one). Write the topic in a circle in the middle of the paper and give them the task of compiling a final mind map that includes all the ideas generated by their individual mind maps.

For more information on teaching mind mapping:

Buzan, T. (1983). *Use Both Sides of Your Brain*. New York: E.P. Dutton.

Buzan, T. & Buzan, B. (1994). *The Mind Map Book: How to Use Radiant Thinking to Maximize Your Brain's Untapped Potential*. New York: E.P. Dutton.

Margulies, N. (1991). *Mapping Inner Space: Learning and Teaching Mind Mapping*. Tucson, AZ: Zephyr Press.

Wycoff, J. (1991). *Mindmapping: Your Personal Guide to Exploring Creativity and Problem-Solving*. New York: Berkley Books.

Closing a Lesson

An outstanding lesson can be spoiled with a poor ending. Remember that students are most likely to remember the first and last things that happen in class. For this reason it is essential to give careful thought to the ending of each lesson. If you think of each lesson as your gift to your students, the ending is the final ribbon on the package. A good ending allows the student to connect what was learned in a lesson with their previous knowledge.

An effective closure provides students with a sense of accomplishment. It helps them reflect on what they have learned in a lesson and to integrate new learnings with their previous knowledge. The ending also provides an opportunity to plant seeds of curiosity for the next lesson. Each activity should be followed by some processing experience to allow students to reflect on what they have learned. The challenge is to present interesting, creative closure activities that keep students actively involved rather than serve as a cue to pack up their books. Here are some suggestions for providing effective closure to your lessons.

➤ Make a commitment to save time to give each lesson proper closure. Shouting the next day's assignment to your class as they rush out the door is ineffective. Allotting five to ten minutes of each class period for closure and debriefing is a valuable investment. Think of your lesson as a gift to your students; the ending is the bow on the package. It ties the whole experience together. It adds the finishing touch to your masterpiece.

➤ Have students draw three balloons on a blank sheet of paper. In each balloon they are to write one important thing they learned in today's class. Have the students then pair with another and share what they wrote. It is a subtle way of encouraging them to review and reflect on what has happened during that lesson. (Of course, don't tell them it is review or they may disengage their brains from the activity!)

➤ If you began the class with a question, you might now solicit their answers. Do they think differently about the topic now than they did at the beginning? Have they reassessed any assumptions?

➤ Design a guided visualization. Leave parts open-ended, such as the best solution to a problem. Process their visualizations in small groups or as a whole-class activity.

➤ Allow one student to interview another about what was learned in the lesson.

➤ Place a cartoon on the overhead projector. Always read the cartoon section of the newspaper with an eye for any cartoons that might pertain to any of your lessons. Enlarge them on the photocopier and make them into transparencies. Let a student color them with colored markers.

➤ Ask all students to jot down one idea from the lesson they most want to remember. Allow a minute for reflection, then solicit ideas from various members of the class. As an alternative you can have them share in pairs or small groups. Or you could give students topics and have them generate answers and use a *Jeopardy* format for teams to generate appropriate questions.

➤ Use a crossword puzzle that incorporates key concepts, names, or vocabulary included in the day's lesson. You can easily create crossword puzzles with inexpensive computer software such as *Crossword Magic* (L & S Computerware) or *Crossword Creator* (Centron Software Technologies). You may let students work in pairs or have them work alone for three minutes, then they are free to help one another.

➤ Connect this lesson with prior learnings. This might be achieved through reflective questions or as a cooperative learning activity.

➤ Provide some opportunity for application. Structure an activity that encourages reality-testing a new skill or concept. Ideally they should receive immediate feedback on their success.

➤ If you have been teaching a controversial topic, have pairs of students do a forced field analysis of the topic. They draw a line down the middle of the page. On one side they list all the arguments for and on the other side all the agruments against the proposition. You might summarize their grids as one large chart on the board.

➤ Let students write a letter to themselves to encourage goal setting and self-monitoring of progress. Have students answer three sentence stems on a sheet of paper: (1) One thing I am doing well and will continue to do is ____. (2) One thing I will start doing in the next month is ____. (3) One thing I will stop doing the next month is ____. You may substitute other questions or statements related to the objectives of your lesson. Students place their completed sentences in envelopes, seal, and write their names on the outside. Collect the envelopes and return them unopened one month (or a longer time period) later.

➤ Have each student write one quiz question about the topic being studied. Collect them and then ask teams of students to respond to the questions in quiz-bowl style.

➤ Provide one or more sentence stems on a transparency or write them on the board. Ones similar to these might be used:

   ➤ I learned…

➤ I was surprised that...

➤ I discovered...

➤ I realized...

➤ I am puzzled about...

➤ I noticed...

➤ I recognize...

➤ I now appreciate...

Give your class two to three minutes to complete any one or two of the stems. Solicit several from volunteers. Be sure to thank contributors for offering their ideas.

Let students draw mind maps summarizing the content from the previous lesson. After individual students have developed their mind maps of the topic, ask them to join another person and combine their two separate mind maps into one. After several minutes redirect each pair to join another pair and again combine their mind maps into one. An option is to finally have all the students then gather around one large sheet of newsprint (or tape four regular sheets of newsprint together to form a gigantic one). Write the topic in a circle in the middle of the paper and give them the task of compiling a final mind map that includes all the ideas generated on their individual mind maps.

Some teachers have employed the mind map as an assessment device. Students complete mind maps to reflect their understandings of complex concepts. All students should be taught the mind-mapping process as an aid to note-taking.

➤ End with a teaser or promo for the next day's lesson. The "Coming Attractions" hook leaves students in suspense, and enhances their motivation to show up next time. Be creative; borrow from television and theater promos. You might pose a couple of startling questions that will be addressed next time. Pose an intriguing problem or challenge. Make a promise. Exaggeration is permitted. Whatever you do, do it with enthusiasm.

➤ Ask each student to write down on a blank sheet of paper one thing he or she learned about the topic today. After everyone has finished writing, instruct them to wad up the paper and throw it across the room. Each person picks up one and reads it aloud. Assign a volunteer to collect all the papers with the wastebasket.

➤ Of course, remind them if there is a test or assignment due or they need to bring special materials to the next class. It is also important to add a word of encouragement if the day's lesson has been particularly difficult for many students. Acknowledge their efforts and successes. Thank them for working so hard. You might even invite them to give themselves a standing ovation.

Putting More Pizzazz in Your Presentations

Making presentations is an inescapable part of the teaching profession: class lectures, inservice workshops, parent open houses, faculty reports, board of education updates, and community service organization speeches. The person who can give a lively, interesting stand-up presentation is in demand.

While lecturing is only one tool in your instructional kit, teacher talk is a vital part of any classroom. Even those who employ a workshop approach must clarify, give directions, help process experiences, and share information. Great speakers are not born but made—through practice, reflection, feedback, and effort. Remember the great Greek orator Demosthenes began with a speech impediment, yet strove to become a competent public speaker. Many actors and politicians overcame shyness to confidently address hundreds. With determination you can become a better public speaker. Here are a few suggestions to help.

VOICE

➤ Tape record yourself teaching a variety of different kinds of lessons. Try to listen to yourself as objectively as possible. Is your voice soft, drowned out by background noises? Is the pitch reasonably pleasing? Note the speed at which you speak. Is the pace so fast that words jumble together? Do you occasionally mumble? Do you fill gaps with "okay" or "you know"? Do you clip the end of some words (e.g., "goin'" for "going")? Is there a nasal quality to your voice?

➤ Varying the pace and pitch of your presentation voice is an effective way to avoid slipping into a monotone style. A current mannerism of many young people is to continually raise the pitch at the end of each sentence, making them all sound like questions. This can be most distracting and makes the speaker sound very unsure of what he or she is saying. Equally distracting is dropping the volume at the end of each sentence.

➤ Be aware of the messages you send simply with your voice, independent of the content you are uttering. Your speaking style may communicate confidence, passion, excitement, enthusiasm, and joy, or it may convey boredom, self-doubt, or fatigue. Always remember that your students will echo your emotional tone.

➤ Is your throat sore at the end of the day? While this is not uncommon among teachers the first couple weeks of school, if it persists it may be a sign that you are using your voice mechanism improperly. Consult with a speech therapist for training in more effective and less harmful use of your voice.

➤ When talking in front of the class, always project your voice as though you were talking to the person in the remotest corner of the room. However, speaking too loudly is also unpleasant for your listeners. Some variation in your voice level is most effective.

➤ Use pauses for impact. Slight pauses refocus students' attention. Do avoid fillers, such as "um," "uh," "duh," and "er."

NONVERBAL COMMUNICATION

All teachers should be students of effective nonverbal communication. A rich understanding of the nonverbal level of expression will allow you to more accurately read students' messages, to remain congruent and accurate in the messages you send, and to avoid negative or incongruent messages you might inadvertently send to others. You are continually expressing nonverbal messages to everyone around you. Indeed, research suggests the overwhelming portion of what you communicate is expressed nonverbally, not verbally. Here are a few tips on using nonverbal communication more effectively in teaching.

➤ Avoid leaning against the lectern or grasping it with a death grip. As much as possible, move away from the lectern. It is generally best to keep moving while providing whole-class instruction, such as lecturing. Not only does that provide better monitoring of student behavior, but you are more likely to be animated while moving than when remaining stationary.

➤ Teaching the whole class while seated at your desk encourages you to speak in a monotone with subdued gestures, two traits that convey a lack of enthusiasm. Move about the room, but don't bound around like a gazelle. You'll wear your students out trying to follow you.

➤ Be aware of using the same gestures repeatedly. Students may begin to mimic such "nonverbal tics."

➤ Strive to achieve a relaxed, natural posture while talking. Too many as well as too few gestures tend to inhibit your message.

➤ Talk facing your class; avoid talking at the chalkboard or the screen. Not only is it ineffective speaking style, but you will be less able to monitor your students' behavior with your back to them.

➤ While there are cultural differences among different ethnic groups, generally it is best to offer eye contact with your audience. Eye contact conveys that you are interested in the listener. Keep your eyes moving around the classroom, holding your gaze upon clusters of four or five students at a time for three to five seconds before moving to the next group. From ten feet away this provides the illusion of individual eye contact, even though you aren't maintaining direct eye contact with any one of the students in the cluster. This is not a natural practice; it takes concerted effort to do it naturally.

➤ When calling upon a student, avoid pointing. Rather, gesture with your palm up, a more inviting message.

➤ A smile is seen by many as a visual hug; it conveys warmth and acceptance. The smile is likely your most powerful social reinforcer. Remember, a genuine smile is conveyed as much with the eyes as with the mouth. Practice in front of the mirror to achieve the twinkle in the eyes.

➤ Occasionally videotape a class. Turn the volume down and just observe your nonverbals. Do you like what you see? Are you directing eye contact equally around the room or only teaching to the students in the front center? Do you look animated or bored? Do you project confidence and enthusiasm through your non-verbal expressions? Do you look relaxed or stiff? Do you exhibit nervous gestures, such as rattling coins in your pocket, lip biting, rubbing your nose, twirling your hair, stroking your beard, popping the top on your magic marker, or playing with your watch or jewelry? These can be very distracting mannerisms. Chances are you have one or more such habits of which you are unaware. That is why videotaping is essential. The camera does not lie. Although you may be unaware of your idiosyncratic gestures, your students aren't. And likely will begin to joke about them among themselves. One of students' favorite pastimes is mimicking the quirks of their teachers. Don't make it too easy for them!

IMPROVING YOUR SPEAKING EFFECTIVENESS

➤ Teach to a variety of sensory modalities. Employ interesting visuals to augment your lecture.

➤ Use vocabulary that all students can understand. While you may want to introduce new vocabulary as part of your lessons, be sure you define unfamiliar terms. Your goal is to help them understand, not impress them with your expansive vocabulary. Simple, direct language usually will be easier to follow.

➤ Consider joining Toastmasters International. There are chapters in almost every community. It is an excellent way to improve your speaking style. They provide outstanding training programs and valuable practice with a supportive audience.

➤ If you are not sure of the pronunciation of a new word you are introducing in your lesson, look it up in the dictionary before class. Remember, you are serving as a model and your mistakes may be copied by your students.

➤ Don't let your dress upstage your message. While wild, flashy costumes may make an individual expression of who you are, your students may be paying more attention to your fashion statement than the content you are trying to teach.

Homework That Helps

Homework, like any other instructional technique, is only a means to an end. Its value is determined by how effectively it enhances learning. If it does neither, it is busy work and serves little constructive purpose. Many critics argue that too little homework is assigned and that learning time can be increased cheaply by requiring more homework. A recent national study emphasized that more than two-thirds of seventeen-year-olds reported spending less than one hour a night on homework. It is not surprising that the same study revealed that higher achieving students spent more time per week on homework than their classmates and that hours of television viewing and time spent on homework were inversely related.

How much homework you should assign is a complex question. The answer depends upon your students' age, abilities, and habits, and your instructional objectives. It is probably reasonable to expect students to spend an hour per day on homework by the end of elementary school. High school students who have study halls should be able to complete two or three hours of work per day out of class. When students have several teachers, some coordination is needed among the faculty on the homework schedule. Otherwise, some students may end up with five or six hours of homework in an evening, which is an unreasonable amount. Students, like teachers, do need some rest and recreation. Merely assigning more homework will not guarantee learning gains. Assignments that are not completed or are done incorrectly are of little benefit. Like seatwork, homework assignments that are too difficult or misunderstood will prove counterproductive.

Activities such as reading the text usually can be done out of class, preserving class time for those activities that cannot be done independently. Homework provides a valuable opportunity to practice and reinforce new skills. It also provides an opportunity to connect new learnings with the outside world. Homework also serves an assessment function, providing the teacher with information on the success of his or her teaching.

Homework can be assigned to provide remedial instruction to students who lag in skill development. When the purpose of homework is to provide remediation, giving the same "blanket" assignment to all students is hardly justified, as students progress at different rates. The assignment of homework provides the golden opportunity for individualization, although it does require advance planning. Although reading assignments, short essay answers, and drill problems comprise the bulk of homework assignments, long-range projects seem to be of greater benefit. Such projects encourage students to use higher level cognitive skills in gathering information, analyzing data, planning sequences, and synthesizing a variety of skills. Another valuable function of homework is to allow parents an active role in their child's education.

Last, do not use homework as a punishment. That practice only communicates to students that homework is an unpleasant activity to be avoided. Such negative attitudes will not benefit either the teacher or the students.

INTERESTING HOMEWORK

Used effectively, homework reinforces practice and synthesis of skills and concepts developed in class. When asked by his father whether he had any homework, a boy replied, "No, the teachers ran out of fluid." This anecdote reveals the lack of imagination of many teachers in assigning homework.

Professional journals, in-service programs, and other teachers are sources for gathering ideas on worthwhile homework assignments. A bit of imagination and planning can yield assignments with high-interest value and can accomplish skill development. Here are a few ideas tried successfully by other teachers.

- ➤ Write a new myth
- ➤ Conduct experiments
- ➤ Do volunteer work
- ➤ Use math skills to measure common objects around the home
- ➤ Plan a trip; include itinerary and costs
- ➤ Develop a budget
- ➤ Write a computer program
- ➤ Observe and record birds, traffic, or weather
- ➤ Plan a week's balanced menu
- ➤ Trace family trees to personalize history

- Interview an older person about a historical event he or she experienced
- Plan and produce a film or skit
- Write new endings to old stories
- Teach someone a skill
- Keep a journal
- Invent a game; teach it to the class
- Write a handbook for consumers
- Research a topic and create a bulletin board display
- Interview people about their jobs
- Develop a creative solution to a problem
- Develop an advertising campaign to promote a product, solution, or idea
- Attend a public meeting
- Design an ideal house, car, school, or government
- Take sides on an issue; prepare a debate
- Design a costume
- Draw a map of the neighborhood or yard
- Develop a case study
- Prepare a photo essay on a community problem
- Collect specimens of rocks, leaves, and wood
- Draw a political cartoon
- Participate in a political campaign

Such "fun with a purpose" assignments can greatly increase students' motivation to learn. The relevance of the skills you are teaching becomes apparent. They must be not only fun but also must have a legitimate educational purpose to justify their use.

MAKING ASSIGNMENTS

The first week of school, clarify your expectations regarding homework. Will work that is not finished in class automatically become homework? If you do not make a specific assignment for the next class, will students be expected to read in their textbooks or review previous work? The procedures for assigning homework must be taught as part of the classroom routine.

Do not compete with student noise when giving oral directions. Stop talking and wait for their attention. Otherwise, you will end up repeating the directions.

Save time and stress by putting directions for assignments on the board. If you prefer, cover them with a map until you are ready to discuss them. Some teachers instruct students to immediately take their seats and copy the assignments into their notebooks, without waiting for the bell to ring. Many teachers choose to put all assignments on ditto sheets for distribution. This minimizes later student remarks such as, "I didn't hear you" or "I didn't know you wanted it done that way." Be sure to write clearly. Save the master copy for use next year. If any problems of understanding arise in completing the assignment, make a note on the master to refine the directions next year. Avoid shouting the next day's assignment over students gathering books as they scramble for the door.

Students are more likely to complete homework assignments when they are highly structured and the directions are very specific. In assigning major projects, displaying completed sample projects will clarify your expectations and save time answering questions. Some teachers take pictures or slides of completed products for next year's demonstration.

It may be helpful to reserve specific days for regular assignments. For example, on Tuesdays students are to read the next chapter in the text; Thursdays they review the drill questions at the end of the chapter. You will have fewer assignments to plan every week and students will be less likely to forget what their assignment is.

Try to be creative in designing some homework tasks that will be fun as well as educationally sound. Experiments, interviews, math games, and active assignments tend to have a higher completion rate. One technique for creating suspense in the next day's lesson is to give students an unusual assignment but not explain its purpose. For example, ask them to count the number of light bulbs in their house or to bring in the next day an empty egg carton or a baby picture. Of course, that activity must be incorporated into the next day's lesson.

Early in the year communicate with your students' parents what role you wish them to play in helping with their child's homework. This can be done in a newsletter and again at any open houses scheduled. Some send a special sheet home to parents on "How to Help Your Child With Homework."

THE HOMEWORK LOTTERY

One strategy used successfully by teachers at all grade levels for motivating students to complete homework assignments is the lottery. The idea is relatively simple and easy to implement, yet can encourage otherwise apathetic students to complete their work. All students who successfully complete their homework for the day put their names on small cards that are dropped in a jar or box. On Friday, a drawing is held, selecting one or more winners.

What the winners receive is quite secondary. Just the recognition of having their names drawn is rewarding for most students. Most will value a privilege, such as being first in line all week or using the tape recorder or computer. Some teachers become proficient at scrounging for freebies such as tickets, posters, coupons, and prizes. Students soon learn that the more times their names are in the jar, the greater are their chances of winning. Of course, you must ensure that the only way to get their names in the jar is to complete their homework. It may be wise to specify a criterion of correctness for work submitted if students begin handing in hurriedly completed assignments.

One prize valued by students is a coupon good for one night of no homework. Instead of handing in homework, the holder may redeem the coupon. If the student did the assignments necessary to win the coupon, one night of missed work will not likely be irreparable.

COLLECTING AND GRADING HOMEWORK

Have homework teams with one student in each team responsible for collecting everyone's work and reporting to the teacher who did not complete their assignments.

HANDLING MAKE-UP WORK

Whenever possible put directions for assignments, projects, or homework in writing, being as explicit in your directions as possible. You might also notify parents that this is the practice as well. This avoids possible misunderstandings as well as saving you time in giving directions to absent students. Be sure to save a copy for next year.

Every teacher faces the challenge of getting students who were absent caught up with missed assignments. Over the course of the year this task can consume huge amounts of time that might better be allocated to other duties. Here are some ideas veteran teachers have found helpful in dealing with this problem:

➤ For each subject or class you teach, attach a clipboard to the wall. Each day hang copies of the next day's assignments on the clipboard. Absent students (or students who lose theirs) can pick them up as needed.

➤ For projects in which a product (e.g., drawing, model, report) is to be produced, first demonstrate what is to be done, then post directions along with a sample. Save some of the best projects to use next year as models. This helps clarify your expectations and gives students an idea of what level of work is expected.

➤ At the beginning of the year assign each student a partner. Have them exchange phone numbers. If one partner is absent, the other is responsible for gathering assignments, handouts, or materials and helping the partner catch up when he or she returns. Ninety percent of your students will successfully handle this. You may still have to help the other ten percent get caught up, but this saves you a huge amount of time dealing with the others.

➤ Make a large calendar with numbers 1 to 31 for the days of the month. Laminate it so it can be reused. Each day write the day's assignments. Absent students can check missed assignments quickly.

➤ As you give oral directions to the class, tape record them. Pencil the day's date and class on the tape and file in a box. Students who are absent that day listen to the taped directions when they return.

➤ If there are handouts involved for make-up work, put the date on them and the student's name. Then, on a designated spot on the bulletin board, tack the handouts and/or any assignment for each student absent that day.

➤ Develop a homework form to record the exact assignments for absent students. The student's partner or another responsible student should fill out the form with the missing assignments.

➤ Keep a homework notebook. Have a separate section for each class. Each day record what work was done in class and any homework assignment with any special directions. Also include copies of any handouts needed. When students return after being absent, they are responsible for checking the homework notebook.

➤ Tape five small cardboard boxes together to make a large mailbox with five compartments. Label the dividers with the days of the schoolweek. As you give out each day's assignment, place any leftover photocopies into that day's slot. When students return from being absent, they are responsible for gathering the necessary materials from the mailbox.

Bulletin Boards

➤ Make two to three covers for bulletin boards at once, placing one on top of the other. When it is time to change displays, simply pull off the top display, revealing the next one beneath it.

➤ At the end of the school year whenever students have some free time, let them create a bulletin board for you. It will be ready for the fall, welcoming the new class back to school. You might want to have them cover it with newspaper to protect it during the summer.

➤ Rather than repeatedly correcting students for the same errors, create a bulletin board display explaining the error and the correct procedures.

➤ From a roll of colored paper, tear a piece to the approximate size of the bulletin board. Mold to the bulletin board by hand and temporarily pin it to the board. With a small pin or razor knife, tear or cut along edges to remove the excess paper. You are ready to place objects and letters on the board.

➤ You need not decorate every bulletin board. Use blank ones for announcements, posters, student work, newspapers, magazine articles, etc. Use some class time to have students brainstorm ideas for bulletin boards.

➤ Generate graphics and letters with computers. Special software is readily available in most schools for printing banners and posters. Use letters of various sizes. Large ones grab the students' attention and get them to read the rest.

➤ Give your students time and materials to cut out bulletin board letters of various styles and sizes. Store these in envelopes for future use.

➤ Project coloring book images onto large sheets of paper taped to the wall. Trace and color the images to make large characters to include in your bulletin boards.

➤ Use some bulletin boards to teach or reinforce a skill or concept.

➤ Reserve one section of a bulletin board for students to use to post interesting articles, invitations, unusual quotations, pictures, cartoons, and other items of interest.

➤ Experiment with three-dimensional bulletin boards. Objects such as feathers, dried flowers, discarded ties, masks, hats, and costume jewelry can all be incorporated into your bulletin boards. Strive to use multiple textures to make the bulletin boards more attractive.

➤ Develop interactive bulletin boards. Use pockets and flaps to hide answers to questions displayed on the board. Post a daily question, riddle, or puzzle for students to explore when they enter the room. Some displays might pose a question to which students write their answers or estimate in a block on the bulletin board. These are especially valuable if they relate to a topic to be studied that day.

➤ Hang a clothesline across one wall of your room. Attach students' papers to the line with clothespins.

➤ Velcro or flannel boards can be incorporated into manipulative boards that invite students to experiment. Bulletin boards can be dynamic, inviting students to interact and reform the display. Self-checking questions can be displayed with answers covered by flaps.

➤ Think of creative materials and ideas to incorporate into unique borders. Discarded fabric, game pieces, silk flowers, ribbons, leaves, greeting cards, or photographs can all be incorporated into attractive borders.

➤ To help maintain interest, alter some part of a bulletin board every day or once a week. Changing a featured quotation or startling statistic each day keeps the students motivated to keep looking at it. Remember, a bulletin board is more than just wall decoration. It can be a great motivational device and instructional aid.

Assessing Student Performance

Some forms of assessment and grading of students' progress are inescapable parts of every teacher's job. Assessment means gathering information about the level of performance or achievement of individual students. Evaluation is the process of making judgments about that information. Evaluation involves comparing a student's achievement with a peer group (norm referencing) or with a set standard (criterion referencing). (*Norm-referenced grades* are those calculated by comparing an individual student's performance relative to the rest of the class. *Criterion-referenced grades* are determined by assessing how well a student has met a specific set of standards, independent of how well anyone else did.) Grading is the subsequent assigning and reporting of a symbol (letter, number, or category) to the evaluation.

Feedback on performance is crucial for improvement. Hence, assessment and some form of evaluation are prerequisites to effective teaching. Teachers' evaluations communicate their judgments of how well their students are performing. Ideally, student assessments also provide teachers feedback on how well they are succeeding and diagnose areas needing additional attention. Some assessment of student progress is essential in determining whether instruction is successful or not in the lesson's objectives.

Grading students' work meets a different set of educational and social purposes. For some students, grades motivate and control behavior (mostly those students already doing well). Grades make categorization of students easier—for promotion, selection, and grouping. Parents also expect feedback from the school on how well their children are performing in school. Traditional grading schemes (A, B, C, D, and F or Satisfactory/Unsatisfactory) still prevail, largely from tradition. There is such variation among teachers, subjects, and schools that deciphering the meaning of a "B" received by one student provides little information about that student's level of achievement.

There are risks in the assignment of grades to student performance. Traditional, norm-referenced grades, approximating the normal curve, probably work very well for the top one-third. They can develop positive academic self-esteem and generally reap the bulk of rewards doled out in schools. The lowest third, however, suffer from overtly competitive grading systems. They enter an environment each day that communicates, "You are a loser. You are valued less than others." Howard Gardner suggests that these students may possess important intelligences (musical, spatial, interpersonal, intrapersonal, or bodily-kinesthetic). Unfortunately, our schools tend to only value and reward the logical-mathematical and linguistic intelligences. It should not be surprising that research reveals students who drop out of school experience an immediate increase in self-esteem.

It is advisable to base student evaluations upon a variety of measures: assignments, projects, exhibits, tests, quizzes, observations, journals, presentations, products, performances, self-evaluations, and peer evaluations.

Though assessment and evaluation play important roles in the learning process, there is little research evidence that grades themselves have much educational value. Yet, the practice persists and most every teacher is mandated to submit a grade (usually a letter) for each student at the end of periodic grading terms. Here are some suggestions to make that process as painless and as fair as possible.

GRADING

Remember that teachers grading the same materials show a variability of grades, especially for essays and other subjectively rated products. Different teachers employ different criteria in assigning grades; even when the same criteria are used, teachers may differ on their judgment of how well those criteria are met.

Teachers' grades reflect many factors besides students' academic achievement: students' efforts, persistence, classroom deportment, and a host of subtle biases that can creep into subjective assessments. Research studies have found each of the following biases to influence teachers' judgments of essays:

➤ Students with neat handwriting get higher marks on essay tests, especially when the teacher has neat handwriting.

➤ A halo effect exists in the assignment of grades. Students who performed well on previous essays tend to be rated higher on subsequent ones, even if the quality diminishes.

➤ Longer essays get rated higher than shorter essays, even when the shorter essays are better in argument, organization, and grammar.

➤ Students with common names (Sally, Mike, Jane) get rated higher than students with unusual names (Elmo, Zeke, Evangeline).

➤ Students deemed "attractive" tend to get rated higher than students rated as homely or unattractive, even when the essays were identical.

An objective view of the research reveals grades do somewhat predict one thing: future grades. And the higher up the educational ladder, the less accurately do grades predict grades at the next level. However, grades have proven of little value in predicting any criteria of post-school success in any field.

➤ Involve students in the grading process to minimize disagreements over grades. Make sure they fully understand how grades are assigned.

➤ Have students immediately grade some in-class assignments for immediate feedback. Sometimes it is valuable to allow them time to improve their effort after the self-assessment.

➤ An elementary school teacher may use recess time for grading the previous period's papers. The teacher goes around to each pupil's desk and grades all the papers at once. Upon returning from recess, the students receive immediate reinforcement of their work. This saves time at night, and also saves the time needed for passing out and collecting papers.

➤ It is not essential for the teacher to correct every student assignment. As much as possible, allow students to swap and grade papers. Spot check to prevent cheating.

➤ For seatwork or some homework, provide scoring keys that the students use to score their own work and add up their point totals for the week. Spot check a few papers.

➤ For checking students' homework, just assign a set number of points to an assignment if it is complete and on time. Let the students check their own answers in class as a whole group. This allows homework to be a learning experience and saves time grading papers.

➤ Require students to keep a page in their notebook on which they record each test or quiz grade when they receive it. That way they always have a tally of their scores and need not continually check with you.

➤ Some teachers find it more efficient to keep the cumulative total of each student's test and quiz points. When entering a score, add it to the previous total. You might mark this new sum on the student's test paper. You'll save time at the end of the semester by not having to refigure each student's grade. This is an especially easy task if you use a computer grade-keeping system.

➤ Stagger the due dates for major projects, papers, and examinations. It can be overwhelming if you receive a barrage of paper. You'll manage your time more efficiently if the assignments are spaced. Students who have you for more than one class will also appreciate it and probably do better work.

➤ It is also a good idea to insist that students keep all graded papers until the end of the term. If there is a discrepancy in what you have recorded in your grade book and what they believe they have earned, they have the final proof.

➤ Some teachers have each student turn in a cassette tape with their name on it along with their writing activities. The teacher records comments about the written work as they read it. Students may take the tape home to listen to it or do so on a recorder in class during free time.

➤ Some teachers assign each student a number. It may correspond to the one appearing beside their name in the grade book. Each assignment or test must have that number included. It is much quicker to find that number when entering scores than to hunt the student's name.

➤ One advantage of seating students alphabetically is that when papers are collected, they are already in alphabetical order, making it easier to record in your grade book.

➤ To keep clear records in the small spaces that are in most teachers' grade books code many events that influence the grade. For example:

"A" in corner of the box means absent

Outlining the box means the work was handed in late

"D" means the assignment was done over

"S" means parent signature on the paper (*Contributed by Betsy Redd*)

➤ Generally it is better to record test and quiz grades as numbers, not letters. Numbers are easier and quicker to convert into grades at the end of the term.

➤ When grading multiple-choice examinations use a computer scoring system if one is available. If not, develop answer sheets and a master key you hold over the answer sheet to facilitate scoring.

➤ Require students to double space all essays or other written assignments. That provides more room for comments than just using the margin.

➤ Develop checklist forms for evaluating essays and other products. List the specific criteria you are assessing and provide a separate rating for each criterion. Some criteria might be weighted higher than others. If you are only concerned with whether the feature is included in the assignment, a simple checkmark beside that item will suffice. Structure the form to minimize the amount of writing required of you.

➤ Teach students to edit and revise their papers before turning them in to save you time of repeatedly reading rough drafts. Let them work in cooperative groups to help each other edit each other's papers.

➤ Some elementary teachers send home a weekly work folder with each student. The parents read the week's projects and then sign and return the folder with the student. This is a valuable way to maintain effective home-school communication.

TESTS AND QUIZZES

➤ The most effective teachers assess student learning often. This discourages student procrastination and cramming and provides a more accurate assessment of student learning.

➤ Strive for higher order levels of thinking in your questions. The biggest disadvantage of multiple-choice questions is the over-reliance upon rote memorization. One research study found that of all the things a student learns, 80% is forgotten in one year. Most of what is forgotten are facts memorized for one quiz or test.

➤ Develop a file for your old tests and worksheets. A large three-ring binder or manila file folder will work. When a test is used, jot notes on the top as to which questions should be replaced because they are too hard or too easy.

➤ If you give diagnostic tests at the beginning of the year, code the test items related to each skill area. Students then receive a checklist indicating their deficiencies. The checklist can also reference pages in the textbook. On the final exam, students only have to complete those areas in which they did not show mastery on the pretest. (*Contributed by Barb Wagner*)

➤ Some teachers choose to make the first test relatively easy to build students' confidence.

➤ Run two-page tests back to back and grade all of the same page at once. When done with the whole stack, just turn it over and begin grading the other side. This way you don't waste time turning all the pages over before you can start grading the second page. Also, you don't have to flip the pages back to page one to begin scoring. Just turn the stack over again. Tests run double-sided do not consume time with collating and stapling. Answer sheets help with multiple-page objective tests. You may only have to grade one sheet instead of flipping through several pages. You can then save the test copies for future use and don't have to run them off again. (*Suggested by Barb Steinhauser*)

➤ Use publishers' textbook tests when possible, but feel free to adapt them to your objectives.

➤ Use as few items as necessary to assess a skill or knowledge. Why use a 50-item test if 20 items will give you the same information?

➤ Some teachers don't give make-up exams except for extended absences. By allowing each student to throw out his or her lowest grade a single missed test does not penalize a student.

➤ Develop a computer test file. A variety of software programs are available to permit the development of a test bank. Tests and quizzes are easily and quickly generated. With some you can even save performance data, allowing you to eliminate ineffective questions.

➤ Do try to include questions of a higher cognitive level. Items merely memorized tend to be forgotten as soon as the test is over.

➤ Provide adequate notice and help in preparing your students for examinations.

➤ Let students review in study teams before an exam.

➤ Set up a self-checking station for students to grade their own multiple-choice quizzes and homework assignments. Have a laminated answer key and colored marking pens available. Students are not allowed to bring their own pens or pencils to the checking station and only one student at a time is allowed at the station. When done, the corrected work is left in a tray at the station. As you record grades, spot check the work for accuracy and honesty. Research shows students are generally quite accurate in their self-scoring.

➤ Use carboned evaluation sheets to rate the student's essay or product. Keep one and return the other to the student to keep.

➤ Experiment with giving collaborative tests. Groups of three students get to work together on the test. You might randomly assign groups each time or carefully select a stratified sample so one high- and one low-ability student get included in each group. To succeed, a cooperative climate must already be established in your room.

➤ Give some attention to reducing test anxiety among your students. One tactic for reducing test anxiety and helping students prepare for an examination is to permit them to ask any question about the test that may be answered "yes" or "no." (*Contributed by Barb Wagner*)

➤ Immediately before an examination lead the class in some relaxation exercises: focused breathing, positive affirmations, stretching, perhaps even shoulder rubs.

➤ Provide adequate feedback on students' test performance. Help them understand where they erred and to correct mistakes and misunderstandings. Any assessment should help a student learn.

➤ Some teachers use cooperative learning groups to take weekly quizzes together and then individual final examinations. The cooperative group may then meet after the examinations are scored to help each other understand questions missed.

➤ If any students are very upset about their exam scores, offer to meet with them the next day. Give them some time to cool off first. Make it a policy to never argue with a student about a grade in front of the class. Nobody wins, and the results usually will only be unpleasant.

➤ If a large number of students do poorly on an exam, reconsider its worth. While it is tempting to blame large numbers of failures upon incompetent, apathetic students, sometimes it is the instruction or assessment that was defective. Try to remain objective.

GRADE CONTRACTS

The grade contract is an option used by many teachers, especially at the middle- and high-school levels. A contract is an agreement between two parties stipulating that when a specified event(s) has occurred, a particular positive consequence will follow. As completion of the grade contract is dependent upon attainment of a preset standard of performance rather than relative position within a group, it is a criterion-referenced form of evaluation, rather than a norm-referenced one.

In its most common form, the teacher specifies a relatively small number of assignments that are required of all students, with each higher level grade requiring one or more additional tasks. Generally, the student signs a contract at the start of the course for an A, B, or C. The students who contract for an A, but only fulfill the required tasks for a lower grade, present a dilemma for the teacher. Should these students be penalized for failing to reach the contracted goal, or rewarded for the performance level that they successfully attained? Another option is to specify the tasks required for each grade category, but not to require students to identify their target grade ahead of time. At the end of the grading period, students receive the grade corresponding with the contract tasks attained.

The contracted tasks reflect the expressed or hidden objectives of the course. There may be other goals the teacher wishes to attain, but students will tend to emphasize the ones being evaluated.

THE MULTIPLE-OPTION GRADE CONTRACT

The multiple-option grade contract is an extension of the grade contract system that maximizes the advantages of a criterion-referenced contract system while eliminating some of the deficiencies encountered with standard grade contracts. The model presented here is a flexible grade contract that has been used successfully at a variety of grade levels and subjects. The multiple-option grade contract is flexible to incorporate the teaching style, needs, and objectives of the teacher, while also incorporating differences in learning styles and individual talents of students.

At the first class meeting, students are given a handout describing the terms of the contract. The minimum number of points needed to qualify for each letter grade is specified. A sample contract might list the following cut-off points:

100 points = A
80 points = B
60 points = C

It is best not to specify a target grade of "D." It often gets a laugh to suggest that those shooting for a "D" should come see you later and you'll negotiate a number. Rarely will anyone ever take you up on such an offer. A grade of "C" is identified as the minimum competency level for your class objectives.

Each week students receive a set of from two to ten activities and projects. These assignments are keyed to the course objectives. Successful completion of each task is accepted as mastery of a particular objective or skill. Some activities, reflecting vital skills or concepts, may be required of everyone. There may be alternate means available for demonstrating attainment of the same skill. Many learning tasks are optional; students choose those that best reflect their individual needs, interests, and learning styles. The fact that students have active choices, even among a limited set of alternatives, enhances motivation.

The total number of points available should exceed the sum required for an A, usually at least double. The contract is cumulative and positive. The student receives points for achievement and effort. Points are not subtracted for poor performance; rather, nothing is added to the student's total.

Students are encouraged to propose assignment options that will demonstrate their learning. Class presentations, reports, book reviews, and interviews are all valid learning experiences that should be encouraged. The student and teacher can negotiate a mutually acceptable point value for such assignments. It is essential that at least an approximate point value be negotiated as part of the contract.

Individual assignments may be evaluated "pass/fail" indicating that minimal criteria were achieved, or a student's assignment may be prorated and thus receive partial credit. If a "pass/fail" assessment is used, you may give students the option of redoing assignments until they fulfill minimum criteria for success. (These criteria can be set quite high as the students have the option of taking more time to attain the level of success.)

It is possible to grade tests and quizzes on a point basis. They are given a specified point value, such as 5, 10, or 20 points. Students are rewarded for high performance. Poor performance is not rewarded, but one bad test score does not doom the student for the duration of the term. As the points are cumulative, not an average, test anxiety is decreased.

The assignments must be clearly specified for the contract to be successful. Students should not have to guess what you expect. What are the minimal criteria for success? It helps to have high-quality sample products or assignments received from previous classes. Students will not perceive the contract as fair if they have to constantly rewrite because they guessed wrong in predicting what you wanted. To discourage procrastination, there should be specific deadlines for all the assignments.

The multiple-option grade contract places the responsibility for grades upon the students. The relationship between performance and grades is apparent. Students always know how many points they have accumulated and how many are needed to attain the grade sought.

The flexible grade contract provides an opportunity to individualize instruction and assignments. A menu is presented to the students. Essential skills of experiences may be required of all students, but in many instances alternative routes to a goal exist. Students may be able to demonstrate mastery of a skill or concept in a variety of ways.

This method of grading forces the teacher to carefully reflect upon the desired course goals. In what way will students be different when they leave than when they entered this class? How will the teacher know whether students have achieved skills or mastered concepts reflected by the course objectives?

Students are competing against themselves, not their peers. No one's grade is dependent upon how well others in the class perform. The student is striving toward a preset standard of performance.

It is fair. Students know where they stand. They are in control of their destiny. The subjective elements of out-psyching the teacher are minimized. This can allow the teacher to be perceived as a resources person. There are no last-minute surprises. This also minimizes disputes over grades earned.

The primary purpose of grades is to communicate a level of performance. The flexible contract represents a fair and consistent method of evaluating academic accomplishment without damaging the students' self-esteem.

AUTHENTIC ASSESSMENTS

In 1935, the distinguished educator Ralph Tyler proposed an "enlarged concept of student evaluation," encompassing other approaches besides tests and quizzes. He urged teachers to sample learning by collecting products of their efforts throughout the year. That practice has evolved into what is today termed "authentic assessment" which encompasses a range of approaches including portfolio assessment, journals and logs, products, videotapes of performances, and projects.

Authentic assessments have many potential benefits. Diane Hart, in her excellent introduction to authentic assessment, suggested the following benefits:

➤ Students assume an active role in the assessment process. This shift in emphasis may result in reduced test anxiety and enhanced self-esteem.

➤ Authentic assessment can be successfully used with students of varying cultural backgrounds, learning styles, and academic ability.

➤ Tasks used in authentic assessment are more interesting and reflective of students' daily lives.

➤ Ultimately, a more positive attitude toward school and learning may evolve.

➤ Authentic assessment promotes a more student-centered approach to teaching.

➤ Teachers assume a larger role in the assessment process than through traditional testing programs. This involvement is more likely to assure the evaluation process reflects course goals and objectives.

➤ Authentic assessment provides valuable information to the teacher on student progress as well as the success of instruction.

➤ Parents will more readily understand authentic assessments than the abstract percentiles, grade equivalents, and other measures of standardized tests.

Authentic assessments are new to most students. They may be suspicious at first; years of conditioning with paper-pencil tests, searching for the single right answer, are not easily undone. Authentic assessments require a new way of perceiving learning and evaluation. The role of the teacher also changes. Specific assignments or tasks to be evaluated and the assessment criteria need to be clearly identified at the start.

In the beginning it may be best to begin on a small scale. Introduce authentic assessments in one area (for example, on homework assignments) and progress in small steps as students adapt.

Develop a record-keeping system that works for you. Try to keep it simple, allowing students to do as much of the work as feasible.

PORTFOLIO ASSESSMENTS

One form of authentic assessment being widely adapted in schools today is portfolio assessment. Hart, 1994 (p. 23) defines a portfolio as "a container that holds evidence of an individual's skills, ideas, interests, and accomplishments." The ultimate aim in the use of portfolios is to develop independent, self-directed learners. Long-term portfolios provide a more accurate picture of students' specific achievements and progress and the areas of needed attention.

Portfolios make it easier to develop grading schemes that emphasize assessing individual student growth rather than competition with other students. As self-evaluation is an integral part of portfolio assessment, a highly competitive climate will prove counterproductive. Students will be reluctant to focus upon their deficiencies if they believe it will put them at a disadvantage in the competition for the top grades. Often portfolios are used to supplement, not replace, traditional assessment procedures.

➤ Remember, portfolios should be developed by the students, not the teacher. Students should have freedom in selecting items to include in their portfolios. It is advantageous to make the whole portfolio process a collaborative teacher-student effort, with the teacher becoming more of a consultant to the student. The teacher functions more as a coach than a director.

➤ Any item that provides evidence of a student's achievement and growth can be included in a portfolio. Commonly used items include:

    ➤ Examples of written work

    ➤ Journals and logs

- ➤ Standardized inventories
- ➤ Videotapes of student performances
- ➤ Audiotapes of presentations
- ➤ Mind maps and notes
- ➤ Group reports
- ➤ Tests and quizzes
- ➤ Charts, graphs
- ➤ Lists of books read
- ➤ Questionnaire results
- ➤ Peer reviews
- ➤ Self-evaluations

➤ Each item in the portfolio should be dated to facilitate the evaluation of progress through the year.

➤ Typically, teachers hold periodic individual conferences with their students to review their portfolios. During this interview it is important to listen to the students' assessments of the items in their portfolio. The focus of the discussion should be upon the products included in the portfolio. The teacher and student work together to set a limited number of objectives for future work. Strive to achieve a dialogue, not a lecture.

➤ Much of the value of portfolios derives from the students' reflection on which items are worth including in their portfolios.

➤ The portfolios may be kept in folders, file boxes, assigned drawers, or other appropriate containers. Whatever the storage container, it must be readily accessible to the students.

➤ Portfolios are especially helpful at parent conferences. Help the parent examine the portfolio, pointing out evidence of progress and areas of needed improvement.

➤ Be patient. Portfolios are a new concept to most students and parents. There is a learning curve involved in adapting to the process. Experiment to determine what works and feel free to modify as needed.

➤ In some schools students' portfolios are made available to their teachers the following year to aid in diagnosis. A few schools are experimenting with the development of a permanent portfolio that follows the students throughout their total school experience. (This would be separate from their cumulative record folder.) Upon graduation the students would keep their portfolios.

➤ Develop your own teaching portfolio as a means of facilitating your professional development. It also can prove invaluable in tenure assessments and future job searches. Your professional portfolio might include videotapes of successful classes, curriculum materials you have developed, course syllabi, sample lesson plans, professional development goals and objectives, workshop classes attended, publications written, student evaluations, awards, certificates, professional affiliations, principal's and supervisor's evaluations, and your teaching philosophy.

➤ A large three-ring binder is a practical way to organize your portfolios. Use tabs to indicate the various categories. You might occasionally share your portfolio with students to model the processes you are urging them to follow.

PERFORMANCE ASSESSMENT

Performance assessments require students to demonstrate mastery of a skill or procedure by performing it. Performance assessment has long been a part of the curriculum in certain courses. Directly evaluating a student's sewing, welding, dancing, typing, piano playing, or woodworking is not a new concept. Direct assessments have the advantage of greater validity as the objective being assessed is observed directly. Indirect measures, such as a paper-and-pencil test on cooking a soufflé, may not accurately predict how well a person would perform baking a real soufflé. Performance assessments are more useful in assessing complex skills and high-level understanding.

Though not new, the trend toward including live performances and products in educational assessment schemes has grown in recent years. The growing interest in performance or authentic assessments is largely a reaction to the limitations and disparities of paper-pencil tests.

➤ The specific events or activities to be assessed are content specific and emerge from the course objectives. The tasks may be very brief or long and complex. The performance tasks may be completed individually or in groups.

➤ Problem-solving tasks related to real-world problems are often used in performance assessments. They may be embedded in a simulated or case study scenario.

➤ Some schools have adapted a "rite of passage" experience, often required for graduation (Hart, 1994). These might consist of mastery exhibits, oral presentations, a résumé, essays, products, artwork, and role plays.

➤ Any performance task can also be evaluated by peers. It is essential to provide a checklist with the evaluative criteria listed with some form of rating scale for each criterion.

SELF-ASSESSMENT

The ultimate aim of education is to produce life-long, independent learners. An essential component of autonomous learning is the ability to assess one's own progress and deficiencies. Student self-assessment should be incorporated into every evaluation process. Its specific form may vary with the developmental level of the student, but the very youngest students can begin to examine and evaluate their own behavior and accomplishments.

➤ Instead of grading all assignments, allow students to correct some themselves. You may choose to randomly collect these and check for accuracy.

➤ Share the specific evaluation criteria (or rubric) students should employ in assessing various tasks or assignments. Provide them with criteria checksheets (or have the class generate them) that specify exactly what constitutes a good product.

➤ Provide models of successful products, answers, or performances. These might be tacked to the bulletin board, in a display case, or on videotape. It is best to share the model before students begin the project. For creative activities, avoid encouraging students to simply copy someone else's product. It is helpful to lead students through an evaluation of the outstanding model, using the evaluation criteria to demonstrate why the model is an exemplar. To minimize peer pressure or harassment, it is generally best to use a previous student's work for the model rather than a current student's.

Attempt to schedule individual sessions to discuss a student's progress. Have the student evaluate his or her own performance. Encourage the student to apply specific criteria in making the self-assessment.

"Independence, creativity, and self-reliance are all facilitated when self-criticism and self-evaluation are basic and evaluation by others is of secondary importance."
—CARL ROGERS

FOR ADDITONAL INFORMATION:

Carey, L. (1994). *Measuring and Evaluating School Learning.* Boston: Allyn and Bacon.

DeFina, A.A. (1992). *Portfolio Assessment: Getting Started.* New York: Scholastic Professional Books.

Fusco, E., Quinn, M.C., & Hauck, M. (1993). *The Portfolio Assessment Handbook.* Roslyn, NY: Berrent Publications, Inc.

Gardner, H. (1993). *Multiple Intelligences: The Theory in Practice.* New York: Basic Books.

Hart, D. (1994). *Authentic Assessment: A Handbook for Educators.* Menlo Park, CA: Addison-Wesley Pub. Co.

Laska, J.A. & Juarez, T. (Eds.), (1992). *Grading and Marking in American Schools: Two Centuries of Debate.* Springfield, IL: Charles C. Thomas.

Marzano, R.J., Pickering, D., & McTighe, J. (1993). *Assessing Student Outcomes: Performance Assessment Using the Dimensions of Learning Model.* Alexandria, VA: Association for Supervision and Curriculum Development.

Miller, P.W. & Erickson, H.E. (1990). *How to Write Tests for Students.* Washington, D.C.: National Education Association.

Mitchell, R. (1992). *Testing for Learning: How New Approaches to Evaluation Can Improve American Schools.* New York: The Free Press.

Robinson, G.E. & Craver, J.M. (1989). *Assessing and Grading Student Achievement.* Arlington, VA: Educational Research Service.

Schurr, S. (1992). *The ABC's of Evaluation: 26 Alternative Ways to Assess Students.* Columbus, OH: National Middle School Association.

Stiggins, R.J. (1994). *Student-Centered Classroom Assessment.* New York: Merrill.

Tierney, R.J., Carter, M.A., & Desai, L.E. (1991). *Portfolio Assessment in the Reading-Writing Classroom.* Norwood, MA: Christopher-Gordon Publishers, Inc.

Fair Use Guidelines for Educational Use of Designated Materials

Material	Copy for Teacher Use	Copies for Class	Number of Uses per Term*
Books (fiction and nonfiction)	1 chapter	1,000 words or 10%	2
Encyclopedias, anthologies, storybooks	1 story	2,500 words or 1 story	3
Poems	1 poem	250 words or 1 poem	2
Periodicals	1 article	2,500 words or 1 article	3
Charts, cartoons, pictures	1 per book	1 per book	3
Lectures, sermons, speeches	1 per book	1 per book	3
Computer programs	Not applicable because of the need to copy the entire program		
Videotapes of TV broadcasts (non-educational TV)	May be shown twice to students within 10 days of broadcast and retained for a maximum of 45 days for evaluation by educators; daily newscasts may be recorded by qualified libraries for research use only		
Videotapes of TV broadcasts (educational TV)	May be recorded and used for educational purposes for maximum of seven days		
Lawfully made videotapes	May be used for educational purposes in face-to-face classroom teaching		

*Total use of reproductions should not exceed nine times per class term.

From: Kenneth T. Murray (1994). Copyright and the educator. *Phi Delta Kappan, 55,* 7, 552-55. Used with permission.

Assignment Record

Name _____ Week _____

Subject	Monday	Tuesday	Wednesday	Thursday	Friday

Skill Assessment Form

Name _____ Date _____

Subject _____

Teacher _____

Skill	Yes	No	No evidence	Comments

Don't Forget!

Test tomorrow

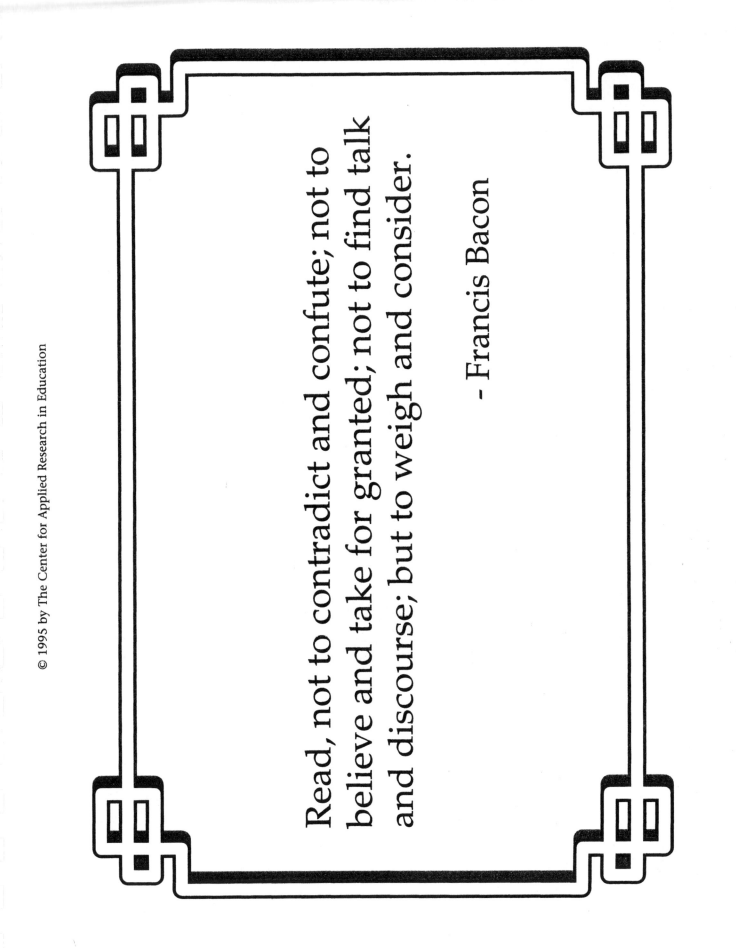

Read, not to contradict and confute; not to believe and take for granted; not to find talk and discourse; but to weigh and consider.

- Francis Bacon

Learning is a treasure which follows its owner everywhere.

- Chinese proverb

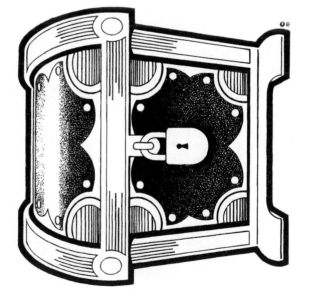

PERFORMANCE RECORD

Class _____ Term/Year _____ Teacher_____

Name																								

CHAPTER 3

Alternatives to Lecturing

As most teachers were taught primarily by lecture, the natural response is to resort to the proverbial "talking head" in front of the class as the favored mode of instruction. Despite a growing body of research evidence demonstrating the limitations of lecture as the primary instructional modality, many persist in the practice. Head nods and whiplash are pervasive in these classrooms as students struggle to stay awake. While lecture can be useful in certain situations, there are many other more valuable teaching tools available. The most outstanding teachers have a variety of instructional techniques in their repertoire.

Hot Tips for Asking Effective Questions

A substantial body of research affirms questions are still the most freqently used teaching tool. However, all questions are not created equally. Some are highly effective; others can be useless or even harmful. There is an art and a science to effective questionning. Here are some tips gleaned from outstanding teachers and research that will improve your use of questions.

➤ As part of your lesson planning, list the processing questions you plan to ask. Effectively worded questions can make a good lesson superb. Develop a logic to the sequence of your questions. Strive for clarity in your questions.

➤ Challenge the total class to make a mental response when you ask a question, pause, and then select the person to respond. Choosing the answerer randomly provides the opportunity for even the shyest child to become involved in the class discussion. The teacher's encouragement and support can reduce anxiety and make it a successful learning experience. It is best for the teacher to build upon small successes by asking open-ended questions rather than factual-recall questions. Unfortunately, it has been observed that teachers ask low-ability students fewer questions and praise them less often when they respond correctly.

➤ Wait three seconds after directing a question before saying anything else. Most teachers allow their students less than two seconds on the average to answer a question. Permitting the student a reasonable amount of thinking time is essential, especially if you are asking for more than recall of a single fact. The length and quality of students' responses increase when teachers allow increased wait time.

➤ Use closed-ended questions when you are seeking information, facts, or a commitment. In attempting to assess student mastery of specific facts, the closed-ended question is most effective. Generally, avoid "yes" or "no" questions in your lessons.

➤ Open-ended questions (beginning with "how," "why," or "what") usually allow greater latitude in the student's response with a variety of possible answers (How can air pollution be decreased? Why do people change careers?) A single correct answer does not exist. Such open-ended questions are most crucial in stimulating students' creative abilities and developing higher level cognitive processes such as evaluation, hypothesis generation, analysis, and synthesis.

➤ What the teacher does after a student responds to a question is going to significantly influence the group discussion process. Students who are insulted and intimidated are going to become increasingly reluctant to become involved in discussions. No constructive end can come from "put downs"—whether they are intiated by the teacher or by other students. People, including students, have a right to make mistakes and a responsibility to learn from those mistakes. A positive class climate is attained when students feel accepted and sufficiently open to take risks—even at the price of sometimes being incorrect.

➤ Encourage students to respond in some fashion, even if they aren't completely sure of the answer. Rephrase the question or provide cues, but don't just accept, "I don't know."

➤ Probe students' responses for clarification and to stimulate further reflection. "Why?" is an effective probing question to force the student to a deeper level of thought.

➤ Avoid multiple questions. Barraging students with a series of questions often only confuses them and obscures the purpose of the lesson. One question at a time posed clearly and concisely will more likely yield a clear and concise response.

➤ Effective teachers keep a balance between calling on volunteers and non-volunteers. Particularly when it is likely many non-volunteers do know the answer, it is better to call on a non-volunteer.

➤ Occasionally have all students jot down an answer to your question before calling upon one person to share the answer.

➤ For variety have all students share their answer to your question in pairs or small groups. Have a few groups report their best answers to the whole class.

➤ For classes of high-ability students difficult and challenging questions seem most effective. For mixed-ability classes, a mixture of higher order and lower cognitive level questions seems to work best. Low-level cognitive questions seem to work best when you are teaching basic skills. Effective teachers ask a combination of both low- and high-level cognitive questions.

➤ Strive to ask questions that yield a high level of correct responses; research suggests around 70% is the optimal success level. There is some evidence that the most successful strategy is to begin a lesson with lower level questions and to use higher level questions as the lesson progresses.

➤ Learn to allow students to talk more. Typically, teacher-talk consumes 70% of class discussion time.

➤ Acknowledge correct responses but be specific in your praise. What exactly was appropriate or creative about the student's response? Avoid the cliché "Very good" in response to every question. Save genuine praise for the response that is truly exceptional.

➤ Occasionally ask the student to repeat the question before replying. This assures they are listening and understand the question.

➤ Give students an equal opportunity to respond to your questions. Research shows students down the middle and across the front of the classroom get called on more frequently. Also, higher ability students tend to get called on more than lower ability students when they raise their hands.

➤ There is research support for permitting call-out answers with lower socio-economic level students, particularly at the elementary level. At higher socio-economic level classes, students should be acknowledged before giving their answers. In the latter students are typically more assertive and eager to respond, creating more chaos. Without having to seek permission to speak, lower ability students are more likely to contribute. A risk of permitting call-out responses is that a few students may dominate class discussions.

➤ Don't accept a clearly incorrect answer. Gently, yet clearly help identify a more appropriate response. Acknowledge if an answer is partially correct but solicit a more complete response from the class before continuing. Have the student reflect a bit more on the question or rephrasing. Don't immediately call on someone else.

➤ Encourage students to ask questions, but don't just do it by saying "Any questions?" Have each student write down one question. Or have them pair up to make a list of questions related to the topic. Real learning is most likely when students are genuinely curious and enthusiastically generate their own questions. Encourage them to ask questions of each other as well as of you.

➤ Be wary of asking "why" questions when used to confront misbehavior. When we ask "why" questions in reference to a person's behavior ("Why did you do that?") we are generally seeking an argument, not an explanation. "Why" questions often put the student on the defensive, yielding a "wise-crack" defensive answer. A "What are you doing?" question is more effective in focusing the student's attention upon his or her misbehavior.

Question and Answer

Questions are a most valuable skill when used effectively. "Question and answer" can be used in a variety of ways in the classroom. Most commonly, teachers ask questions and students answer. This can be a useful technique. The Socratic method of stimulating the creative thought in students through skillful questioning can be especially valuable. On a lower level it may take the form of rote drill, with the teacher firing a barrage of questions around the room soliciting answers. This form of question and answer is most effective when the content is fairly concrete. See the previous section on questions for tips on the effective use of teacher questions.

"Question and answer" may also consist of students asking the teacher questions. The least effective method of doing this is to simply ask "Are there any questions?" especially at the very end of the class period. Most students are hesitant to openly ask questions in front of the whole class, even if they do have them in mind. One useful technique is to have each student jot down one question about the topic on a sheet of paper. Then you might collect them and respond to a few. Another possibility is to have small groups generate a list of two to five questions that are submitted. Rather than answering these questions, direct some of them back to the class, to consider either as a whole-group discussion or in small groups.

In facilitating question-and-answer sessions, try to stand across the room from the student speaking. This forces the student to speak in a louder voice, allowing everyone else to hear him or her. This will require you to keep moving during the discussion, but will pay off in better interaction. As you call on students you might nonchalantly pace toward the opposite side of the room. A secondary benefit of maximizing your distance from the student speaking is that it broadens your range of vision, allowing you to better monitor the rest of the class.

Brainstorming

Brainstorming, first introduced by Alex Osborne in the advertising industry, can be a valuable technique for stimulating creative thinking in groups. It can be incorporated into almost any lesson. Brief, one- to four-minute brainstorms are a quick and effective way to re-energize a group when you find their interest waning. Some advance training on the principles of effective brainstorming is essential. You might display the four basic rules of brainstorming (listed below) as a poster or transparency. When you first explain brainstorming, discuss the following rules:

➤ Generate as many ideas as possible. (The more ideas a group has, the greater the probability of discovering a good idea. The emphasis for now is upon quantity, not quality.)

➤ Delay evaluation. (Later we will evaluate our ideas, but for free and open brainstorming, students must not be worried about whether others are going to criticize their ideas. Innovation only occurs when we are able to see with fresh eyes, stripping away the tubular vision that usually limits our creativity. Positive evaluation is prohibited as well, as those not receiving positive comments from the group will assume their ideas are inferior. Record each idea without evaluation. You might introduce the idea of "Creativity Crunchers" (see the handout) that we commonly use to squelch each other's creativity.

➤ Encourage wild, zany, half-baked ideas. (Even if it doesn't quite make sense now, it might be the stimulus for a great idea. Record it; later it may blossom into something worthwhile.)

➤ Build upon others' ideas. (Listen to the ideas of others and springboard from them.)

Someone should be appointed to record on paper the ideas as they are generated by the group. All ideas should be recorded, ideally on a large sheet of newsprint for all to see. After the initial brainstorming exercise, you might assign the group the task of discussing their ideas and selecting (and possibily ranking) their top five or ten solutions.

When you first introduce brainstorming, give your students an opportunity to practice applying it to unusual, interesting, and novel problems. Generating lists of unusual uses for common items is often used. You might even hold up an object when assigning the brainstorming task. Here are some possibilities of objects for brainstorming unusual uses:

➤ Chalkboard eraser
➤ 10,000 unmatched socks
➤ Softball
➤ Used auto tires
➤ Soda straws
➤ Pie pan
➤ Cafeteria tray
➤ Wallpaper sample book
➤ Carpet scraps
➤ Empty paper towel tubes

Another technique for practicing brainstorming is to encourage students to project what would likely happen if some major change occurred. How would the world be different? "Just suppose..."

➤ All people looked the same
➤ Everyone had the same voice
➤ We no longer had trees
➤ Televisions were banned
➤ Men could not vote
➤ Everyone was given a million dollars
➤ There were no telephones
➤ We had no thumbs
➤ There were no traffic laws

➤ Curriculm expert and teacher trainer Cerylle Moffett suggests an interesting adaptation of the brainstorming technique that she calls "Carousel Brainstorming." Several topics are listed on newsprint and posted on the wall around the room. The class is divided into an equal number of groups. Each group gathers at a different post. Give the groups three to five minutes to brainstorm and record their ideas on the topic written on the sheet in front of them. When time is called, everyone rotates clockwise around the room to the next post. Give them a set time limit to read the ideas written by the previous group and to continue the brainstorming process, recording their ideas on the sheet. Repeat the cycle until each group has considered each of the ideas posted.

➤ Another technique, sometimes called "Rapid Brainstorming," involves posting a variety of topics on separate sheets of newsprint posted around the room. A group is assigned to each topic and gathers in front of their sheet of newsprint. All groups brainstorm all the responses they can in two to three minutes. The ideas from each group are then shared with the total class. Another variation is to have each group rotate to the next topic and spend two minutes trying to add ideas to those already posted. Continue rotating until each group has brainstormed on each topic. Another variation is to have the groups remain seated in their groups and to pass the sheets of paper around the groups.

➤ Another idea borrowed from Cerylle Moffett is the "Mail Call." This technique works well in considering several related problems. Break the class into groups of four to five. Identify several problems for brainstorming. Each group needs a set of envelopes with each problem written on a different envelope. Place all the envelopes in the center of a table. Each person in the small group writes one idea on a note card and puts it in each envelope. Use newsprint or the chalkboard to record the various brainstormed solutions generated in each group.

➤ Another variation of brainstorming is to direct students to silently brainstorm their ideas for a minute. Each student jots down his or her ideas on a sheet of paper. Then, in the small brainstorming groups, each shares two ideas. Afterwards the group follows normal brainstorming procedures.

Brainwriting

Brainwriting is a variation on the brainstorming technique. It assures that everyone has an opportunity to participate and minimizes the effects of premature evaluation of each other's ideas. A topic or problem is assigned to a small group (four to seven members) and each student is given three note cards (or small sheets of paper). Upon being assigned the problem, each student is to write a different idea on each card. These are placed face down on a table or desk. When all cards are face down, the students take turns drawing one card and reading it aloud. It is then placed face up on the table for all to see. As similar ideas are read, they are grouped into clusters. After all the groups have read and grouped their ideas, they can be shared with the total class and recorded on the board or newsprint. This is a useful technique for generating class rules at the beginning of the school year.

List Making

List making can be combined with several other techniques, such as brainstorming or brainwriting. It may be done individually, in small groups, or as a whole class. Here are some ideas for possible lists:

➤ Causes (economic depressions, the Civil War, fights, fires, success, trust, decay of organic matter, substance abuse, the civil rights movement)

➤ Effects, real or projected (of chemical fertilizers, unemployment, alcohol abuse, global warming, soil erosion, television, decline of communism, of Watergate on American politics and society)

➤ Characteristics or traits (properties of organic matter, components of a healthy diet, parts of an airplane, forms of mental illness)

➤ Criteria for judgments (selecting a college, choosing a friend, a good novel, successful employee)

➤ Members of sets (countries of Africa, religions of the world, elements of the periodic table, 19th-century American authors, species of birds, proverbs)

➤ Solutions (for decreasing crime, lengthening our lifespan)

Lists are easily incorporated into consensus-building activities. Students are assigned the task of first individually ranking the list in priority. Afterwards small groups discuss their lists and attempt to arrive at a final group ranking. It is important to prohibit simple voting; the issues must be presented and negotiated.

Class Discussions

Class discussion is a useful strategy for stimulating thought and encouraging students to re-examine their attitudes. To be effective the students must possess some general information about the topic under consideration, unless you are using the discussion as an advance organizer to introduce a new topic.

The teacher's role in a class discussion is as a moderator. You pose the initial question, facilitate thinking with follow-up questions, and assure that everyone has an opportunity to participate. You can also introduce bits of information, but generally it is best if you refrain from offering your opinion. If you do choose to take a position, it is probably wise to wait until the end. It is essential that you merely facilitate, not dominate, the discussion.

➤ Whole-class discussion is best facilitated with the group seated in a large circle or a horseshoe. They are more encouraged to respond to each other rather than a series of successive dialogs with the teacher if they can see each other.

➤ Do give some forethought to the stimulating questions you will ask. It is best to write them down. Overall, the less you have to participate to keep the discussion going, the better. It is also essential to establish the procedures for taking turns speaking. Does the student need to be acknowledged by the teacher before speaking?

➤ Begin the discussion by introducing the topic. Students need to be aware of the general theme of the discussion and have a sense of its purpose. A couple of sentences and an opening question may suffice.

➤ Discussions can serve a variety of purposes. They may focus upon examining a problem, analyzing its causes, effects and potential solutions. A discussion may be used to debrief an activity such as a simulation, role play, or experiment. Discussion may focus upon predicting some future event or explaining some past phenomenon. For any of these aims to be met, the discussion must progress beyond the knowledge level. Higher level cognitive questions must be asked.

➤ The class may be broken into small groups to stimulate discussion. Each group might discuss the same topic or have separate topics to consider. It is helpful to provide the groups a written list of questions, either as a handout or displayed on the overhead projector or chalkboard. Without a clear purpose and a task for which they will be accountable, the discussion will quickly degenerate into a conversation. It is usually a good idea to appoint a group leader who is responsible for keeping everyone on task, recording the group's ideas, and reporting back to the whole class. (See the page at the end of this chapter listing creative ways to appoint group leaders.)

➤ To facilitate only one person talking at a time, bring a sponge ball or other soft object to class. To speak a student must be in possession of the ball. When students want to contribute to the discussion, they must raise their hand. Once the previous speaker has tossed them the ball, they may speak.

➤ Avoid over-including high-ability students in an effort to keep the discussion going.

➤ A tactic commonly used to prevent several persons from dominating the discussion is to allocate each student three or four poker chips or other tokens. Each time a student makes a comment, he or she must turn in one token to the teacher. Once their chips are gone, they may add no more comments to the discussion. Another way to control the monopolizer is to first break into small groups and designate a reporter from each group to share the group's conclusions. Another option is to appoint the monopolizer to a role that inhibits his or her participation; for example, as a process observer or recorder.

➤ Don't allow the discussion to deteriorate into a shouting match. Emphasize the value of free and open discussion and supporting positions with facts. Emphasize that reasonable people may sometimes make differing interpretations of those facts.

➤ End the discussion before it begins to stagnate. Do something different: have each student take one minute to write an answer to a question, introducing some relevant facts.

➤ Provide some structure to the discussion so it is not too divergent. It must have focus to encourage serious reflection. An exchange of unexamined opinions is of minimal educational value.

➤ Provide closure to the discussion. One way is for the teacher or volunteers to summarize the main points emphasized. Another is to have students reflect and/or write on how the discussion may have changed their view of the topic.

➤ Thank students for their contributions. It generally works best to reinforce but not grade participation in discussions.

➤ Provide a transition to the next phase of the lesson. Point out how the discussion fits into the overall lesson objectives.

➤ Occasionally it is helpful to lead a post-discussion review of the process and techniques of the discussion. Encourage the class to analyze what went well and which areas might need improvement. Encourage reflection on the level of thinking that occurred during the discussion. Sometimes appointed observers can provide feedback on the group dynamics.

Fishbowls

A fishbowl consists of a small group that discusses an issue while seated in the center of the classroom with the rest of the class seated in a larger circle around the fishbowl. This technique is most effective for topics in which students have a lot of interest and some disagreement exists. Often an empty chair is included in the fishbowl. Anyone in the outer circle who wishes to inject a comment may temporarily join the fishbowl. Once that student has contributed a comment, that student returns to his or her seat on the outside, leaving the chair vacant for the next volunteer.

It works best to prepare a list of questions in advance to structure the discussion and keep it on task. It is essential that those in the outer circle remain quiet during the discussion. They may only talk if they join the fishbowl in the empty chair. Observers should take notes during the discussion (e.g., recording the pros and cons related to the topic). One option is to have the fishbowl participants and observers reverse roles and continue the discussion. Time should be allowed for debriefing at the end of the discussion. The fishbowl technique can also be used as a lesson in group processes.

Another option is to break the class into several smaller discussion groups to examine a controversial topic. Each group then selects a representative to participate in the fishbowl and express his or her group's concerns on the issue. After 15 to 20 minutes of discussion, the representatives might rejoin their groups for feedback and new "ammunition" to share once they rejoin the fishbowl.

Artwork

Most students still love to draw, especially if they are not being evaluated. For variety, experiment with art media in your regular classes. Crayons, colored markers, colored pencils, and chalk seem to immediately grab students' attention. Students who otherwise find self-expression difficult may be able to communicate deeper ideas and feelings through artistic media. Art has been used successfully to build students' self-esteem and self-confidence. It can tap the creativity and imagination of all students.

➤ Experiment with inserting a five-minute art activity into a lesson. Rather than having students write out their responses to a discussion question, have them draw a depiction of their answer. It provides a re-energizing break from the left-brain focus of most lessons.

➤ Added motivation comes with the use of scented markers (Mr. Sketch® is one brand) available at most office supply stores.

➤ Play music in the background while students are doing their artwork to further stimulate creativity.

➤ Encourage students to use drawings in their journals to represent some of their ideas. Have them take a sketch pad along on field trips to record their observations. Drawing helps students focus their attention and to process their perceptions.

➤ Cooperatively drawn murals can enrich students' reflection about the academic content while developing social skills.

➤ Discourage competition among students in their artwork. Be cautious of effusive public praise for obviously talented students. It may discourage less artistically inclined students. Private praise is probably much more effective.

➤ Have students draw a vertical and a horizontal line to create four equal boxes. In each box the students draw a different item in response to four different questions about the topic being studied in your class. (For example, it could be four causes of the Civil War, four kinds of clouds, four effects of inflation, four career possibilities). Or each box might be used to address a different question. (For example, the first box might show a cause of some problem being studied. An effect and two possible solutions might be drawn in the other three boxes.)

➤ Keep the directions to any art assignments general. Let the students use their creativity and imaginations to construct their vision of reality. Give them as much freedom as possible to choose the form and media they believe best expresses their ideas.

➤ Encourage the use of color by having assorted markers, pens, crayons, or pencils available for students to use if they do not have to provide their own.

➤ Incorporate the construction of advertisements into your lessons. Ads may take the form of posters or magazine layouts. Their ads should express some relevant concept related to the topic being studied.

➤ Collages can be adapted to a great many purposes in non-art classes. Though most art collages consist of pictures and captions clipped from magazines, most any item that can be pasted to a piece of posterboard can be included in a collage (e.g., photographs, fabrics, drawings, leaves, buttons, ribbon).

➤ Collages can be composed by individuals or in groups. Ask students to bring in a variety of old magazines as sources of pictures to be cut out. Have students attach titles to their collages.

➤ Check out Betty Edwards's excellent book, *Drawing on the Right Side of the Brain* (Los Angeles: J.P. Tarcher Publishers, 1989) for many practical ideas for incorporating drawing into your lesson plans.

Music

Music has many uses in the classroom. It can be used in the background to set the mood for a lesson, to energize, relax, inspire, cue transitions, focus attention, reinforce a theme, or for fun. Music affects our physiological systems, our emotions, and our spirit. Music can influence the mood and behaviors of your students.

It is generally best to select instrumental music, although vocals might be used during breaks or if the lyrics pertain specifically to the lesson. Pay special attention to the beat of the musical selection. A march is hardly going to soothe and calm a group of hyperactive, rowdy students. Baroque and soft New Age instrumentals work well as background music during individual seatwork.

➤ Special effects or emphasis can be achieved by using themes from famous movies or television programs. (The theme from *Jeopardy* during a spelling bee or oral quiz lightens the atmosphere.) Continually be aware of the purpose you want to achieve with each musical selection.

➤ Incorporate humorous novelty songs into your lessons. This is especially effective if the theme of the somg relates to the topic under study.

➤ Put a part of your lesson to music. If you are bold, try singing an announcement or assignment to a rap beat.

➤ Allow students to bring a favorite tape to play before class begins or during lab or project work. The privilege of selecting the tape for the day can be used as a reward for outstanding performance.

➤ If you play a musical instrument, bring it to class and feature a brief selection as part of the lesson or use as a novelty reward. It reinforces the value of music.

➤ Some teachers play music before the class. Stopping the music is a cue that it is time to begin class.

When words leave off, music begins.
—HEINRICH HEINE (1797-1856)

Be sure your recordings are cued at the appropriate spot and volume adjusted before class begins. You'll lose momentum and effect if you have to waste class time searching for the segment you want to use. Have them out of their boxes and clearly labeled and ready to use.

Guided Imagery

Guided imagery can be used effectively to stimulate students' problem solving, goal setting, and hypothesis building in studying complex issues. In affective education guided imagery is also used to help students explore their feelings and attitudes. The intent of the guided imagery lesson is to immerse the students in the subject. It is the "next best thing to being there." It is an active, not passive, instructional strategy.

Careful thought must be given to the topic chosen as the focus of a guided imagery. The students' prior experience and knowledge about the topic must be considered in designing the lesson. It may be necessary to present some background information before the introduction of the imagery. The questions to be included must be given careful thought.

➤ It is best to allow students the option of not participating in fantasy trips or visualizations. Though rare, some students might not wish to participate for religious or emotional reasons. Don't make a big fuss, but avoid forcing student participation. Provide an alternate assignment, perhaps a written theme on the same topic.

➤ When you introduce the visualization, make it clear that no one will be forced to share their thoughts or feelings afterwards. In debriefing, only call on volunteers for responses.

➤ Introduce the visualization by encouraging students to make themselves comfortable, to take several deep breaths, and to relax. You may choose to turn the lights off. Some may prefer to close their eyes to eliminate distractions, but do not insist that they do so.

➤ Carefully script the visualization the first time. Pause after each line to allow time for students to create their fantasy response.

➤ Design visualizations that encourage students to use all their senses as they progress through the visualization. For example, "What sounds are outstanding?" Or "What do you see from the top of the hill?"

> In debriefing the visualization, invite students to share whatever observations they choose. This might be perceived as safer if done in pairs or small groups. A large-group discussion might then elicit any generalizations or conclusions.

To imagine is everything.
—**ALBERT EINSTEIN**

Journal Keeping

A valuable instructional device for encouraging reflection, review, application, and creativity is the student journal. As most commonly used each student periodically makes entries into a spiral-bound notebook, which is occasionally handed in to the teacher. The teacher scans the journals, making relevant comments in the margin or a separate column. Student journals can serve a variety of purposes: to improve writing skills, to remind the student of important things to remember, or to strengthen self-reflection skills.

> Learning logs or journals function as course diaries. Students enter summaries of the major content they have been studying. These might be major points from class lectures, formulae and other important pieces of information that need to be memorized, or procedures and directions. It might be kept in the form of a mind map.

> Reflective journals serve as a medium to stimulate and record thinking about what is being experienced in the class. This form of response journal may be turned in to the teacher and returned with the teacher's comments, creating a teacher-student dialogue. Each can in turn ask the other questions.

> Journals can also serve as logs, helping the students and the teacher track the books read, experiments completed, learning centers done, or objectives attained. Journals can also help students monitor their progress.

➤ Experiment with assigning specialized journals, such as a conflict journal. Students would record instances in which they encounter conflict in their daily lives, their response to the conflict, the outcome of their reactions, and other options they might have taken. Other topics for specialized journals might include: stress, use of time, successes, anger, joys, positive and negative consequences, nutrition, or exercise. Of course, the journals you require should be relevant to the subject you are teaching.

➤ Journals can also function as field notebooks for recording observations of processes or phenomena you want students to examine over time. Students can keep journals on weather patterns, wildlife observed, progress of experiments, social/psychological observations (e.g., violence on television, smiles), child development, political developments, books read, or field trips.

➤ Provide instructions as to the format of their journals, what medium (spiral notebook, notebook paper, computer disk) may be used, how frequently they will be writing in it, the minimum amount they should write, and if and when it will be read by the teacher.

➤ In assigning a journal-keeping assignment, be sure to explicitly describe its purpose. A frequent purpose of journals is as a learning log to record new knowledge gained each day. This is especially valuable with experiential learning.

➤ When emotions become aroused during heated discussions, it is often helpful to call a time out for students to reflect on the issue at hand and enter their thoughts and feelings into their personal journals. It is a useful way of encouraging them to summarize the main points on both sides of an issue.

➤ Another strategy for using journals is to have students list the three most important points or ideas from the day's class that they think will be most helpful to them. You might then encourage them to share these thoughts in pairs or seek volunteers from the class at large. This facilitates review of the day's lesson and encourages application.

➤ To stimulate students' journal writing, ask specific, open-ended questions that are to be answered in their journals.

➤ As part of the introduction of a new topic, particularly ones of natural interest to students, ask each student to enter in their journals two or three questions they hope will be answered during the upcoming lesson. Near the end of the lesson you might ask students to check their list of questions for any that remain unanswered.

➤ Have students assume a role related to the topic being studied (e.g., antebellum plantation owner, colonial merchant, entrepreneur, union organizer, underground railroad conductor, or explorer. Students make their journal entries as though they were the person in the role they are assuming. Or the student might be assigned to study a real person, such as George Washington, Clara Barton, Eleanor Roosevelt, Madame Currie, or Albert Schweitzer. Students are to make their journal observations as they believe their assigned persons would have responded.

➤ Some teachers have successfully employed the use of team journals. Teams of five students are each given a journal. Periodically the teacher assigns a topic for the class to consider and enter their reactions in their team journal. The team leader, which is a rotated position, enters the first entry in the journal. Other members are then responsible for adding their comments. Each student, except for the team leader, is supposed to comment upon at least one previous entry. The teacher then reads each journal and adds his or her own entry to the journal. It encourages students to write regularly and to assume a position and defend it.

Field Trips

All the world is a learning resource if a knowledgeable guide shows the way. Well-planned, organized field trips can be one of the most valuable ways of helping students apply their textbook and classroom learning to the greater world. Here are some practical tips for making field trips into profitable learning experiences.

➤ Any class trip should have a meaningful purpose that is explicitly communicated to the students. It is also essential to communicate that purpose to any off-site presenters and any parents or others serving as chaperones. Any field trip should have a legitimate aim, directly related to the subject being taught. A class trip cannot be justified if its sole purpose is to entertain or fill time. It should enrich and expand your regular curriculum.

➤ Clarify your school's procedures and requirements before you begin planning a field trip. Will parental permission be required? If so, is there a special form you must use? (See the sample permission letter included at the end of this chapter). When and where must the permission forms be filed? Will chaperones be required? How many? Always notify your building administrator in writing.

➤ How will transportation be provided? Busses are generally preferable to traveling in private automobiles. It is simpler, easier to control students' behavior, and less likely to bring up liability issues.

➤ If chaperones will be accompanying you on the trip, be sure to communicate your expectations of what role they should take. It is best to send a note to each chaperone detailing when they should be at school and exactly what you expect of them. Are they only to monitor student behaviors? Which behaviors are unacceptable? How should rowdy students be handled? Will the chaperones have a role in the learning associated with the trip?

➤ Send information to the parents about your field trip, describing its purpose and specifics of the travel arrangements. If you are seeking parents to accompany the class, be sure to give ample notice (ideally, at least two weeks). Are any costs involved? If so, how are they to be handled? Will lunch be provided?

➤ Be sure the proposed visit is age-appropriate for your students. Is this site used to having visits from students? Will a guided tour be provided? If so, are they used to talking to students of this age group? Will cameras be allowed? Is any special attire required?

➤ Strive to make the field trip an active learning experience. The more hands-on the experience is, the better. If it is a guided tour (e.g., a factory or battlefield) provide students (either individually or in cooperative groups) specific tasks to accomplish during the visit. In some way the class should be accountable for learning that occurs during the trip. This can be in the form of word puzzles, word scavenger hunts, or a study guide to help direct their attention and reflection. It is often useful to break the class into learning teams, each with a different task to accomplish. The next school day they can exchange their insights and completed tasks.

➤ As much as possible, the field trip should be integrated into a sequence of planned class activities. Before the trip, prepare the students with background information about the topic of the field trip. The day after the visit, allow class time for reflection and discussion of the experience. Plan a lesson that allows them to apply this new knowledge.

➤ Be reasonable in what you can accomplish on a field trip. Often teachers try to accomplish too much, especially if it is a day-long trip. Once students become bored or fatigued, less learning and more misbehavior are likely.

➤ Try to arrange for your parents to meet with you 15 minutes before the group is to leave so you may share any last-minute details and coordinate efforts. It's generally a good idea to have one more chaperone than you think you'll need. If parents will be driving, be sure to give each one a map of the route you will be taking.

➤ Adequately prepare your students before the day of the trip. Clarify your expectations for both appropriate behavior and any learning assignments associated with the trip. Are there special dress requirements? Will seats be assigned on the bus? What should they do if they get separated from the group?

➤ If possible, give your planned trip a dry run. How long will it take to get there? Try to meet any guides or presenters who will be leading your group. Will eating arrangements need to be made en route or on-site? Make note of details, such as locations of bathrooms, parking, etc. Is the site fully accessible for any handicapped students? Determine precisely where and when you are to arrive with your group. How will any admission fees be handled?

➤ Count noses before you leave the school and again when you meet to return home.

➤ With older students identify a landmark where all should meet should they become separated.

➤ Carry a notepad or cards with you on the field trip. During the excursion jot down ideas for process questions or points to emphasize back in the classroom.

➤ It is probably wise to take along a small bag with some emergency supplies including adhesive bandages, tape, safety pins, needle and thread, tissues, and coins for emergency phone calls. On a long bus ride carry a couple of bags for students who experience motion sickness—and hope you don't need them.

➤ During a tour carry an easily identifiable object, such as a colorful umbrella, that you can hold up for students to easily find their group. With small children some teachers use a rope the children are instructed to cling to in a single file throughout the walking tour.

➤ After the field trip send a thank-you note to the organization or person who facilitated the visit. If appropriate, you might encourage your students to draft a letter to send.

➤ Evaluate the field trip. Did it fulfill your educational purposes? Solicit feedback from the students. What would have improved the experience?

➤ If you plan to use that field trip site in the future, jot down any reminders of changes that would make the trip more profitable next time. You might file these along with copies of your form letters and permission slips, student activities, and any promotional brochures.

IDEAS FOR POTENTIAL FIELD TRIPS

Airport	Law enforcement agency
Amusement park	Legislative session
Aquarium	Library
Arboretum	Military base
Art exhibit	Museum
Artists' studio	Neighborhood
Battlefield	Newspaper office
Botanical garden	Observatory
City council meeting	Park (local, state, national)

College & university	Planetarium
Concert	Political rally
Conservatory	Presidential library/home
Court house	Science museum
Cultural fair/festival	Seashore, river, lake
Factory	Ship
Farm	Special exhibition
Fire department	State capitol building
Geological site	Television/radio station
Historical museum	Theatrical performance
Historical site/building	Train ride
Hospital	Weather station
Laboratory	Zoo

Guest Speakers/Panels

The use of guest speakers, either individually or as a panel, can provide valuable educational opportunity. Outside presenters can enrich a lesson, provide special expertise, stimulate interest, and help students connect classroom learning to "real world" applications. Guest speakers provide variety: a different voice and a new face. A bonus benefit is the public relations value of inviting parents and community members to share their wisdom, skills, and views with young people.

However, as with any instructional approach, planning and preparation are crucial for success. A poor speaker is worse than none at all. Not only can precious educational time be lost, but the speaker may leave with a lower opinion of schools and your students.

Sources of potential speakers:

➤ Anyone who has traveled to a foreign country
➤ People representing different careers
➤ Persons with unusual hobbies or interests
➤ College and university professors
➤ Elected officials
➤ Local citizens of other nationalities
➤ Area business owners, executives
➤ International students attending local schools/colleges
➤ Governmental agency employees
➤ Someone with an interesting collection
➤ Physicians, lawyers, and other professionals
➤ School alumni
➤ Representatives of trade associations, unions, service organizations
➤ Local radio/television/newspaper celebrities
➤ Federal government employees

➤ Local newsmakers

➤ Better Business Bureau, consumer agencies, advocates

➤ Why is the speaker (or panel) being used? What benefit do you expect students to gain from being exposed to this speaker or panel? Communicate without jargon your objective to the speakers when you invite them.

➤ Give careful thought to whom you invite to participate in your class. What are their credentials? Parents, senior citizens, local "celebrities," civic leaders, skilled artisans, artists, professors, and local business persons can potentially contribute much to your students.

➤ When you extend an invitation, be specific as to the date, topic, and time limits. What format are you suggesting: lecture, demonstration, question and answer, a panel discussion? Have they spoken before in front of groups this age? How will they relate to students? Some persons are more comfortable participating as a member of an informal panel discussion than as the sole presenter.

➤ Give your speakers as much support as possible. Tell them about the kinds of students you have. Alert them to potential behavioral problems they might encounter and how you plan to deal with such disruptive students. See if they need any special equipment or supplies. Encourage them to use props and to involve students as much as possible.

➤ Short presentations are generally preferable, at least the first time you have a speaker present on a specific topic. If it is well received, more time can be allotted the next time.

➤ Prepare your students for the speaker(s). Before the speaker arrives, clarify who is coming and why. Clarify what behaviors you expect from your students. You might suggest they formulate some questions ahead of the presentation. Make it an active learning experience.

➤ Ask permission to video the speaker's presentation for use in the future or with students who were absent.

Be sure to send thank-you notes to your panelists/presenters. If students express high interest in the subject, invite them to write thank you notes, either individually or all signing one big one.

Persons who have some expertise in the subject under discussion might be invited to share their knowledge in a panel discussion. These might be parents, community members, or representatives of a particular organization, occupation, or interest group. Most people feel more comfortable participating as a panel member than giving a stand-up solo presentation. Generally three to five participants are included. The panelists might discuss the topic among themselves as well as respond to questions from your students. Another option is to select a group of students who study a particular topic and present it to the rest of the class as a panel discussion.

To stimulate questions it is often a good idea to give students a few minutes in class (or as homework) to write one or two questions they could submit to the panel. This might also be done as a small-group exercise. You serve as a moderator, posing questions when the discussion lags. Avoid dominating the discussion, however.

Arrange chairs at the front of the room so that the panelists can see each other and be seen by all the class. Keep track of the time and try to allow for some closing thoughts by each panelist.

Another useful variation is to allow 15 to 20 minutes at the end for the panelists to meet with small clusters of students and permit individual questioning and discussion.

Debates

The debate can be a powerful motivational and instructional device. Though formal debate has perhaps become a "lost art," seldom practiced outside of law schools, the debating process can successfully be adapted to any educational level. Informal debates can be used in almost any subject. They are an effective tool for honing students' thinking skills. The debate also reinforces data gathering, persuasion, public speaking, and listening skills. The ability to analyze a position and persuasively present a case for or against that position will benefit students throughout their lives. One of the most valuable gains from debates is the appreciation for more than one way of viewing issues.

Informal classroom debates need not follow all the procedures of a formal debate, though some basic rules need to be taught to structure any debate. Each side should have the same amount of time to present its case. They take turns presenting their arguments with time to rebut the points made by the opponent.

Any topic on which people might disagree can be selected for a debate assignment. This might include local or school-related issues, national or even international events. Most any proposal for change meets resistance with advocates for both sides. Though some students may initially be reluctant, most really do find classroom debates exciting and even the academically less-talented students can become involved. Debates frequently are quite lively and do elicit post-debate discussion on the issue.

➤ The first time you use the debate in class, keep it fairly simple. With experience your students can successfully take on more complicated issues. The more complex the issue, the more time needed for preparation. Adjust your expectations to the intellectual level of your students.

➤ Present some of the basic principles of effective argumentation, such as distinguishing opinions and emotions from facts. If you aren't familiar with these skills, find a book from the library (see the suggestions below). Invite a lawyer or a debate coach to speak to your class about effective debating.

➤ Debates generally work best as a cooperative learning activity. Students will feel much more comfortable as a member of a panel than as a sole debater. Emphasize the collaboration within each team more than the competition against other teams.

➤ Another adaptation of the debate is to assign a variety of debatable topics to pairs of students. Each pair works collaboratively to identify the best arguments for and against their assigned proposition. The teacher then randomly assigns one student to present the pro and another student to present the con position in a five-minute presentation. Allow two minutes to review their notes before the presentation to the whole class. Everyone in the class gets to speak, but the time is brief enough not to arouse undue anxiety in most students.

➤ For variety, debate with yourself in front of the class. Choose a stimulating issue and argue one point of view, perhaps in a relevant hat or shirt. Then quickly don the other costume and argue the other position. Switch back and forth for rebuttal. With a bit of practice you can present a most entertaining as well as enlightening debate. The hat serves as a cue that the roles are shifting back and forth.

➤ Provide the option for your students to demonstrate their debating skills by presenting their argument to an outside audience, perhaps the board of education, city council, the school administration, or on the local cable television channel. This would require students to carefully research the issue, analyze the supporting data, and rehearse their presentations.

FOR ADDITIONAL READING

Branham, R.J. (1991). *Debate and Critical Analysis: The Harmony of Conflict.* Hillsdale, NJ: L. Erlbaum Associates.

Freeley, A.J. (1993). *Argumentation and Debate: Critical Thinking for Reasoned Decision Making.* Belmont, CA: Wadsworth Publishing Co.

Towne, R. (1975). *Establishing Belief: The Process of Proving.* Skokie, IL: National Textbook.

Vancil, D.L. (1993). *Rhetoric and Argumentation.* Boston: Allyn and Bacon.

Ziegelmueller, G.W., Kay, J., & Dause, C. (1990). *Argumentation: Inquiry and Advocacy.* Englewood Cliffs, NJ: Prentice-Hall.

Films and Videos

Films and videos can be a tremendous asset in some lessons. The challenge facing teachers using films or videos in class is that their students have been over-exposed to the medium at home. Most students spend more time facing a television or movie screen each year than they do in class. And much of what they have seen is action-packed, lusty, and very professional. Educational films, which are usually low budget and often of low technical quality, can be weak competition for students' attention.

Yet, when used effectively films and videos can be a powerful learning aid. The visual media can take students places they could never visit, help them see things they could never see or experience, and make the things they have read about come alive. Good films and videotapes can be very effective in arousing interest and motivating students. Many excellent documentary videos are available via commercial or educational broadcasting stations. *The Civil War* series produced by Ken Burns demonstrated the power and appeal of well-done video-broadcasting. (See Chapter 2 for copyright laws and fair educational use of videotaped programs.)

Selecting the right film or video is crucial. It must clearly fit into the lesson, not simply be an add-on or time-killer. It is only a tool for helping you attain your instructional objective. A good film or videotape does not replace good teaching, it complements it.

➤ Check with your local library or television station about the availability of these programs. Many commercial organizations lend free films and videos. Colleges and governmental organizations are also sources of free or inexpensive films or videos.

➤ Whatever the source, the cardinal rule in using any audio-visual material is to preview it first to determine its appropriateness. You don't want any surprises in class! Evaluate the film or video for accuracy, age-appropriateness, cultural or gender bias, relevancy to your class, and production quality. A bad program is worse than none at all.

➤ As you preview a film or videotape, jot down potential processing questions and main points you want to stress in the debriefing. If only portions of the film or video are worth showing, observe the timer to determine when the desired segment begins and ends.

➤ The biggest risk of audio-visual media is that it can become a passive learning experience for students, little more than a recorded lecture. Successful learning from films and video hinges upon the teacher's ability to actively engage students in the experience. One way is to assign students a task to accomplish while viewing the presentation. This may take the form of two or three questions to answer, behaviors to count, words to define, or examples to observe.

➤ Another way to keep students actively involved in visual media is to stop the film or video occasionally and ask questions about what they've seen or to predict what they think will happen next. In affecting learning, the subsequent processing of the film or video is as important as what is seen and heard. Ask questions that stimulate reflection about the experience. Help students connect what they have learned in this presentation with prior knowledge and skills.

➤ Do not put on a film or video and then leave the room while students watch it, even if you have seen it 50 times. Apart from the liability issues of leaving an unmonitored classroom, your absence suggests to students the film is just being used to fill time and really isn't very important.

➤ Don't feel compelled to rewind the film immediately. Proceed directly to your debriefing activity and rewind the film later.

➤ Experiment with just using small clips from films and videos to augment lectures. A brief two- or three-minute segment illustrating an important point adds variety to any lesson and can enhance attention and retention. It is crucial that the desired segment be cued up and focus and volume levels set before the lesson begins. It is also imperative to adjust the lighting for optimal viewing of the screen.

➤ After the film or video, solicit candid feedback from your students as to how helpful it really was. If it gets low marks, don't use it again. You might even have them complete a brief rating form. Don't just ask if they liked the film, ask what they learned from it.

➤ If you have not learned how to work the VCR or thread the film projector, find someone in the school to teach you. It is much better to know how to do this than to always depend on finding someone else to do it.

One last tip: Be sure you know where to quickly locate a projector replacement bulb and how to change it if help is not immediately available.

HELPFUL RESOURCES FOR MORE INFORMATION

Emerson, A. (1993). *Teaching Media in the Primary School*. New York: Cassell Educational.

Film & Video Finder. 3rd ed. Medford, NJ: Published for the National Information Center for Educational Media, a Division of Access Innovations, Inc.

Lankford, M.D. (1992). *Films for Learning, Thinking, and Doing*. Englewood, CO: Libraries Unlimited.

Resch, K.E. & Schicker, V.D. (1992). *Using Film in the High School Curriculum: A Practical Guide for Teachers and Librarians*. Jefferson, NC: McFarland & Company, Inc.

Slides

Slides are a relatively inexpensive way to add visuals to your class presentations. You can take slides as you travel to places related to your subject or with a copy stand take slides of photos in books. Take slides of outstanding student projects for use in future classes. Take slides of students working in class on different active learning activities. Use these to prepare a slide presentation for use at open houses or to show your students at the end of the school year. Of course, many commercially prepared slides are available for almost any topic. Discarded filmstrips can be cut into individual frames and placed in cardboard or plastic slide mounts.

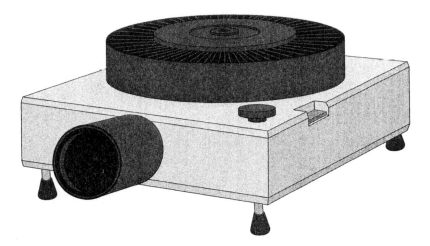

➤ With a copy stand slides can be easily taken of pictures from books and maga-zines. Inexpensive title slides can be made by constructing them on a computer and photographing the layout directly from the monitor. You will need to mount your camera on a tripod and tilt the camera to assure the lens is parallel with the monitor screen. Another option is to print (preferably with a laser printer) your title slides on colored papers and photograph these on a copy stand. Either way use large size fonts (at least 36 point).

➤ Be sure you know how to take a carousel off a projector if a slide jams. By plac-ing a coin in the slot in the center of the slide tray and twisting you can release the carousel from the projector.

➤ It is better to use carousel trays that hold 80 slides than the ones for 140. They are less prone to jamming.

➤ Students in the furthest corners of the room must be able to clearly read your slides. Using too small a font is perhaps the biggest mistake in using slides.

➤ A horizontal format is best. It fits the screen better. It is visually distracting to alternate back and forth between horizontal and vertical formats. Fill up the screen with the largest image possible.

➤ The lower quarter of the screen is difficult to see from the back of the room. For that reason it is best to project only onto the upper three-quarters of the screen.

➤ Insert black slides at the beginning and end of your slide program. Avoid blind-ing your students with a white, light-filled screen.

➤ The biggest disadvantage of slides is that the room must be sufficiently darkened that they project sharply on the screen. Turning out or dimming some of the room lights will usually suffice. Avoid totally dark rooms as they are conducive to sleeping and mischief.

➤ Preview your slides to make sure they all are placed in the correct position and sequence.

➤ Have a spare bulb available and know how to change it.

➤ When showing slides, stand off to the side so you do not block the view of any students.

➤ Use a remote control with an extension cord to allow you freedom to move away from the projector.

Videotaping

Camcorders and VCRs are widely available in schools and homes. Used wisely video recording can be a versatile, powerful, instructional tool. It can also motivate reluctant students. Current models of camcorders are simple to use, requiring little experience to operate. As with any other instructional technique, the key to success is careful preparation and planning.

➤ Before you attempt to use a camcorder in class, be sure you have practiced using it. Double check that the battery is fully charged.

➤ If you use the same videotape repeatedly, mark on the label the length of time the tape consumes. That will make planning the class time to allot easier the next time. Also file processing questions and any related student activities with the tape for easy access.

➤ One teacher videotapes parts of the opening day discussion of rules, routines, expectations, and grade policies. If the principal has an opening presentation, that might also be included on the tape. Students joining the class after the first day sign out the video to view it in the library or at home in the evening. This can also be a useful option for assisting hearing-impaired students or others for whom English is not their primary language. Any student who wants to review the first day might choose to check out the tape overnight. Some parents might even be interested in viewing it to learn more about your class.

➤ Take the camcorder along to tape field trips, special speakers (with their permission), or other interesting lessons.

➤ Videotape class activities to send to students who are absent with extended illnesses.

➤ Record various interesting class experiences throughout the year to show at the parents' open house or when making a presentation at a Parents/Teachers Association meeting.

➤ Use a camcorder to record various activities and events throughout the school year. On the last day of the year show the videotape in your class. Students will love seeing themselves and recalling some of the highlights of their year.

➤ As more schools turn to portfolio assessments, videotaping will be incorporated as part of their student evaluation process. Each student might have his or her own videotape that is periodically updated.

➤ Some high-quality class-produced videotapes might be shown on the local cable channel. While providing a valuable educational service you are also creating good public relations for your school.

➤ Videotape students involved in successful lessons. Send these home with students to show their parents. Most parents will love the opportunity to see their kids involved in schoolwork.

➤ Don't overlook the value reviewing videotapes of your own teaching as a means of self-improvement and professional development. The videotape creates a truthful memory of the lesson. Use the videotape to stimulate reflection on your teaching. Retain videotapes of successful teaching experiences to include in your professional portfolio.

FOR MORE INFORMATION

Artesani, M. (1994-present). *Teaching's* "videoclub exchange" (a monthly column), *Teaching K-8.*

Cates, W.M. (May 1989). "Making more effective use of films and videotapes in the classroom." *The Clearing House, 62,* 401-407.

Eckart, J.A. & Gibson, S.L. (1993). "Using camcorders to improve teaching." *The Clearing House, 66 (5),* 288-292.

Matson, M. (1989). *Using Your Camcorder.* New York: AMPHOTO.

Merrill, J. (1992). *Camcorder Video: Shooting and Editing Techniques.* Englewood Cliffs, NJ: Prentice Hall.

Nourie, B.L. (April 1990). "Camcorders and classrooms." *The Clearing House, 63,* 363-365.

Dyadic Encounters

A dyadic encounter is a structured dialog between two (or occasionally three) students. It works best to prepare a sheet or a small booklet. A booklet of 10 to 20 pages works better than a single sheet as the students are more likely to fully focus upon one question at a time and not race ahead. (**Hint:** Make mini-booklets by cutting an 8-1/2 × 11-inch sheet of paper into four smaller sheets.) On the first page include a brief paragraph giving directions on how to proceed through the stimulus questions.

A dyadic encounter can work with any topic in which you want students to reflect on their experiences, opinions, or attitudes. The booklet may contain questions (e.g., "What qualities do you most value in a friend?" or "What do you think are the most pressing problems facing our country today?") or sentence stems (e.g., "One thing I would like to be better at is..." or "The character in *Moby Dick* most like me is..." or "If I could have dinner alone with one historical character it would be..."). Both students respond to each question or stem and take turns going first. Encourage students to ask each other questions and to help clarify each other's responses. The intent of the dyadic encounter is to stimulate thought about a specific topic.

A variation on the dyadic encounter is the Talk-Walk exercise. Students conduct their dyadic encounter while walking around. This can work well on a nice day when you can take the class outside. Establish restrictions on where they may roam. As they walk together, they discuss the assigned topic. At a whistle or other cue, they all return to the classroom.

Demonstrations

Demonstration is an essential step when you are teaching a skill. It provides an opportunity for students to see the task modeled. Adequate preparation is the key to effective demonstrations. Have any needed equipment or materials readily available. Pay attention to the details in your preparation. Assure that all students can clearly see the demonstration. If necessary, allow those in the back to stand to gain an unobstructed view. One option is to have someone who has mastered the skill demonstrate it while you narrate the process.

As you introduce the demonstration, be sure to explain its purpose and to focus students' attention on each step as you proceed. You might choose to demonstrate a task or skill at regular speed and then repeat the demonstration in slow speed, stopping to discuss each step in more detail. Explain why you are doing each step as you proceed. You might occasionally ask students questions at crucial points in the demonstration. In most instances it is best to keep your demonstration short, probably no longer than five minutes. Attention will begin to wane if it drags on much longer.

Ideally, your demonstration should be followed by an opportunity for the students to practice the skill you have just demonstrated. Supervise their practice and permit opportunities to receive feedback from the teacher or from peers.

Boardwork

Math teachers have traditionally had students work through problems at the chalkboard. While this can be an effective means of giving students practice at problem solving and assessing progress, with some creativity it can be even more instructive and fun. Some teachers have problems already written on the board before the class begins. As students enter the room they might be assigned to work on these problems at the board in pairs. The teacher can offer hints to pairs who are having difficulty. Students who are not working at the board are called upon to analyze the completed problems.

Action Research

An effective learning device for teaching the process of scientific investigation and systematic problem solving is "action research." This may take the form of a case study, an experiment, a survey, or interviews. Students learn how to "ask the right questions," gather data, tabulate results, draw conclusions, and present findings. Action research can be conducted in cooperative teams or as a whole-class project with various delegated tasks. Guest speakers may be invited to provide the class with some background information on the problem under investigation. The final report might be presented orally or in written form to a group or organization, such as the city council or board of education.

Interviews

Many lessons can be enriched with the use of interviews. Best used as a homework assignment, potential targets of interviews might include parents, grandparents, local government leaders, peers, civic leaders, neighbors, or business persons. Besides enriching the students' knowledge and motivation through "active learning," interviews are also a good public relations tool. People in the community, especially parents, generally enjoy being asked about their experiences and opinions. It invites parents and others to have discussions with young people which might never otherwise occur.

It is best to have students develop in class a set of questions that will be used to structure their interviews. Give them sufficient time and specific instructions on whom to interview and a deadline for reporting their results. The interview results can be submitted as a written assignment or discussed in class as a large group or in small groups.

One variation of the interview is to conduct them as mock press conferences in which one or more class members assume the role of a person or group being studied in the class (astronaut, president, explorer, author, scientist, etc.). They should be given time to research their role and instructed to answer all questions from the point of view of their assigned character. The rest of the class assumes the role of television or newspaper reporters who then interview the "celebrity." A moderator or panel can also be appointed and a *Meet the Press* format can be used.

Construction

Building or making things is an integral part of many courses. Examples include baking cakes, building models, sewing a tie, constructing a house, making a stained-glass window, reconditioning a piece of furniture, taking and developing photographs, reproducing a chair, making a clay pot, composing a song, making a quilt, or constructing a poster.

Such hands-on projects are among the most valuable learning experiences. They closely approximate reality or rehearse activities actually used in the world outside schools. Students tend to become highly motivated when involved in real-life tasks.

It is important to clarify the boundaries of the assignment, including any evaluation criteria. Deadlines must be specified. For very large projects it is often desirable to have several checkpoint deadlines prior to the final due date.

Tell students what help they may receive from others. There are many advantages to using group projects where feasible.

See that particularly outstanding products are publicized, with the student's permission. Some might be exhibited in government buildings, malls, fairs, festivals, local cable television, or school open houses. Consider inviting the local newpaper or television to do a feature story on noteworthy accomplishments of your students.

Almost daily, local and national newspapers, television, and professional journals highlight outstanding learning activities. Keep an idea notebook of ones you might adapt to your class.

Card Sorts

Card sorts are a useful device for helping students narrow a range of options, clarify criteria, or set priorities. Potential topics for a card sort might include career options, life goals, interests, criteria for selecting a career or college, or funding priorities. Any choice in which more than a dozen alternatives are available can be adapted to a card sort.

The first step is to generate a list of alternatives. This can be done as a large-group brainstorm, listing the alternatives on the chalkboard or newsprint. After the list is constructed each student prints each option on a separate card or slip of paper. (It works well to precut or have students cut 8-1/2 × 11-inch sheets of paper into eight equal slips, 4-1/4 × 2-3/4 inches each.) After each student has a complete "deck" of cards, directions for the card sort are given. Instruct the students to sort their cards into three piles: "yes," "maybe," and "no." After the initial sort have them count the number of cards in the "yes" pile. If they have more than ten or twelve, ask them to sort through one more time, sorting that stack into two more piles: "those they feel red hot about" and "those they feel lukewarm about." The goal is to get the options down to less than ten.

Once the cards in the top "yes" pile are down to ten, instruct the students to spread out all the cards in their "yes" pile so they can see them all at once. Direct the class to study their cards carefully. After a pause, instruct them that they may only have one card. "Which one will it be? Pick it up and hold it in your hand." After everyone has made their selection tell them they may have one more card, to pick it up and place it behind their first choice. After everyone has made their second choice, instruct them to continue picking up their cards one at a time until the whole stack of "yes" cards is in their hand. They should then record the list in order on paper.

Once the card sort is completed, you may process the activity in a large-group discussion or in small groups. Another option is to construct a large grid on the board revealing the top priorities of the group. Experiment with variations on the card sort. It can be used successfully in almost any subject.

Rating Scales/Questionnaires

Instruments such as questionnaires and surveys can serve a number of valuable purposes: to enhance interest and motivation in a topic, to introduce a new lesson, or to assess prior knowledge, attitudes, and experiences. Students should be told whether their answers will remain private or they will be asked to share them. Experiment with using soft music in the background while students are completing the instrument.

You can construct your own survey or questionnaire or you can easily adapt them from newspaper and magazine articles, especially those reporting survey results pertaining to topics you are teaching. Many teacher guides also include brief surveys or questionnaires.

A variety of follow-up activities can be used with the survey or questionnaire. A large-group discussion might be held to process the students' answers. Students can talk about and compare their answers in pairs or small groups. Tabulate the answers on a chart or graph to synthesize the group data. A small fishbowl discussion in the middle of the class can be used to facilitate examination of the content. If comparison data are available from other groups it might be shared with the class.

As an introduction to a new topic, construct your own questionnaire to include significant facts related to the subject. Be clear that it is not a quiz and will not be graded. As each question is scored, you are reinforcing the information included in the questionnaire.

Oral Presentations

Oral presentations have long been used as an instructional strategy in American schools. At their worst they are frightening to give, boring to watch, and time-wasting. Used effectively oral presentations can be stimulating and motivating learning aids. To be of maximum benefit the teacher must appropriately structure the oral presentation assignment. Most students do not know how to give a brief, focused presentation. When making the assignment it is important to provide adequate coaching on the "why," "what," and "how" of the project. The following suggestions might be adapted to improve your students' presentations.

➤ To reduce the anxiety of talking in front of the group, begin with safe topics the students know well. Themes such as "my dream vacation" or "my favorite game" tap a student's experiences. Permitting students to teach a skill they know or talk about a favorite possession are topics students can present with little extra study.

➤ Letting two students do a presentation together is less anxiety-provoking.

➤ Assign students to read magazine articles related to an assigned subject area. The students should take notes summarizing the key points of the article and prepare a four- to five-minute talk. Specify the main parts of their presentation. The talk could be split between two students, dividing the content between them.

➤ In most instances individual oral presentations should be limited to ten minutes. Few students possess the skills and enthusiasm to hold their listeners' attention longer. Little is gained and much precious time is lost if your class must endure a succession of long, boring reports. It probably wouldn't be too exciting for you, either.

➤ It is helpful to demonstrate the oral presentation you are assigning. Model the parts of the demonstration and process the presentation afterwards, providing a written outline of its parts. Another option is to videotape your five-minute presentation and to replay it, pointing out the different parts of the talk. Encourage the class to critique the presentation. It is best if it is not perfect. If you can point out your own errors or deficiencies, they will realize they don't have to be perfect.

➤ If students have some experience in giving oral presentations, allow two to three minutes at the end of the talk for the rest of the class to ask questions of the presenter. This develops the ability to think on their feet and to speak extemporaneously.

➤ Sometimes teachers provide an opportunity for the class to offer feedback to the presenter. This may be done in writing, responding to such criteria as, "List one thing the speaker did well" or "One part of the presentation that needs improvement."

➤ Another tactic for developing oral presentation skills is to develop a persuasive speech. This assignment requires students to take a stand on an issue, to research it, and to develop a brief persuasive presentation.

➤ It is best to set a time limit for student presentations. The time should be appropriate to the age and developmental level of your students. Seldom should a solo presentation exceed ten minutes, even for high school students. For elementary students, three to four minutes are generally sufficient, especially if everyone in the class is assigned to do one.

➤ The debate format is also a most useful alternative for developing the skills of oral persuasion.

➤ Require students to speak from note cards. Don't let them write out a verbatim script and discourage them from trying to memorize the whole speech. Encourage them to use a visual aid or prop. This serves as a cue, creates added interest, and gives them something to do with their hands.

➤ Oral presentations can also be incorporated into cooperative learning activities, with each team member presenting a different part of the program. It is easier to stand in front of the class as a member of a supportive group than alone.

➤ Having students interview a student can be a valuable learning experience. The focus of the interview must be established ahead of time. Again, it is easier if the topic is one the student already knows. Another option is to assign students to various historical or fictional roles. The students then study the lives and times of the characters they are playing. The class then interviews them as reporters with the role player answering in character.

➤ It is sometimes helpful to videotape the presentations and allow students to review them later either alone, in teams, or with the teacher. Students might be allowed to check them out overnight to show their parents. Some of the better ones might be saved for use at the parent open house.

Role Playing

Role plays are a valuable technique for simulating real-life situations. They provide a safe environment for students to experiment with new behaviors and skills. The role play can arouse interest in a topic, as well as encourage students to empathize with differing viewpoints. Because students become totally involved in their roles, the learning is holistic, involving their emotional and psychomotor domains as well as the cognitive. The role play is one activity in which students don't have to be anxious about coming up with the single right answer. Giving them permission to make mistakes even encourages more risk taking and experimentation. Even low-ability students can experience success. The creativity of all students can be unleashed through role-playing activities.

Role plays are typically very short, seldom more than 15 minutes. In a role play, two or more students improvise a specific, assigned scenario. These roles may be ones that are familiar (e.g., introducing a new student to a friend) or beyond their realm of experiences (e.g., a World War II resistance fighter, a nuclear scientist, or a U.S. President). The actors receive only a sketchy outline of the scenario. Role plays may be set in the past, present, or future. The directive may be no more than a sentence or two. For example, two students in a French class may role play a job interview or ordering a meal from a menu.

Here are some suggestions for using role plays effectively:

➤ Plan role plays to support your instructional objectives. Depending on their function, role plays can be used in the beginning to introduce a new topic, in the middle of a lesson to help teach a skill or concept, or at the conclusion of a lesson to tie together and reinforce the whole lesson. Whenever used, role plays should have a sound educational purpose.

➤ Generally, the purpose of the role play should be clearly explained ahead of time. In some role plays where the purpose is to sensitize students to their attitudes, it would be detrimental to fully explain the intent beforehand. In such instances, seek their cooperation by explaining that you'd like their help in an experiment. It is important to avoid forcing students into roles that will prove embarrassing.

➤ To overcome some of the initial resistance to role playing, it may be best not to use the word "role play" the first time it is used. Many students have preconceived notions about role plays. Describe it as an experiment or simply say, "Assume for a moment you are _____." or "Respond as though you really were _____."

➤ It's usually best to seek volunteers for the role play unless everyone is going to be participating. You will likely encounter less resistance to role plays if everyone participates in small groups. (Groups of three seem to work well.) By having people assume roles, they must talk: there is no place to hide as in group discussions.

➤ You must provide a safe climate for students or they will not get into the roles. After students have gained some experience in small-group role plays, some (but not all) will feel more comfortable role playing in front of the class. Do invite and encourage participation by the introverts as well, but it's probably best not to force very shy children to role play in front of the whole class.

➤ Explain the roles or give brief written descriptions to each role player. Keep the scenarios and role descriptions brief. A sentence or two is usually sufficient. Assign non-participants to make structured observations of the role play. An observer's worksheet is helpful in focusing their attention. Rearrange the room to enable everyone to see. If several simultaneous role plays are occurring, spread out the groups so they do not interfere with each other.

➤ Students are more receptive to role plays if they have some freedom in choosing how to play it.

➤ Keep the introduction to the role play simple. The more you build up the role play, the more anxiety you are likely to create. Succinctly convey the essentials. One tactic used by some teachers is to wave a wand and say, "You're a __(role to be played)__!"

➤ Giving the role players props, a costume, or a hat sometimes adds a touch of realism and increases their motivation to assume the role. Having something in their hands seems to also reduce anxiety.

➤ At least the first time you use role plays, assign roles they can easily play. You may have to provide some prompts for initial dialogue.

➤ Have students use fictitious names rather than their own. It makes getting into the role a bit easier. It adds a touch of humor to make up funny, nicknames for them to use.

➤ One tactic often used is to interrupt the role play and have two people reverse roles. Or have another student step into a role and continue the role play.

➤ Immediately after one group completes a role play, have a second group repeat the same role play with a different twist.

➤ Another option is to have the audience participate by giving the role players directions. For example, in a foreign language class they might suggest a scenario or responses to help structure the role play.

➤ Adapt the "empty chair" technique used by Gestalt therapists in exploring conflicting situations. It is a good way to look at two sides of an issue. Only use this technique with content that is "safe" and doesn't evoke strong feelings in the student. A student volunteer sits in a chair facing an empty chair. The student begins by arguing for a particular issue or course of action (e.g., compulsory education, banning cigarettes, curfews). After 15 to 20 seconds, say "Switch." The student then moves to the other chair and argues the opposite point of view. After another 15 to 20 seconds, again call "Switch." Repeat three to four times or until the student runs out of things to say. A safe way to introduce this is to have everyone in the class do it simultaneously, or break the class into groups of three with one volunteer in each group who engages in the "empty chair."

➤ A commonly used role play is the "press conference." One or more students assume roles, such as famous historical characters, scientists, explorers, or authors. The rest of the class act as reporters and interview the "celebrity." As a variation, use a *Meet the Press* format with a panel of two to four journalists who conduct the interview with a moderator.

➤ Videotape the role play. As it is played back, occasionally stop it to process significant points. This is especially valuable in introducing new skills. Students might even take the video home to study their own progress.

➤ Don't allow the role play to run on. Try to cut it off at a high point. If the scenario has run its course, cut off the role play and debrief. If it isn't working, cut it off but don't belittle the actors for their efforts.

➤ Thank students for participating in the role play. If they have been asked to take a special risk, such as performing in front of the class, praise or a small reward is sometimes appropriate.

➤ Don't criticize students' role-playing performances (unless it's a theater class). The threat of evaluation will surely stifle students' willingness to engage in role plays. Keep the focus on the actions, not the acting.

➤ Be sure to always allow time afterwards for processing the role play. This is the most important part of the role play; don't rush it. Debriefing is absolutely essential if conflict or negative emotions are evoked as part of the role play. Ideally, it should immediately follow the role play. Feedback should be solicited from the observers as well as the role play participants. Ask questions that explore content as well as feelings. It is important to help students make connections between the role play situation and real-world events.

➤ Morry van Ments, author of the revised *The Effective Use of Role-Play* (East Brunswick, NJ: Nichols, 1989) suggests the following steps in debriefing a role play:

1. Bring players out of the role.
2. Clarify what happened (get the facts).
3. Correct any mistakes or misunderstandings.
4. Dissipate any anxiety or tension.
5. Elicit the assumptions, feelings and changes that occurred during the role play.
6. Give the players an opportunity to develop self-observations.
7. Develop observation skills.
8. Relate the outcome of the role play to the original objectives.
9. Analyze why things turned out as they did.
10. Draw conclusions about the behaviors observed.
11. Reinforce or correct learnings.
12. Draw out new points for consideration.
13. If appropriate, deduce ways of improving behaviors.
14. Generalize to other situations.
15. Link with prior learning.
16. Provide a plan for future learning.

➤ Be patient. Role playing may be a new experience for some students. As a more trusting class climate emerges, students will feel more comfortable taking risks and less inhibited.

➤ If the role play went well and you would like to use it again with future classes, make notes on any refinements you might want to make the next time.

Dramatization

In dramatization students act out a skill or situation before the class. It may be done with or without the use of scripts. A dramatization is a mini-play. The roles are much more defined than in a simple role play. Each character is given instructions as to the role they are to demonstrate and suggestions as to the behaviors and techniques to be included. The dramatization will usually be rehearsed prior to presentation to the whole class.

Strive to minimize the potential embarrassment of participants by matching the roles to the personality of the students as much as possible. Creating a safe atmosphere for the dramatization is important so that all participants feel at ease. Generally, it is best to explain what you will be asking the students to do before soliciting volunteers. Don't force anyone to participate.

Some dramatizations will require advance preparation. Generally it is best not to use verbatim scripts but to assign roles and provide guidelines for the roles to be assumed. Occasionally you may employ improvisation to encourage students to develop their creativity.

Experiment with using puppets to create your dramatization. Most students find it much easier to invest themselves in a role through a puppet. Costumes, props, hats, or masks can also arouse students' enthusiasm for the skit.

The group-processing of the experience is an integral part of the learning process. Give careful thought to developing good open-ended processing questions. Help the class clearly understand the purpose and different aspects of the dramatization.

Here are some examples of dramatization used by teachers in various subject areas.

➤ Some foreign language teachers have students enact soap operas in their new language.

➤ Conduct a mock constitutional convention.

➤ Present past or current Presidential debates.

➤ Conduct a press conference of famous scientists, artists, explorers, or inventors about their accomplishments.

➤ Present a public hearing of an agency on some social or environmental issue. Each side has to prepare testimony and present it to the panel who must ask questions of the witnesses.

➤ Conduct a mock trial. It could be over some fictitious character from literature or a real person from history.

Simulations/Games

Games and simulations can be powerful learning strategies. However, only use them when they have a sound educational purpose related to the topic you are teaching. Academic games should require some use of intellectual skills, rather than chance, to succeed. The skills used in this game should have application to the real world. Academic games may be very brief, requiring only a few minutes of class time, or may continue over a number of days, perhaps stretched out over several weeks or longer.

➤ Besides using games to build skills, they can also be used as rewards for good performance.

➤ It is best to avoid games that end with only one winner. While the winner feels good, the negative emotions experienced by the losers make it an unpleasant experience for most students. They will have plenty of opportunities outside the classroom to confront defeat and to know how it feels to lose. Team competition is preferable to individual competition.

➤ As with all learning activities, explain the purpose of the game or simulation. There may be some affective learnings you expect to explore and may not be overtly described ahead of time.

➤ Some form of scoring system should be included in the structure of the game. To score well one must be required to use the academic skills, rather than luck.

➤ Ask the following questions in considering a game for use in your class:

  ➤ Is it fun?
  ➤ Is it challenging for *your* students?
  ➤ What is the purpose of the game?
  ➤ How will this game further my learning objectives?
  ➤ What skills does this game develop?
  ➤ Is this game age-appropriate?
  ➤ Are skills, rather than luck, required to win?
  ➤ Are the rules relatively simple? Do they need modification?
  ➤ Is team rather than individual competition used in this game?
  ➤ Will the game reward inappropriate behavior?
  ➤ How will scores be determined and recorded?

➤ Consider redesigning an existing game to fit your classroom needs.

➤ Robert Slavin promotes the use of Teams/Games/Tournament (TGT) as a cooperative learning activity. Students are broken into heterogeneous teams allowing students within each team to collaborate in mastering new content. The teams then compete against each other in academic contests. For the tournament phase, students compete against students of similar ability and their success contributes to their teams' score.

In simulations students assume roles and make choices as though they were the person in that role. It is more complex and evolving than a role play which focuses upon a single incident. As a structured activity the simulation provides consequences for the choices the players make. For a simulation to succeed students must be convinced to realistically act out their roles. They must try to think and act like a real-world person in that role.

Simulations are categorized by Margaret Gredler according to the types of tasks and nature of interactions of the participants. Tactical-Decision simulations require students to interact in resolving a complex problem or crisis and to arrive at a logical, safe resolution. The participants must interpret data, develop options, and implement strategies. Simulations that require management of economic resources fall under this category. In contrast, the Social-Process simulations encourage students to interact to address social challenges or to attain a political or social goal. Participants must interact and react to each other in a social milieu. Such simulations often involve interviewing, negotiating, cooperation, questioning, or persuasion. Communication or empathy-building simulations are of this variety.

The most important learning occurs after the simulation when the participants reflect on what happened during the game. This debriefing should encourage them to examine their thoughts, feelings, and actions that were elicited by the simulation. Generalizations of these insights for future real-world application should also be examined. This reflection must be facilitated by the teacher, not left to chance.

Processing done in small groups may assure that more people actively participate. A good way to facilitate small-group thinking about the game is to provide several written questions for each group to discuss. Each group should have a recorder. Later, the group answers are discussed as a whole class.

The latest development in the world of academic games and simulations is the wide availability of the computer. Thousands of computer games and simulations are now available. Much of it is commercial, although many good free or shareware programs are also available and easily accessible through the Internet or computer user clubs. There are indeed some pearls in this sea of computer simulations and games. There is also a lot of garbage. While the potential of computer applications with multigraphics, sounds, and instantaneous feedback are attractive and possess a great deal of potential, the teacher must use sound criteria in selecting those games and simulations to use in class. A risk is that the eye-catching graphics can distract the player from the real purpose of the game. Don't just use a game because you have it. Use as rigorous criteria in selecting a computer game as you would a board game. Is it worth class time? A major disadvantage of most computer games is that only one or two persons at a time can usually participate.

For suggestions in designing original effective simulations see one of the resources listed below, particularly Margaret Gredler's book.

➤ To keep track of small game pieces, store them in plastic sandwich or freezer bags.

➤ Laminate any paper game items that will be used repeatedly.

➤ One kind of game students love is the television quiz show. Adapt the format of *Jeopardy, The College Bowl, Family Feud,* or other popular television programs to entice students into review, reinforcement, and assessment of your classroom content. Such activities add variety, energy and enthusiasm to your curriculum. Although some element of competition is involved, try to structure the game so everyone wins or downplay the competitive aspect.

➤ Read the group energy level. When the enthusiasm for the game begins to wane, end the game and proceed to the debriefing phase.

HELPFUL RESOURCES

Bell, R. C. (1988). *Board Games Round the World: A Resource Book for Mathematical Investigations*. New York: Cambridge University Press.

Bright, G.W., Harvey, J.G., & Wheeler, M.M. (1985). *Learning and Mathematics Games*. Reston, VA: National Council of Teachers of Mathematics.

Cornelius, M. (1991). *What's Your Game?: A Resource Book for Mathematical Activities*. NY: Cambridge University Press.

Gredler, M. (1994). *Designing and Evaluating Games and Simulations: A Process Approach*. Houston, TX: Gulf Publishing Co.

Cruickshank, D.R. (1977). *A First Book of Games and Simulations*. Belmont, CA: Wadsworth Pub. Co.

Ellington, H., Addinall, E., & Percival, F. (1981). *Games and Simulations in Science Education*. New York: Nichols Pub. Co.

Jones, K. (1988). *Interactive Learning Events: A Guide for Facilitators*. New York: Nichols Pub. Co.

Kaye, P. (1987). *Games for Math: Playful Ways to Help Your Child Learn Math from Kindergarten to Third Grade*. New York: Pantheon Books.

Salvner, G. (1991). *Literature Festival: Ten Cooperative Learning Games Designed to Stimulate Literary Analysis*. Lakeside, CA: Interaction Publishers.

Scott, M. (1983). *Games for Teaching World History*. Portland, ME: J. Weston Walch.

Scott, M. (1984). *Games and Strategies for Teaching U.S. History*. Portland, ME: J. Weston Walch.

Slavin, R.E. (1991). *Student Team Learning: A Practical Guide to Cooperative Learning*. Washington, D.C.: NEA Professional Library, National Education Association.

Cooperative Learning

The traditional argument for adhering to the bell-shaped normal curve in distributing class grades was that students needed to be prepared for the competitive, "dog-eat-dog" world of work. However, the dramatic changes in the global economy has forced a revolution in the workplace. The emphasis is upon teaching employees to work cooperatively. Quality circles and work teams are now utilized almost universally. Employers realize that to be competitive in the world economy, their employees must be skilled in working collaboratively.

Cooperative learning is comprised of a variety of techniques that requires students to work collaboratively in mixed-ability groups to help each other learn the material. Students are taught to take greater responsibility for their own learning. The ultimate goal of cooperative learning is to enable each student to become more successful in school.

The essential focus of cooperative learning is that students are not competing with other students for success. They are seeking to top their own level of achievement. By helping each other, students can all attain improvement. Success is no longer defined by how many people the student defeats in the grade-race. Cooperative learning succeeds when students become convinced that their success is determined by how well they help each other. They must become interdependent in their use of the available learning resources.

Numerous research studies have found cooperative learning does work. It results at achievement gains in every grade level, for both high- and low-ability students. Research has found cooperative learning to enhance student self-esteem, mutual helping, and more positive attitudes toward teachers and learning. Contrary to the fears of some, high-ability students do not suffer when they work cooperatively with middle and lower ability students.

Direct teaching of the interpersonal skills necessary to work cooperatively is an essential component of cooperative learning.

Cooperative learning is widely used across all grade levels and subjects; probably every school in America has some teachers using cooperative learning. The major spokespersons for cooperative learning have been Roger and David Johnson and Robert Slavin. These educators are among those offering outstanding training programs on the use of cooperative learning. A thorough presentation of cooperative learning is beyond the scope of this book, but you are urged to take a course or workshop to learn more about implementing the various cooperative learning strategies available.

➤ Merely participating in a group activity will not assure success. Several conditions must exist. The students must be working toward a common goal and their success in attaining that goal must be dependent upon working interdependently. Ideally, they must also have to depend upon each other to share resources as well. There is evidence that the use of group rewards enhances cooperative learning efforts of students, but only if the rewards are contingent upon the individual learning of all group members.

➤ Cooperative learning activities can only succeed if a supportive class climate is established. Students must feel free to take risks and to make mistakes.

➤ Be creative in how you form groups. For most temporary groups randomly dividing the class into the desired number of groups will assure a sufficient degree of mixed abilities in each group. Simply counting off and grouping the ones, twos, threes, etc., is the most common tactic. Inject some humor and interest by using unconventional ways of forming equal-size groups. For example, have students line up against the wall in order of their birthdays, without talking. Then break them into the desired number of groups.

➤ The size of the groups will vary with the objective of the activity. Generally, a maximum of five seems to be advisable. Heterogeneity in gender, ability, and ethnicity are desirable. The research shows students involved in cooperative learning become much more accepting of other students, including those different from themselves.

➤ Clear directions are essential for the success of cooperative learning groups. Provide written instructions in assigning any complicated tasks. Give careful thought to the completeness and clarity of your directions. Encourage students to ask questions if they do not understand what they are to do.

➤ Each person in a group has a job. The number of jobs required to complete the assignment determines the size of the cooperative learning group. Sometimes the teacher may assign the specific jobs of each member; other times the group may decide how to break up the functions.

➤ Cooperative learning develops the social skills necessary to work with others: seeking and giving help, listening to others' points of view, and resolving conflicts. Special training has to be provided to students to develop the skills needed for collaborative work. Assessment of each student's social skills is an essential component of successful cooperative learning. Training in the constructive management of conflict is vital for success. For many students cooperation may be a new classroom mode of learning. Patience and guidance will be necessary.

➤ Cooperative groups can be especially valuable in editing each other's written compositions. Students should be provided with a checklist of criteria that are used to evaluate each other's compositions. The peer editor places his or her signature on the criteria checklist. At each step of the writing process—from conceptualization through polished product—the cooperative team aids each other. Ideally, everyone submits a high quality written product while saving the teacher much time reading and re-reading rough drafts.

➤ Some teachers have their students explain and grade their homework assignments in cooperative learning groups. An efficient routine must be established for the procedures to follow, with several roles assigned (accuracy checker, grade recorder, coach, explainer). An advantage of this group approach is that students have the opportunity to help each other understand why they made the errors they did and to obtain corrective feedback.

➤ Cooperative learning groups are sometimes permitted to take examinations or tests together. The day prior to the test, groups may help each other review. It is essential that the groups be heterogeneous in ability. On the test day students may take individual examinations. After the answer sheet is turned in, the students meet with their cooperative learning group and collaborate on the examination. A second answer sheet is turned in, with performances on both exams being recorded for each student.

"The reason cooperative learning is so successful is that the context of a work group is more important than the content of the group. If you have a group of people who care for and are committed to one another, they are going to achieve the goal of the activity much more quickly than if each were to attempt the task alone."
—HARRY WONG, 1991

"Cooperative learning methods are creating a classroom revolution. No longer is a quiet class thought to be a learning class; we know now that learning is often best achieved in conversation among students. Teachers all over the world are breaking up the rows in which students have sat for so long, and are creating classroom environments in which students routinely help each other master academic material."
—ROBERT SLAVIN, 1994

FOR ADDITIONAL READING

Bennett, B., Rolheiser-Bennett, C., & Stevahn, L. (1991). *Cooperative Learning: Where Heart Meets Mind*. Bothell, WA: Professional Development Associates.

Breeden, T. & Mosley, J. (1992). *The Cooperative Learning Companion*. Nashville, TN: Incentive Publications, Inc.

Forte, I. & Mackenzie, J. (1991). *Pulling Together for Cooperative Learning: Cooperative Learning Activities and Projects for Middle Grades.* Nashville, TN: Incentive Publications, Inc.

Hamm, M. & Adams, D. (1992). *The Collaborative Dimensions of Learning.* Norwood, NJ: Ablex Pub. Corp.

Johnson, D.W. & Johnson, R.T. (1994). *Learning Together and Alone: Cooperative, Competitive, and Individualistic Learning.* Needham Heights, MA: Allyn and Bacon.

Kagan, S. (1994). *Cooperative Learning.* San Juan Capistrano, CA: Resources for Teachers.

Kessler, C. (Ed.), (1992). *Cooperative Language Learning: A Teacher's Resource Book.* Englewood Cliffs, NJ: Prentice Hall Regents.

Lyman, L., Foyle, H.C., & Azwell, T.S. (1993). *Cooperative Learning in the Elementary Classroom.* Washington, D.C.: NEA Professional Library.

Rybak, S. (1992). *Cooperative Learning Throughout the Curriculum: Together We Learn Better.* Carthage, IL: Good Apple Inc.

Salvner, G. (1991). *Literature Festival: Ten Cooperative Learning Games Designed to Stimulate Literary Analysis.* Lakeside, CA: Interaction Publishers.

Sharan, S. (Ed.), (1994). *Handbook of Cooperative Learning Methods.* Westport, CT: Greenwood Press.

Slavin, R.E. (1991). *Student Team Learning: A Practical Guide to Cooperative Learning.* Washington, D.C.: NEA Professional Library, National Education Association.

Slavin, R.E. (1994). *A Practical Guide to Cooperative Learning.* Boston: Allyn and Bacon.

Stahl, R.J. (1994). *Cooperative Learning in Social Studies: A Handbook for Teachers.* Menlo Park, CA: Addison-Wesley.

Sample Letter to Parents—
Beginning of School Year

(Date)

Greetings:

Do you have a special talent? Do you enjoy an interesting hobby or activity? What skills do you use in your work? Have you traveled to an interesting or exciting place? Have you had a significant life experience from which young people might learn something? Please consider sharing any of these special abilities or events with my class sometime during the school year.

If you will complete and return the section below, I will contact you to arrange a mutually convenient time when you might visit my class. This is a valuable opportunity to become a part of the school community and to show your child you are interested in his/her education.

Sincerely,

(Your name)

- -

Name _____

Phone _____

Address _____

_____

_____

What talent, experiences, or hobby would you be willing to share with my students?

RULES FOR CREATIVE BRAINSTORMING

- Generate as many ideas as possible

- Delay evaluation

- Encourage wild, zany ideas

- Build on the ideas of others

150

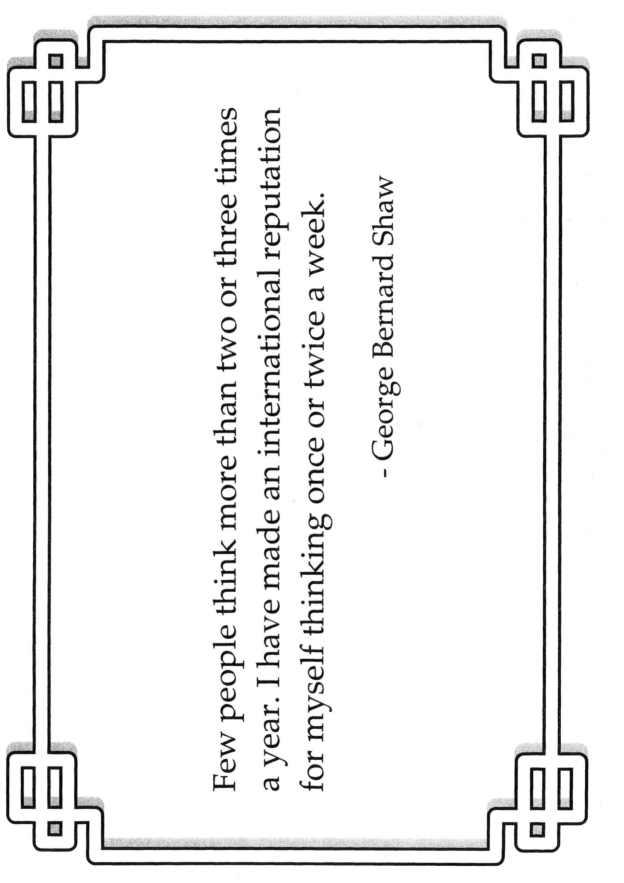

Few people think more than two or three times
a year. I have made an international reputation
for myself thinking once or twice a week.

- George Bernard Shaw

Strategies for Selecting Group Leaders

First person to stand up
Smallest high school graduation class
Got up earliest this morning
Tap person on your right, congratulate
Drives the oldest car
Lowest last two digits in their phone number
Whoever has marker under the desk
Draw cards
Youngest/oldest in group
Born furthest/closest from workshop site
Stayed up the latest last night
Most or least brothers
Traveled the farthest to get here
Has the most animals
Been to the movies the most recently
Nearest birthday
Shortest pinky
Number of siblings
Newest employee
Most seniority on the job
Traffic tickets/least
Wearing the most jewelry
Number of children
Last name comes first in alphabet
Moved most recently
Most exotic vacation
Most recent vacation
Born earliest in year/month
Who has the most colors on
Most children

Went swimming most recently
Person to left of the last group leader
Has the most pennies with them
Came into the room last
Has the most eyelets in their shoes
Changed jobs most recently
Is wearing the smallest watch face
Ate broccoli most recently
Has the largest purse with them
Is using the shortest pencil/pen
Has moved the most times
Married the longest
Mowed the grass most recently
Rented a video most recently
Baked bread most recently
Most years in the profession
Appointed by the last leader
Shortest/tallest
Has the biggest shoe size
The most letters in name
Bought a (_____) most recently
Lives closest to where they were born
Most recent airplane ride
Longest/shortest hair
Had a child most recently
Sitting closest to the door
Sitting nearest the instructor
Graduated most recently
Last person to talk
Everyone point to the next leader at once

Field Trip Checklist

Site: _____ Date of Trip: _____

Contact person: _____ Phone: _____

Departure Time: _____ Return Time: _____

Chaperones: _____

Done

Before the Visit

❑ Identify the purpose of the trip

❑ Contact site to arrange date and time

❑ Obtain administrative approval if necessary

❑ Distribute permission forms

❑ Letter to parents describing details of the visit

❑ Solicit chaperones

❑ Arrange transportation

❑ Make any necessary lunch arrangements

❑ Develop active learning worksheets

❑ Collect and turn in permission forms

❑ Construct map/directions to the site

❑ Discuss behavioral and academic expectations with students

❑ Remind chaperones and students the day before the trip

Day of the Visit

❑ Meet chaperones a few minutes early

❑ Give drivers maps if necessary

❑ Distribute any worksheets

❑ Remind students of when and where to meet

After the Visit

❑ Debrief students and help students connect the visit with prior learning

❑ Write thank you note(s) to chaperones and site coordinator

❑ Note any changes to be made in next field trip

❑ File forms, brochures, lesson plans to use next time

Field Trip Permission Form

We are planning a class field trip on _____

to _____ . We are seeking your

approval for your child to participate. We will be leaving at approximately

_____ and will return to the school at _____ .

We will be traveling by _____ . The trip will be appropriately

supervised. I believe this visit is of sound educational value. Please call me if you

have any questions. I need this form returned to the school by _____ .

The above student has my permission to participate in the above field trip.

_____
(Parent or guardian)

Field Trip Permission Form

We are planning a class field trip on _____

to _____ . We are seeking your

approval for your child to participate. We will be leaving at approximately

_____ and will return to the school at _____ .

We will be traveling by _____ . The trip will be appropriately

supervised. I believe this visit is of sound educational value. Please call me if you

have any questions. I need this form returned to the school by _____ .

The above student has my permission to participate in the above field trip.

_____
(Parent or guardian)

© 1995 by The Center for Applied Research in Education

Audio-Visual Request Form

To: _____   Today's Date _____

From: _____   Room No. _____

Equipment	Date Needed	Time	
		From	Until

TEAM RECORD

TEAM NAME _____

CLASS _____

Team Members	1	2	3	4	5	6	7	Totals
Team Score								
Average Score								

Tasks:

1)_____

2)_____

3)_____

4)_____

5)_____

6)_____

7)_____

CHAPTER 4

Building a Learning Community

Working with Other Teachers

The isolation of the classroom is well known to most experienced teachers. In many schools, a teacher can go through an entire day with little more than superficial contact with other adults. What happens behind the closed classroom door is still guarded as private in some schools. In the past, beginning teachers entered the profession with full responsibility from the first day, learning to teach largely on their own through "trial and error" or "sink or swim." Fortunately there are signs that the school culture is opening up. Increasingly, teachers are collaborating, working in teams, and engaged in peer coaching. Attention to developing collegial relationships and nurturing positive school climates is growing.

➤ If you are a beginning teacher or having difficulty, find a mentor. Identify a teacher whom you respect and whose style and personality is simpatico with yours. Seek someone who is genuinely enthusiastic about teaching and is an exemplary instructor. Share your difficult problems with them and listen openly to their advice.

➤ Talk about teaching with your colleagues. This should involve more than complaining about insufficient supplies or how terrible kids are these days. Nor should conversations be limited to trading "war stories." Encourage a positive focus upon sharing strategies for improving classroom teaching, solving school problems, or seeking innovative ways of doing old tasks.

➤ Experiment with peer coaching. Invite teachers you respect to observe your teaching and provide suggestions for improvement. Let the observer know which areas you are seeking to improve. Of course, if you solicit their feedback, listen to it objectively. Don't discount their views and become defensive.

➤ Ask for help from colleagues. Share your concerns about what you would like to do better. In every building there are successful teachers. Seek them out and learn from their experiences.

➤ Acknowledge the successes of your fellow teachers. Relay positive comments you hear from students about other teachers.

➤ Send special notes and cards to your colleagues recognizing their successes or offering words of comfort during difficult times. Eschew jealousy over the success of other teachers. Your value as a teacher or person is not diminished by the accomplishments of others. To be appreciated is one of the most fundamental human needs.

➤ Share curriculum resources or creative ideas you bring back from professional workshops or read in journals.

➤ After school in-service programs, discuss the content with other teachers. Try to remain open-minded in examining new ideas, always seeking new ways to improve your teaching. Convey to your colleagues that you value improvement and appreciate their ideas.

➤ Avoid joining the staff saboteurs whose main function is to prevent any efforts at improvement. Their primary activities are complaining, gossiping, nit-picking, whining, and ridiculing. Rarely do they offer positive solutions or acknowledge their own deficiencies. They blame all their problems on others. Often they will be found sitting in the back at faculty meetings or clustered in faculty lounges before and during school. Treat them cordially, but resist their venomous game. They are an emotional and economic drain on their schools, taking far more than they contribute. It is unlikely they find much joy in teaching.

➤ Avoid gossiping about other teachers, students, or the administration. It serves no constructive purpose and poisons the school climate. It is unprofessional as well as destructive. If you hear gossip, don't spread it. Be especially careful in what you say about students or faculty outside of the school.

➤ Organize or join a study group or peer support group. Peer coaching is gaining acceptance in many schools. Do whatever you can to nurture mutual support and the development of collegial, professional relationships.

➤ Participate in professional improvement activities with your colleagues. Attend workshops, classes, or conferences together. Watch videotapes or discuss education-related books. Nurture each other's professional development.

➤ Strive to develop connections with teachers beyond your area or grade level. Much can be learned from all good teachers, regardless of the subject or grade level they teach.

➤ Observe outstanding teachers in their classrooms. The truly effective ones will welcome your presence. They are not threatened by having visitors in their classrooms.

➤ Never criticize fellow teachers in front of students. Such unprofessional conduct serves no constructive purpose. Always assume that whatever you say about a colleague will eventually get back to that person. Communicate directly with the other teacher if you believe his or her behavior creates a problem for you or the students. If the grievance is serious pursue it through your building principal. Remember, you will probably be working with that teacher for some time.

➤ Be willing to do your share of the work. Volunteer for some committee assignments, chaperoning dances, organizing events, or supervising students.

➤ A friendly "hello" or "good morning" plant the seeds of an inviting relationship with your colleagues, even those you don't know very well or who treat you coolly.

➤ Help create good will. Celebrate special occasions by bringing cookies, fruit, or other treats to a faculty meeting or to the lounge in the morning.

➤ Avoid associating only with a favorite clique. Try to develop cordial relationships with all teachers, even the ones with whom you disagree. Try to get to know them as people. Discover their interests, family news, and achievements.

➤ Respect the rights of your colleagues. Avoid causing students to be late to their classes. Don't undermine colleagues' authority and credibility with their students. Remain considerate of the needs of your fellow professionals.

➤ Don't borrow materials, books, supplies, or equipment without asking. If you do use someone else's things, be sure to return them promptly.

➤ Be extremely cautious of reprimanding other teachers' students, especially while the students are under their supervision.

➤ Try to resolve conflicts in a mature, assertive fashion. In any school there will occasionally be disagreements over policies, perceptions, solutions, or actions. Feelings can get hurt, intentions misperceived. Seldom is one person right and the other absolutely wrong. Colleagues are rarely evil; occasionally they may be thoughtless or inconsiderate. Don't overreact. The first step is to let the person know, in an assertive, not hostile way, that you perceive a problem to exist. Seek collaborative problem solving. Really listen to their point of view. Avoid petty squabbling.

➤ Be patient with your colleagues. Like you, your fellow teachers are humans. They will have bad days and will make mistakes. Don't expect them to hold the same values and perspectives as you.

➤ Treat all colleagues as professionals, even if you don't believe they are treating you with full respect. Work at being tolerant of those who have views different from yours. Treat all others decently. Your initial perceptions of people can be wrong; you don't know all that is happening in their lives beyond school.

Guidelines for Collaborative Teams

The ability to arrive at group decisions has become a vital skill for today's teachers, as increasingly schools incorporate site-based management, collaborative teams, and shared decision making. The opportunity to participate more broadly in the school decision-making process has several potential benefits. Giving teachers a greater voice in the school decision-making process, like the quality circles being adapted by businesses, assures that decisions are made by those having the best available information and who are responsible for the implementation of the decision. Participatory decision making also gives the participants a greater sense of control and is more likely to yield a commitment to the resulting decisions.

The ability to effectively arrive at good group decisions requires a set of learned skills that has been only rarely included in teacher education courses of study. It is risky to assume that all members of a team possess the skills of group problem solving. Unfortunately, most persons assume everyone knows how to arrive at group decisions. A substantial body of research suggests this is a most erroneous supposition. To be effective, specific training in collaborative decision making should be available to any staff moving toward greater use of teams. The preponderance of evidence also shows training in group problem-solving skills leads to more creative ideas, both in quantity and quality.

Whenever two or more persons must jointly arrive at decisions, two conditions can assuredly be predicted: (1) It takes more time and (2) There will be friction. While any group can arrive at a decision, the barometer of success is whether the group considered the best available information in making its choice. When groups effectively tap the resources possessed by all their members, they are capable of achieving synergy, meaning the group product is superior to anything any one individual could have achieved alone.

➤ Be sure everyone clearly understands the issue to be decided. Occasionally, group members discover they have been arguing over different issues. Early in the group process some agreement on their mutual mission, problem definition, and goals must be attained.

➤ Ask open-ended questions to elicit all points of view. Some participants are going to be more reluctant to share their views openly without encouragement. Paraphrasing for understanding and clarity is another valuable communication tool for group decision makers.

➤ For clarification occasionally ask for examples and specifics. Don't necessarily assume you know what another person means.

➤ In the early stages of searching for possible solutions, employ the strategy of group brainstorming. To succeed, brainstorming must adhere to four rules:

> ➤ Elicit as many ideas as possible. The focus in this stage is upon quantity, not quality. The more ideas you have, the greater the possibility of discovering a good idea.

> ➤ Delay evaluation. Later you will apply criteria of judgment to your ideas, but premature criticism nips creativity in the bud. People will be less reluctant to suggest an idea in a climate of skeptical criticism.

> ➤ Wild, far-out half-baked ideas are to be encouraged. It may be the diamond in the rough.

> ➤ Listen to the ideas of others and springboard off them. Let their ideas stimulate your search. For this reason it helps to record the group ideas on newsprint for all to see.

➤ Different points of view must be elicited. View such disagreements as a healthy part of the group search for the optimal decision. The avoidance of conflict is not productive in arriving at good group decisions. Research shows the most effective decision-making groups encourage minority opinions to be aired. It is important to discuss sources of resistance openly than to let them fester and later sabotage the implementation of the decision.

➤ The goal should be to arrive at a win-win consensus, rather than a compromise about which no one is particularly enthusiastic. For that reason such conflict-reducing techniques as voting or averaging should be avoided. While they may save time, they often yield inferior decisions that lack the commitment of all members.

➤ It is also important for groups to arrive at their own definition of consensus. It could mean that everyone must enthusiastically endorse any group decision (which is virtually impossible to achieve), that everyone agrees the solution might work and should be tried and later reevaluated, or simply that everyone can live with the recommendation.

➤ Concensus building is most likely when all group members seek to identify areas of disagreement and the common ground. The advantages and disadvantages of all possible solutions should be fairly analyzed.

➤ Don't change your mind merely to avoid conflict. It is a legitimate part of the group process that persons with different needs and assumptions disagree. Conversely, it is important to challenge the ideas of others, especially when there is little support offered for that position.

➤ When conflicting views emerge, strive to identify the needs and interests rather than merely the positions of the opposing group members.

➤ Show your respect for others by listening to their ideas. When you share your opinions try to be non-confrontive. Present your point of view without putting down those who disagree. Focus upon issues, not personalities.

➤ If necessary, leave the decision for a later time. This permits some incubation time. New, more creative solutions may emerge from this reflection. Such a delay is especially warranted if the discussion has become excessively volatile or if the group lacks information necessary to make a sound decision.

➤ Groups have very limited attention spans and tend to digress from the issue at hand. Gently refocus the group's attention with such open-ended questions as, "What additional information do we need?" or "Are there any other options we have not considered?"

➤ Be sure to have a team recorder keep a written record of your team's decisions. Such a "group memory" helps the team keep focused on its task and assures a future record of what has been decided by the group.

➤ Create opportunities to celebrate your team's successes. It might be through a gag gift, funny ritual, special meal, or a party.

➤ A team must assume responsibility for decisions that don't succeed. Part of the price of the freedom to make decisions is accepting the consequences of those decisions.

➤ Capitalize on the strengths and talents of each team member. Match the tasks required with the skills possessed by your team members.

➤ Training should be available on group roles, group problem solving, planning, and stages of group development. Some of the resources below might be read and discussed by the group.

➤ The group should be conscious of and occasionally examine its group process to see if it is working effectively. By enhancing its group process, the team can arrive at better choices. Some teams find it helpful to take five minutes at the end of each meeting to complete a group-process evaluation form such as the one included at the end of this chapter.

HELPFUL RESOURCES

Erb, T.O. & Doda, N.M. (1989). *Team Organization: Promise—Practices and Possibilities*. Washington, D.C.: National Education Association.

Maeroff, G. I. (1993). *Team Building for School Change: Equipping Teachers for New Roles*. New York: Teachers College Press.

Quick, T.L. (1992). *Successful Team Building*. New York: American Management Association.

Rees, F. (1991). *How to Lead Work Teams: Facilitation Skills*. San Diego: Pfeiffer & Co.

Working with Your Principal

A principal who truly serves as an instructional leader is of immense value to any school. The role of the building principal and the nature of school leadership are being redefined as increasing numbers of schools turn to site-based management, total quality schools, teaming, restructuring, peer coaching, decentralization, and other paradigm shifts.

Whatever the exact configuration of leadership functions in a specific building, teachers and their principals are locked in an interdependent relationship. They need each other to succeed. The less friction and stress between principal and teacher, the more enjoyable both will find their jobs. There is also evidence that the quality of the teacher-principal relationship greatly influences the overall school climate, which in turn affects the success of students in the classroom.

Investing in a positive, professional teacher-principal relationship should be a top priority for any beginning teacher. While some principals are more talented leaders than others, students are ultimately the winners when building principals and teachers can work in harmony. No one gains and ultimately students lose when a poisonous, adversarial relationship exists between principal and teachers. Successful teachers strive to develop partnerships with their principals.

➤ Keep your principal informed of both budding problems and your triumphs. Don't wait to surprise them with major problems. It is best for them to have ample information directly from you, before they hear about a problem from others. No decision can be better than the information upon which it is based. Take time to communicate your interests and needs.

➤ Avoid only visiting your principal when you have problems. Share some good news or ask his or her advice. Invest time in nurturing a positive relationship. If you are experimenting with a new instructional technique or a novel assignment, alert your principal and seek his or her support. Only through frequent interactions does mutual trust evolve.

➤ When your principal has done something considerate or particularly helpful, drop him or her a note. Let the principal know his or her efforts are appreciated. Like department stores, principals often only hear the complaints.

➤ For special achievements send an unsolicited letter of recognition or support for your principal to the superintendent. Anytime you want to give someone major recognition, don't just tell them; tell their superior.

➤ Avoid dumping your problems on your principal. Especially avoid sending kids to the office for misbehavior unless it involves persistent or serious infractions, such as fighting. You will be creating an impression that you cannot control your own classroom if you have to rely on the principal to solve your student behavior problems on a daily basis.

➤ Avoid backbiting or ridiculing your principal, even if he or she falls short of your expectations. It simply isn't professional and it really doesn't accomplish anything positive. Don't join in the game even if others are playing.

➤ If you have a complaint or disagree with the principal on an issue, communicate your case clearly and rationally. This never calls for yelling, name-calling, or sarcasm. Stick to the facts. If you have difficulty controlling your emotions in direct conversation, articulate your position in a letter. Remember, you still have to work with him or her tomorrow. Your aim is to influence the principal's decision, not to alienate him or her. In all contacts act maturely and professionally.

➤ Choose your battles carefully. In any relationship you only have a limited amount of credit available in the other's emotional bank account. Don't squander your assets on minor skirmishes; save it for the truly important issues. If you rarely complain, you are more likely to be heard when you do.

➤ When you take a problem to your principal, prepare at least one or two possible solutions. Anticipate the consequences of each, the risks, and the resources needed. Be succinct in your presentation. Be rational in what you expect the principal to do to solve your problems.

➤ Find opportunities to make your principal look good. Publicizing in the community the outstanding achievements of students is one way this is attained. Any noteworthy school accomplishment reflects positively upon the building principal.

➤ Don't make the principal's job more difficult than it needs to be. Submit grades, attendance records, and reports on time. Some amount of paperwork has to be done to make a school work smoothly. It may sometimes be inconvenient, but must be done. Avoid using the principal's time for petty problems.

➤ Try to see things from the principal's point of view. It is not an easy job; they have many interests to please: teachers, non-certified staff, boards of education, central office, students, parents, and taxpayers. Most every decision they make irritates someone, especially with the limited resources available to most schools. They are also sometimes obliged to enforce school policies they may not like. Be a bit empathetic. That doesn't mean you have to sacrifice your principles, that you shouldn't advocate for those issues to which you are passionately committed. However, recognize you won't always get what you want when you want it.

➤ Take the initiative in inviting your principal to visit your classroom. If you have a particularly interesting or successful lesson coming up, try to schedule an observation. Strive to view the principal as an instructional ally, even if you do disagree on your teaching effectiveness.

➤ Avoid interpreting criticisms of your teaching effectiveness as personal attacks. No teacher is perfect. Avoid becoming defensive. Reality-test any criticisms by asking other administrators or teachers to observe your teaching. Invite the principal to observe you again to reassess your teaching. A goal you both should share is to provide the best instruction possible to all your students. Build on that common purpose.

➤ Avoid asking for special privileges. It unfairly puts the administrator on the spot. If you have a request for special resources or exemption to school policies, consider how your fellow teachers will accept that request if it is granted.

➤ Share articles you read on school improvement practices with your principal. Occasionally, ask his or her opinion on an educational trend or innovation.

➤ A good time to get to know your principal better is during the summer. Most are on an extended schedule. Stop by to see the principal during the summer. She or he will have more time than during the school year when her or his time is so consumed dealing with daily crises.

➤ Show your principal you are thinking of him or her. Small considerations such as a birthday card, a holiday card, homemade cookies, or a vacation postcard are fruitful investments in a positive relationship.

Improving Parent-Teacher Relations

You have much to gain from developing a constructive working relationship with the parents and guardians of your students. If invited, parents can play a valuable role in your teaching success. They can offer support and reinforcement for your academic and behavioral goals. They can provide assistance in a variety of ways, both in your classroom and from their homes. Many possess talents, interests, and ideas that can augment what you offer. Many parents (and other community members) aren't more fully involved in their schools simply because they haven't been invited.

➤ Before the school year begins, send notes home to your students' parents or guardians introducing yourself and inviting them to become a part of the school community. Some teachers include a checklist of hobbies, talents, and interests the parents might be willing to share with your class at some time during the year. Emphasize that you believe they play an important role in their child's education.

➤ Send periodic notes to parents recognizing positive achievements or behavior of their children in your class. Typically, parents only hear from the school when their children are in trouble. Set aside ten minutes each week to send two or three notes to different parents. Don't just acknowledge the students who are getting A's. Recognize the student who has been reluctant to participate but is now contributing in class or the student who did an outstanding job on one project, or the student who had been getting C's and is now getting B's. It will pay dividends!

➤ Occasionally call parents to communicate some good news about their child's accomplishments. It will catch them off guard, but they will likely be most appreciative.

➤ Develop home-school contracts with the parents of students having difficulty in completing homework or behaving inappropriately in class. If the student fulfills the contract, the parents offer a special privilege or reward. You might have a checksheet that both you and the parent must sign each day or week. This forestalls students from reporting "I didn't have any homework" and other similar "inaccurate" communications that are sometimes related to parents.

➤ Invite parents to become involved in your classroom. Tap their talents as special volunteers, not only for field trip supervision and class parties, but as teacher's aides and to give special presentations. You might send a survey home to obtain information about their skills and interests and willingness to help.

➤ If feasible, make home visits to meet the parents of your students. Not only will you learn much more about your students through these visits, but you will also be communicating to the student's family that you genuinely are interested in their child.

➤ Be sensitive in making assumptions about the constellation of your students' families. It is likely that some of your students reside with only one parent (not necessarily the mother), or with grandparents, older siblings, aunts, uncles, non-related guardians, or foster homes. It is also possible that some of your students have parents who are deceased, incarcerated, or hospitalized. Tactfully determine the child's living arrangements before contacting the home. You can avoid potentially embarrassing situations.

➤ Let parents know early if their child is having difficulty in your class. Don't wait until grades are sent home.

➤ Consider sending parents a class newsletter several times a year to let them know what is happening in your class. Your students might even be given responsibility for writing, editing, and printing it. Content to be included might include news of field trips, special class projects, guest speakers, birthdays, and features recognizing achievements of individual students.

➤ Sponsor a family fun night in which parents and their children come to school to participate in some fun, interesting activities together. These might be related to your subject area or simply a chance to interact and have fun together. Some schools are very successful in offering workshops on topics of interest to parents, anything from flower-arranging to parenting skills. If your faculty cannot teach the workshop, find someone in the community who can.

➤ Designate one evening a month as an informal open session to which all parents are invited to visit your room to discuss any concerns or to learn more about what their children are learning. Provide coffee, tea, or cookies. If no one shows, you can get some extra work done.

➤ Some schools sponsor a "Grandparents' Day." Students are invited to bring their grandparents to school for a visit. You might even encourage grandparents to participate in the lesson of the day (e.g., a discussion of the 1950's or how technology has changed). Grandparents are also a valuable, though under-utilized, source of school volunteers.

➤ Send special cards or notes to parents for special family celebrations: birth of a new child, a new home, special award received, etc. Clip newspaper articles featuring any family members and send them to the parents with a note of congratulations.

Parent Conferences

The prospect of a parent-teacher conference can arouse intense emotions in both the teacher and the parent. Beginning teachers can be especially anxious about meeting parents for the first time. For parents whose memories of school are less than pleasant, the parent-teacher conference can be intimidating and dreaded. However, the reality is that most parents really do want their children to have a positive school experience and prefer to develop a cooperative home-school relationship. Professionally conducted parent-teacher conferences can prove a most valuable strategy for improving student classroom behavior as well as enhancing learning. Here are some ideas used by successful teachers to reap the maximum benefit from parent-teacher conferences:

➤ Before the conference, plan what you hope to accomplish. What information do you want to share with the parent? What problems need solving? Do not overwhelm the parent. Settle on no more than two or three concerns to be addressed. A laundry list of complaints will only discourage or alienate them.

➤ If you are requesting the conference in response to a specific problem with the child, allow some time to cool off before meeting with the parent. You'll be less emotionally charged and more objective after a couple of days. Remember, you are a professional educator.

➤ When a student begins to misbehave in class, begin to keep an index card recording specific disturbances noted. Include the name, date, description of problem behavior, and action taken. Make your notes as soon after an incident as possible. It helps you to identify patterns and gives more credibility to your complaint when talking with the child's parent.

➤ If possible, clarify ahead of time who will be attending the conference and their relationship to the child. Is this the child's mother, father, guardian? Also verify from the school records the person's name. Do not assume their surname will be the same as the student's. Don't make a big point of it in front of the parent, but a bit of advance checking can help avoid potentially embarrassing gaffes during the conference. Some teachers have mistakenly assumed that an older parent was the student's grandparent.

➤ Within reason, try to accommodate the parent's schedule. Many parents cannot readily take off work to attend school conferences. If parents have more than one child, attempt to coordinate their appointments so they only have to come to school once. Such small considerations can reap significant cooperation.

➤ Consider sending a reminder of the time, date, and place to the parent a couple of days before the scheduled conference. If special directions are needed for parking or for finding your room, include those as well. If you are seeing several parents back-to-back, inform them how much time is allotted for their appointment.

➤ Put your name on the door to make it easier for parents to locate your room.

➤ Create an inviting room atmosphere. Displays of students' work, projects in progress, bulletin board displays, posters or learning centers, and "Welcome Parents" signs can all help create a warm atmosphere.

➤ Arrange the room setting to minimize potential distractions or interruptions during the conference. Close the door if necessary.

➤ Assemble samples of the student's work and a list of his or her grades before the conference. It will save you the time of having to look them up during the conference. Some teachers have their students assemble a work portfolio in a folder. This might include a greeting from their child. You might also include a page where the parent can return a positive note to their child about their schoolwork.

➤ Many teachers keep a note card for each student, recording points to discuss at the parent-teacher conference. Try to anticipate any questions a parent might ask and note your thoughts related to that issue.

➤ Greet parents cordially when they arrive, again being sure to verify their names immediately. Ideally, try to greet them at the door. Thank them for coming to see you.

➤ Be the gracious host. Some teachers set up coffee, juice, or snacks for parents, especially if they might have to wait in the hallway while you finish a prior conference. If they must wait in the hall, provide some chairs and perhaps copies of your textbooks or other materials to scan while waiting.

➤ Practice the very best of manners, treating each parent with full respect and dignity. Whatever their occupation or socio-economic status, treat all parents as you would the president of a corporation or a physician. Strive to make them feel as welcome and comfortable as possible.

➤ Address all parents by their last names preceded by the appropriate Mr., Mrs., or Ms. until you are invited by them to use their first name.

➤ Don't hide behind your desk. It can be a barrier to developing a working relationship. If possible, sit beside the parent at a table. Also avoid seating parents in small children's chairs.

➤ Begin the conference on a positive note. Think of two or three positive descriptors for each student (e.g., "Michelle is so eager to help" or "Braedon seems well liked by his classmates"). You might jot these down on each student's card or file to stimulate your memory. It is important to find something to praise with each student.

➤ Establish rapport with the parent. This need not take long, but try to establish a personal connection and create an inviting atmosphere. If you know about the parent's job, hobby, or special interest, make a brief inquiry (e.g., "Matt tells me you've been working on your family genealogy"). Help put the parent at ease.

➤ Do question the parent about the student's special talents, interests, or accomplishments. Express a genuine interest to better understand their child's successes and strengths as well as challenges.

➤ Be specific when discussing difficulties the student is experiencing. It is generally better to be candid, yet non-blaming. It is unwise to mislead the parent into thinking all is well if there is a problem with their child. Stick to the facts, giving concrete examples, rather than broad generalities.

➤ Don't dwell on any student's attributes that are unlikely to change or over which the parents have little control.

➤ It is best to avoid getting emotional in discussing problems you may be having with the student. Remember, your goal is to enlist the parent's cooperation in resolving any difficulties the student may be experiencing in your class.

➤ Actively listen to the parent. Practice the reflective listening skills discussed earlier in this book. Respond empathically to feelings expressed by the parent (e.g., "You are disappointed Laurie isn't getting more individual attention in class"). This communicates that you really are trying to understand the parents' perspective; it does not imply you necessarily agree with their view. Such active listening is an especially effective way to handle the angry parent.

➤ Encourage parents to ask questions and respond fully yet tactfully. Avoid jargon, "educationese," or psychological labels. Allow parents time to talk.

➤ Inquire about home routines (responsibilities, homework habits, play, etc.). Seek information that might help you gain a better understanding of the student's talents, interests, and challenges.

➤ Try to offer two or three specific suggestions for the parent to implement at home that might help the student. Offer them not as commands, but as ideas that have worked with other students.

➤ Invite the parents to contact you with any future concerns about their child's classroom progress.

➤ Some traps to avoid: discussing family problems, discussing other teachers' classroom treatment of the student, comparing the student with siblings, arguing with the parent, attempting to psychoanalyze the student, blaming the parent for the student's misbehavior.

➤ End the conference in a hopeful tone. Summarize the main points discussed and any steps to be taken to resolve identified problems. Again commend them for coming to the conference.

➤ Do follow up with notes or a phone call, especially if a particular problem has been identified for attention.

➤ If other parents are waiting, be sure to end the meeting at the scheduled time. Ideally, allow yourself a few minutes between sessions to permit time to note any major points discussed during the conference. If necessary, offer to schedule another conference with the parent.

If you promise not to believe everything your child says happens at this school, I'll promise not to believe everything he says happens at home.

—ENGLISH SCHOOLMASTER
THE WALL STREET JOURNAL, JANUARY 4, 1985

The only reason I always try to meet and know the parents better is because it helps me to forgive their children.

—LOUIS JOHANNOT
HEADMASTER, INSTITUT LE ROSEY
SWITZERLAND
LIFE, MAY 7, 1965

The Successful Open House

Many schools sponsor "Open Houses" for parents and guardians. The open house can be a valuable opportunity to get parents more involved in their child's education.

➤ Videotape several interesting learning activities in your class. Have these playing on the VCR as parents enter the room. You might play selected segments to give them a flavor of what your class is like. It is best to edit your tape first to avoid having to fast-forward. Five or ten minutes of videotape is sufficient.

➤ Avoid getting into prolonged discussions with individual parents about their child's progress. Do offer to arrange appointments with any parents who would like to discuss their children's work in more detail.

➤ Create an especially inviting atmosphere. Remember, some parents do not have fond memories about school and may be a bit anxious about being in a classroom.

➤ Greet parents at the door. If you do not already know them, introduce yourself to each as they enter.

➤ Some teachers have each student create a folder of exemplary work throughout the term. Have these available for parents to examine as they first enter.

➤ Create a welcome sign with your name and subject clearly posted on the door to avoid confusion as to whether parents are in the appropriate room.

➤ Attractive bulletin board displays featuring student work is a plus. If students create projects or build projects, have these on display.

➤ If parents are visiting several rooms, do not keep them past the time they should be moving to the next class.

Substitutes

Substitute teaching can be a challenging experience, but you can help assure a constructive experience for both the substitute and your students. It is essential that learning continue even in your absence. Advance preparation can make a substitute's visit run more smoothly and assure that useful learning occurs.

➤ Early in the year inform the students of your expectations of acceptable behavior when a substitute is present.

➤ Agree with a nearby teacher to help the other's substitute when one of you is absent. The teacher can help the substitute get settled and become familiar with your procedures.

➤ Develop a substitute's notebook that includes all information he or she will need to make the experience successful. Be sure your notebook is clear and precise, avoiding special codes or abbreviations the substitute may not understand. Here are items many teachers include:

  ➤ Lesson plans.
  ➤ Daily schedule of activities.
  ➤ Class roster(s). The substitute can make notes on these (for example, checking off homework completed).

> ➤ Attendance forms and procedures.

> ➤ Hall passes and procedures for going to the rest room, library, guidance office, etc.

> ➤ The names of teachers, administrators, clerical staff, or students they can turn to for help with special problems or questions.

> ➤ Seating charts for each class.

> ➤ Classroom rules. It is helpful if the students already have a copy and they are posted for everyone to see.

> ➤ If you have established any special classroom routines or behavior management programs, be sure to leave details about these. Also inform the substitute of any students with special needs who will require attention.

> ➤ Any special non-teaching duties you must perform (e.g., playground or lunchroom supervision).

> ➤ Bus information. Times and procedures for dismissal and getting students to and from their busses.

> ➤ A map of school building.

> ➤ Student handbook.

> ➤ Instructions on where all textbook manuals and supplies are kept.

> ➤ Teacher handbook.

➤ Don't forget to inform the substitute of any special scheduled interruptions (assemblies, class pictures, field trips, homerooms, etc.).

➤ If you know ahead of time you will be absent, leave a lesson plan to cover the material you want taught. It may not be the same lesson you would have taught, but it should be something of instructional value. It is a good idea to have a couple of special learning activities that can be plugged into the schedule at any point in the year. Keep these in a special place with all the necessary materials and directions. Try to help the substitute by including something you know your students will enjoy. Don't just use tests and seatwork on the days substitutes are covering your class.

➤ If you know ahead of time you will be absent, make a videotape for the substitute to show at the beginning of class. In this presentation you can give the students instructions on what you expect them to do that day. You might also videotape and save demonstrations or some lectures from previous years for the substitute to use.

➤ Expect the day to be used constructively. Most substitutes are qualified professionals with the training and motivation to do a good job. Treat them as professionals and with due respect.

➤ If you know you will be absent several days, invite your substitute to visit your class beforehand to be introduced to your class and to discuss your lesson plans and classroom procedures with you.

➤ Ask your substitute to leave a note describing how the day went. It helps to remind your students ahead of time that you will be soliciting feedback from the substitute. You might express your appreciation to your students (through praise or special privileges) if the report is favorable.

➤ If you have a substitute who does perform particularly well, drop him or her a note to express your appreciation. Let your principal know as well. Specify that individual to take your place when you are absent. That will permit that substitute teacher to become more familiar with your routines and your students. If you will have frequent absences, it also alleviates the stress of getting the students accustomed to another person. Trust them to provide a meaningful learning experience for your students (with your help).

Working with Support Staff

Successful teaching is a team effort. Teachers will be much more successful with the support of other competent professionals: counselors, secretaries, nurses, custodians, aides, cafeteria workers, and librarians. Each has a valuable function to play in creating a smooth-running and effective school. Special efforts should be made to make them feel included and valued as part of the school community.

➤ Learn the names of the support staff. Ask them how they would prefer to be addressed. Don't assume they want to be called by their first name.

➤ Attempt to discover what is important to them. Their jobs and needs are different from yours. Wherever possible, help them get their needs met.

➤ Acknowledge their contributions. An occasional "thank you" note for any special assistance or a particularly outstanding contribution will be most appreciated. Offer verbal comments that convey you do value their efforts. Seek genuine opportunities to offer sincere compliments.

➤ Let others know what is happening. If you are planning a special activity that is going to affect someone else's job, check it out with them first. Try to minimize any disruption of their work. Seek their advice on how to proceed. Even if they don't have any suggestions, they will appreciate being asked.

➤ Always treat support staff (and all other persons) with courtesy. Accompanying requests with a "please" or "thank you" will plant the seeds of a cooperative, mutually respectful relationship. Always greet them with a smile and pleasant acknowledgment in the morning.

➤ Whenever someone puts forth an extra special effort to help you, acknowledge it with a note, small gift (cookies, bread, flowers from your garden), or even a note to their supervisor.

➤ If you see a positive news article about any staff members or their family, clip it out and send it to them with a note of congratulations.

➤ Treat all, including those with less education, as equals. Never assume that more education makes you a superior human being. Chances are that persons having less education than you possess experiences, talents, or knowledge you do not.

➤ Sooner or later, you are going to need a favor from a support staff member. You are much more likely to gain his or her compliance with your request if you have invested in a collegial relationship.

Working with Volunteers/Aides

Time is the teacher's most precious resource. There is always too much to do in too little time. Many essential tasks could be completed by someone other than a teacher, if such help were available. Using aides, either paid or volunteer, is one valuable way to get more help in the classroom, freeing you to spend more time on the most important teaching tasks. One estimate is that over five million persons volunteer to help in schools each year; and probably many more would help if they were invited. Many adults in your community have valuable talents that could be tapped to enrich your instructional program.

One benefit of using aides, whether paid or volunteer, is that they share the challenges and achievements of your school with the greater community. They can become valuable public relations spokespersons simply by sharing their experiences with friends and neighbors. These paraprofessionals from the community are more likely to become advocates for their schools. There is also evidence that student achievement improves in schools where volunteers are used extensively. Teachers who are freed from many of their non-instructional tasks have more time and energy to focus upon their teaching responsibilities. Additionally, individual students gain more of the teacher's attention, as well as the added contact and reinforcement from the paraprofessional helper.

The paraprofessionals working in their community schools also gain. Many feel a greater sense of social responsibility and personal enrichment from using their time to aid the development of children. Many feel more positively about themselves, knowing that their talents and knowledge is valued and needed. For others, especially college students, it provides an opportunity to develop skills and knowledge that may enhance their employment prospects. All classroom assistants gain a greater appreciation and insight into the inner workings of their local school.

Volunteers can help in a variety of ways, depending upon the age group of the students, the skills and knowledge of the volunteer or aide, and the willingness of the teacher to delegate tasks and train the paraprofessional to assume these duties. Some of the more common tasks assigned to aides and volunteer helpers include the following:

- ➤ Take attendance or lunch count
- ➤ Help students get on the bus
- ➤ Tutor individual students
- ➤ Supervise field trips
- ➤ Escort students through the hall
- ➤ Demonstrate an experiment
- ➤ Listen to students read
- ➤ Grade objective tests and quizzes
- ➤ Collect and distribute materials
- ➤ Find materials in the library
- ➤ Make phone calls
- ➤ Monitor students
- ➤ Converse with individual students

- ➤ Facilitate small-group activities
- ➤ Supervise recess
- ➤ Complete certificates for students
- ➤ Praise students
- ➤ Filing
- ➤ Set up displays
- ➤ Record grades
- ➤ Type
- ➤ Operate instructional equipment
- ➤ Administer quizzes and tests
- ➤ Photocopy
- ➤ Help with computer software
- ➤ Laminate materials
- ➤ Supervise learning centers
- ➤ Compute grades
- ➤ Use desktop publishing on the computer
- ➤ Order free materials
- ➤ Help organize games
- ➤ Requisition supplies
- ➤ Routine first aid, taking students to the nurse
- ➤ Help returning students make up missed work
- ➤ Assist with club meetings
- ➤ Paint murals
- ➤ Help with seatwork
- ➤ Prepare instructional resources
- ➤ Record observations about students and classroom activities
- ➤ Proofread
- ➤ Housekeeping chores (water plants, arrange desks, clean, etc.)
- ➤ Put up bulletin boards
- ➤ Direct a play
- ➤ Provide enrichment activities
- ➤ Make costumes
- ➤ Restock supplies
- ➤ Share a hobby
- ➤ Monitor computer use
- ➤ Prepare visual aids
- ➤ Mediate student disputes
- ➤ Conduct storytelling
- ➤ Coordinate volunteers
- ➤ Share career guidance information

➤ If aides are not regularly provided by your school, discuss the idea of using volunteers with your principal. There are concerns such as legal limits and liabilities and delegated responsibilities that will need to be considered. You might want to start small at first to determine how best to use classroom assistants.

➤ Send out a call for all potential volunteers, not just to the parents of your students. An announcement in the local newspaper or through the PTA newsletter may encourage others to volunteer. Senior citizen groups and grandparents of your students are also potential sources of volunteer aides. College students, especially teacher trainees, may value the opportunity to work in a classroom. Elementary teachers sometimes use high school students. You might also survey local businesspersons to determine if they might be willing to help on an *ad hoc* basis. Some companies provide released time for their employees to help in the schools. The regular school open house is an excellent recruiting opportunity. Create and prominently display a recruiting poster describing the specific ways parents can help. Follow up the open house with a letter inviting parents to volunteer. Make a special effort to recruit parents who speak languages other than English.

➤ Parents and others are generally reluctant to volunteer because they are unsure they have anything to contribute. Be sure to list specific tasks parents are capable of handling. Where possible provide options, allowing parents to choose those activities they find most attractive. While some parents may be able to work every week, let parents know that you value their help even if it is only a one-time visit to share some talent or their jobs with your class or help with one activity. It's possible some parents might be able to help even if they cannot come to school. Many tasks can be done in their homes: typing, sewing, baking, or computer data entry.

➤ Interview each volunteer, preferably in person. Assess whether you think you can work comfortably with each individual. You likely will need more than one volunteer to cover the week. Determine how much time each day you want an aide or volunteer in your room. You'll also need to decide whether to schedule volunteers for specific tasks as needed or for the same time-block each week. Some persons might wish to help weekly; others will only be able to assist occasionally. Be sure to call everyone who volunteers.

➤ Appropriate training is essential for effective use of paraprofessional help. Allow time for them to observe you interacting with students and doing tasks you will expect them to fulfill. They will also note the routines you have established. If you are using several volunteers, you might schedule an orientation session where you can provide training for all at once. Also provide ample time for them to ask questions. It is helpful to let them just observe for a day before you have them work directly with students.

➤ Develop a handbook for your assistants. It should describe tasks to be done with samples when possible, disciplinary procedures, rules, and responsibilities. It is also important to emphasize confidentiality, that volunteers shouldn't gossip about the problems of individual children.

➤ Do try to get to know your classroom helpers. Ask about their families and interests. When appropriate, seek their suggestions on how to make improvements in the classroom.

➤ Develop a file, tray, or box in which you place work to be done by your aide or volunteer when time is available. This prevents them from having to interrupt you to get instructions on what to do. A desk or table designated as their work station would be helpful. Be sure to provide an adult chair if you teach young children. Also designate where they can store personal items and clothing.

➤ Construct and post a chart depicting the schedule for your assistants. Ask them to call when they are not able to come. It is helpful to send reminders to volunteers who are coming for a special project. If you are scheduling a parent to help with one class, remember it is easiest for most parents to come first thing in the morning or late afternoon. Be considerate of their schedules.

➤ Make sure you always have something useful for them to do. They will get bored or discouraged if they arrive to find they really aren't needed. Keep a running list of things for your helpers to do. Try to give them meaningful, interesting tasks at least part of the time.

➤ Design a system so that you need to spend only minimal class time supervising your aide/volunteer.

➤ In front of students, always address your aide or volunteer as you would any other professional in the building, generally by title (Mr., Mrs., Ms.). Insist that students also address them as they would a teacher and that they treat any paraprofessionals with courtesy and respect.

➤ In the beginning, delegate tasks you are quite sure the paraprofessional can handle, assuring initial success. As they gain confidence and your trust, assign more challenging duties. Provide an opportunity for your assistants to learn and to grow. Encourage them to ask questions if they are not sure how to complete a task.

➤ Remain tactful, yet clear, in providing suggestions and feedback to your assistants. Always treat them with respect. Show them that you have confidence in their ability to fulfill their duties. When appropriate, seek their opinion on items related to classroom success.

➤ Allow your classroom assistants an opportunity to work with all students, not just the ones having difficulties. Discourage parent volunteers from only working with their child.

➤ Give ample recognition and appreciation to your aides. Never take them for granted; strive to always make your assistants feel needed. Here are ideas some teachers have used to show their appreciation to their paraprofessional helpers:

  ➤ Certificates
  ➤ Plaques
  ➤ Verbal praise
  ➤ Special thank-you notes
  ➤ Newspaper features on volunteers
  ➤ Invite them to lunch
  ➤ Recognition ceremonies
  ➤ Small gifts
  ➤ Invite them to a staff development program

- ➤ Buy them a soft drink, coffee, or tea
- ➤ Send them a birthday and/or holiday card
- ➤ Delegate additional responsibility
- ➤ Seek their opinion
- ➤ Take them to the faculty lounge
- ➤ Introduce them to other school personnel
- ➤ Offer to write letters of recommendation
- ➤ Celebrate their achievements
- ➤ Nominate for volunteer awards
- ➤ Smile
- ➤ Send letter of appreciation to their boss
- ➤ Treat them as a professional
- ➤ Bring a cake for their birthday
- ➤ Praise them in front of your principal
- ➤ Greet them by name
- ➤ Take time to listen to their ideas
- ➤ Give them a space of their own

While volunteers do save the teacher time and having parents in the classroom may enhance parent-teacher relationships, the bottom line is that extra help in the classroom benefits students.

Invitation to Open House–
Sample Letter to Parents

October 3, 199_

Greetings,

Kalida Elementary School will be holding its annual open house on Monday, October 12. We ask all parents and guardians to first meet in the school auditorium at 7:00. After a brief introductory program, you are invited to join me in Room 68.

I will have several samples of your child's work available for you to examine. While we will not have time to discuss your child's performance in detail, I would be willing to schedule a private conference if you desire. I do hope to briefly explain some of the activities we will be doing this year and to respond to any questions you might have about our classes.

I very much value the help and support my students receive at home. Together, we can assure that your child has a successful year. I hope to see you at our open house.

Sincerely,

Mrs. Ritter

Parent Survey

I believe the parents in our school community possess a great many talents and skills that would be of benefit to our students. I would like to invite you to become involved in our class activities during this year. To help me identify what special interests or skills you might possess that would be most helpful, please complete this survey and return to me at school. If you are willing to help in any fashion, I will contact you later to determine when you would be available to help.

Name _____ Child's name _____

Address _____

Phone _____ Job _____

What special hobbies or interests do you have that you might be willing to share with my class?

With which of the following activities would you be willing to help?

Supervise field trips

Teach a hobby or skill (Describe: _____)

Create a bulletin board

Tutor individual students (Subject: _____)

Assist in the classroom (Filing, tutoring, monitoring, grading, etc.)

Help with computer hardware/software

Other (Specify)

Team Process Assessment

At the end of the team meeting each member should indicate his or her assessment of how that meeting went. Circle the number that represents your rating of each dimension. The group should then spend a few minutes discussing the group's responses.

Participation

1	2	3	4	5	6	7
Some did not participate at all						There was significant participation by all

Group Focus

1	2	3	4	5	6	7
The group tended to digress from the session agenda or objective						The group stayed on task throughout the meeting

Listening Process

1	2	3	4	5	6	7
It seemed participants were not fully listening to one another						Outstanding efforts were made to fully hear each other

Commitment Check

1	2	3	4	5	6	7
I am not supportive of the meeting outcome						I am very supportive of the group decision

Quality of the Group Effort

1	2	3	4	5	6	7
The session did not produce an effective outcome						The final outcome was excellent

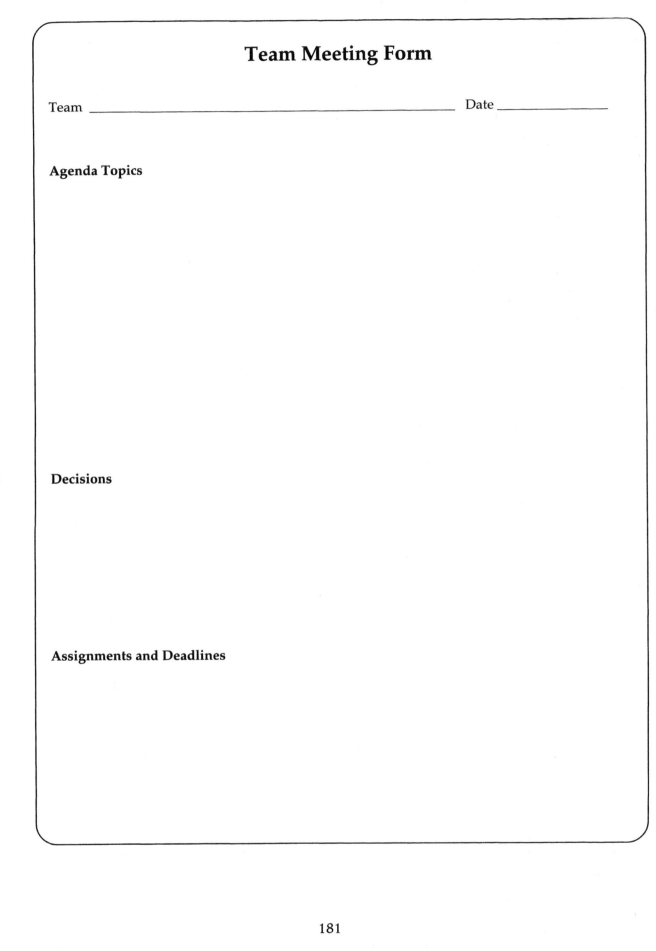

Team Meeting Form

Team _____ Date _____

Agenda Topics

Decisions

Assignments and Deadlines

CREATIVITY CRUNCHERS

No way!
Don't be silly.
It's too risky.
We tried that before.
It would take too long.
The administration will never go along.
We don't have the money.
Let's form a committee.
You've got to be kidding!
It will never work.
Yes, but...
They'll never let us.
It'll never sell.
That's not our problem.
The time isn't right.
The main office won't let us.
It's too new.
Put it in writing.
We'll discuss it later.
Why do it now?
It will never be approved.
What for?
Nobody needs it.
It's against our rules.
The union won't go along.
It's too faddish.
What will the community think?
Let's table it for now.
Don't rush into things.
It's politically unwise.
Too radical.
We're too small.
It's too much work.
Let's wait and see.
Let me think about it.
What good will it do?
We already have enough problems.
It'll never happen.

You're dreaming.
It's a nice theory, but...
You don't understand.
We're too big for that to work here.
Why?
Maybe someday.
It'll never fly.
They'll laugh at us.
We have too many obstacles.
It's reactionary.
We don't have proof it will work.
It will offend someone.
It's too late.
It's not our policy.
Are you serious?
We need more data.
It didn't work the last time.
Costs too much.
Baloney!
Someone else should do it.
They aren't ready for it yet.
There's no use trying.
It's not our job.
Dud!
Nobody cares anyway.
We don't have enough details.
Don't you think there is a better way?
Too corny.
It's too soon.
That's not new.
It's illogical.
Get practical.
Here we go again.
That's fine, but...
Whose idea is that?
It's too simple.
It's too complicated.
That's just plain dumb.

Parent Conference Record

Teacher_____ Date_____

Student_____ Parent(s)_____

Objective:

Suggestions for improvement:

Signed:_____   _____
                                                Teacher

_____
Parent(s)/Guardian(s)

                                        _____
                                                Student

CHAPTER 5

In Search of
Educational Excellence

Becoming an Effective Teacher

"Great teachers rely not on charisma. Instead, they rely on the inner qualities of love, integrity and commitment."
—ERIC JENSEN

While teaching is a complex and challenging profession, some teachers are more successful than others. Their students perform better on achievement tests, are more likely to succeed in future grades, and remember their teachers more fondly. There are many outstanding teachers who are creative and successful in facilitating the academic as well as personal growth of their students. We need not search only for those gaining national recognition, such as Jaime Escalante featured in the real life drama, *Stand and Deliver*, or Kay Tolliver, the East Harlem teacher touted in the P.B.S. production *Good Morning, Ms. Tolliver*. In every school building, exciting, creative, and effective teaching is happening. A growing body of educational research has focused on what these exemplars are doing that makes them successful. Use every opportunity to observe outstanding teachers in action; you can learn much from them. Listed below is a compilation of the characteristics of these effective teachers as discovered by a number of researchers:

➤ The A+ teachers tend to have realistic, yet high expectations for their students. They require students to use higher level mental processes, such as critical thinking, deeper understanding, creativity, and problem solving. They present the appropriate level of challenge in their lessons.

➤ They incorporate student questions and comments into their lessons. Their classes tend to involve significant amounts of class discussion and group exploration. This is especially important in teaching high school students.

➤ The best teachers actively involve their students in the learning process. Their students spend less time doing seatwork, passively watching, or waiting. When they do employ seatwork, it is more interesting and varied.

➤ Much thought and planning go into their instruction, yet they remain flexible in their teaching to allow for spontaneous discovery as opportunities present themselves. They are especially sensitive to cues that their lessons are not working and must be adapted on the spot. They continually seek ways to improve their teaching. They produce lessons that enhance student mastery.

➤ The best teachers tend to conduct their lessons in a businesslike, task-oriented style. They maintain a strong academic focus in their classrooms. They are effective in designing lessons that enhance student mastery.

➤ Effective teachers match their instructional activities to the developmental level of their students and then gradually lead them to higher levels of mastery. This involves recognizing and remediating deficiencies in students' skill level.

➤ They employ structuring comments or advance organizers at the beginning of their lessons. They are also careful to use language appropriate to their students.

➤ Teachers rated highest by their students tend to use more humor in their classrooms. This humor does not typically come from joketelling, but rather from the good-natured banter they carry on with their students. This contributes to developing good rapport with their students.

➤ They genuinely believe in the value of their subject matter. Almost without exception they exude enthusiasm for what they are teaching and they teach in a manner that exhibits that passion. You can sense the energy and animation in their teaching. The research suggests this is especially important at the junior high and high school levels.

➤ The best teachers possess a "can do" attitude, sometimes referred to as efficacy. Although they face the same problems as less effective teachers, they have confidence in their ability to cope with the challenges they face. They feel their efforts can make a difference in the lives of their students.

➤ The memorable teachers exhibit empathy toward their students striving to see the world from their point of view. Such caring and desire to genuinely understand their students is sometimes characterized as "teacher warmth." This includes a sensitivity to the cultural background of the students as well. One opportunity to do that is by arriving at class early to chat with students as they enter. These teachers' classes are more student-centered than subject-centered.

➤ Top-performing teachers seek help from others. They discuss teaching ideas with colleagues and seek input from parents, students, administrators, and educational specialists. They also read more educational magazines and books and are more likely to attend professional development programs.

➤ They provide opportunities for students to seek extra help if they fall behind. They are approachable. They are also observant of cues that individual students are not learning or are uninvolved. They more frequently check the progress of students and proceed only when students have shown mastery of the content being taught.

➤ The A+ teachers avoid embarrassing students and do not resort to intimidation to gain their cooperation. They avoid showing favoritism toward selected students. Not surprisingly, the better teachers tend to have more positive opinions of students, as well as fellow teachers and administrators. Research shows ineffective teachers are more prone to use sarcasm, shaming, ridicule, shouting, and scolding. High-achieving classrooms are cooperative, warm, and convivial.

➤ The top teachers give clear instructions in assignments and demonstrate clarity in their presentations. They also attend to the nonverbal cues that might suggest students are not comprehending and make mid-lesson adjustments as needed.

➤ Excellent teachers are more likely to incorporate a variety of instructional strategies into their lessons. They tend not to do the same thing in the same way for too long. They possess a broad repertoire of teaching skills.

➤ They use more encouragement than criticism. Indeed, criticism has been found to be negatively related to student achievement. However, they do provide corrective feedback whenever necessary to help students rectify mistakes.

➤ The most effective teachers are in control of their classrooms, but are not obsessed with the idea of control. They invest time and effort into prevention of discipline problems by developing positive student relationships and planning well-organized, interesting lessons. To the outside observer, these teachers seem to exert relatively little effort to maintain an orderly environment. They are more apt to intervene to "nip problems in the bud" before they escalate into major disruptions. They are also less likely to send students to the principal, punish their students, or call parents to complain about students' misbehavior.

➤ The effective teachers continually monitor their classrooms; they are aware of what is happening at all times. They often do this by moving about the room and maintaining frequent eye contact with all students.

➤ Good teachers teach their students "classroom routines," such as what to do when they finish an assignment early or how to obtain extra help.

➤ Not surprisingly, effective teachers actually spend more time teaching. They use class time to maximize student learning time and try to minimize distractions, chaos, and interruptions. Indeed, teachers who are less able to manage their time well tend to leave the teaching profession.

➤ The truly outstanding teachers are not necessarily charismatic, dynamic individuals, but enjoy and believe in what they are teaching, work hard at it, and spend time planning well-organized lessons.

"Effective teachers let students know they are somebody, not _some body_."
                    —WILLIAM PURKEY

A man reported to his friends that he had taught his dog to whistle. His friends coaxed the dog to whistle. Despite their fervent pleas, nothing happened. In exasperation one finally retorted, "I thought you taught him to whistle."
    The man replied, "I did. But he just didn't learn."

"Successful teachers are vital and full of passion. They love to teach as a writer loves to write, as a singer loves to sing. They are people who have a motive, a passion for their subject, a spontaneity of character, and enormous fun doing what they do."
                    —THOMAS CRONIN, 1991

SUGGESTED READING ON THIS TOPIC

Burden, P.R. & Byrd, D.M. (1994). *Methods for Effective Teaching*. Boston: Allyn and Bacon.

Frase, L.E. (1994). *Creating Learning Places for Teachers, Too*. Thousand Oaks, CA: Corwin Press.

Goodlad, J.I. (1994). *Educational Renewal: Better Teachers, Better Schools*. San Francisco: Jossey-Bass Publishers.

Kretovics, J. & Nussell, E.J. (1994). *Transforming Urban Education*. Boston: Allyn and Bacon.

Seymour, D. & Seymour, T. (1992). *America's Best Classrooms: How Award-Winning Teachers Are Shaping Our Children's Future*. Princeton, NJ: Peterson's Guides.

Zehm, S.J. & Kottler, J.A. (1993). *On Being a Teacher: The Human Dimension*. Thousand Oaks, CA: Corwin Press.

Effective Teacher Checklist

DO YOU...

____ Listen to your students?

____ Know your students' names by the end of the first two weeks of school?

____ Try to see things from your students' point of view?

____ Smile in class?

____ Believe all your students are capable of learning your subject?

____ Convey your enthusiasm for what you are teaching?

____ Continue to improve your teaching effectiveness?

____ Believe in the value of what you are teaching?

____ Have clear objectives for each lesson?

____ Clearly communicate your expectations to your students?

____ Strive to create an inviting room environment?

____ Establish routines the first week of school?

____ Try to get to know all your students as individuals?

____ Encourage cooperation in your classroom more than competition?

____ Demonstrate a sense of humor in working with your students?

____ Praise your students for specific accomplishments?

____ Fairly and consistently enforce your rules?

____ Use more positive statements than negative statements in your classes?

____ Vary your seating arrangement according to your teaching needs?

____ Communicate the positive achievements of students to their parents?

____ Make positive comments on students' papers?

____ Permit your students to make mistakes?

____ Avoid overreacting to minor misbehaviors?

____ Create interesting lessons that actively involve students?

____ Encourage students to ask questions when they don't understand some part of your lesson?

____ Capitalize upon spontaneous learning opportunities when they occur?

___ Attend workshops or classes to continue improving your teaching skills?

___ Maintain at least an 80% on-task rate in your classes?

___ Compliment students, individually and as a group?

___ Create a sense of family among your students?

___ Make effective use of class time?

___ Strive to link current lessons to students' prior knowledge?

___ Provide reflection time for all students?

___ Give students guided practice?

___ Provide appropriate pacing for your lessons (neither too slow nor too fast)?

___ Employ a variety of instructional techniques besides lecture?

___ Regularly communicate with the parents of students having difficulties?

___ Consider the variety of learning styles of your students in planning your lessons?

___ Incorporate students' questions and comments into your lessons?

___ Adapt your lessons on the spot when they aren't working?

___ Provide opportunities for students to seek extra help if they fall behind?

___ Feel confident in your ability to handle the challenges you face in the classroom?

___ Greet your students as they enter the classroom?

___ Avoid the use of sarcasm or ridicule in interacting with students?

___ Have everything ready for the day when you enter the building in the morning?

___ Are you in control of your classroom, but not obsessed with the idea of control?

___ Are you able to effectively nip behavior problems in the bud before they escalate?

___ Are you constantly aware of what is happening in your classroom through continul monitoring?

___ Strive to minimize distractions, chaos, and interruptions?

___ Love teaching?

SCORING DIRECTIONS

Count the number of items you checked and find your score in the categories below.

41-50	Outstanding	A master teacher. Others can learn much from you.
31-40	Good	You're on the way to success. There are a few areas needing attention.
21-30	Challenged	It's not too late to seek help in improving your classroom effectiveness.
0-20	Struggling	Teaching is probably not very enjoyable. Considering a career change might be wise.

Why Teachers Fail

Teachers sometimes fail. In a survey of school administrators seeking reasons for teacher failure (dismissal, reprimand, reassignment), Professor Jack Riegle found teachers are more likely to get fired because of poor human relations skills than lack of knowledge about their subject matter. The following reasons were most frequently mentioned:

➤ 1. Inability to organize and control a classroom of students

➤ 2. Lack of knowledge concerning how children grow and develop as pertaining to pupil-teacher interactions

➤ 3. Inability to work effectively with other educators

➤ 4. Inability to work effectively with parents

➤ 5. Subject matter inadequacies

➤ 6. Other (immorality, insubordination, absenteeism, child abuse, senility, drugs and alcohol)

Source: Riegle, J.D. (1985). What administrators say about why teachers fail. *The Teacher Educator, 21* (1), 15-18.

Effective Schools

In the past two decades substantial attention has been given to studying effective schools (see the work of Ron Edmunds, Larry Lezotte, and John Goodlad). While no universal blueprint exists, some generalizations can be drawn from the myriad of research studies available. The exact causal nature of these characteristics is difficult to determine. However, the presence of certain specific traits are found in the most outstanding schools. The following characteristics have been identified as exemplifying the most effective schools:

➤ The professional staff is committed to the belief that all students can learn.

➤ Teachers hold high expectations for their students. Teachers also believe their efforts do make a difference in the lives of their students.

➤ Students believe their success in school is related to how hard they work.

➤ The principal functions as an instructional leader. The principal is able to set high goals for the building and to inspire the staff to move toward those goals.

➤ A safe and orderly school environment is provided.

➤ Continued professional development is encouraged and facilitated.

➤ Firm, consistent, and fair enforcement of appropriate student behavior is emphasized. Disruptive and dangerous behaviors are not tolerated. Rules and expectations are clearly communicated to all.

➤ A climate of cooperation exists among the staff. The faculty works as a team. Collaboration becomes part of the school culture. Mutually supportive relationships exist between the principal and the staff.

➤ Students exhibit a high level of school spirit. They identify with their school and feel good about attending their school.

➤ Academic learning time is safeguarded. Frivolous interruptions of class activities are minimized.

➤ Parents feel welcome in the school. The community is supportive of their schools.

➤ Student progress is systematically monitored.

➤ Staff input into instructional decisions is invited.

➤ Students' level of on-task behavior is relatively high.

➤ An emphasis is placed upon developing basic academic skills in students.

➤ Continuity of instruction from one grade level to the next is emphasized.

"Faced with the choice between changing one's mind and proving there is no need to do so, almost everyone gets busy on the proof."
—JOHN KENNETH GALBRAITH

FOR ADDITIONAL READING

Block, A.W. (1983). *Effective Schools: A Summary of Research.* Arlington, VA: Educational Research Service.

Bryant, B.I. & Johnes, A.H. (1993). *Seeking Effective Schools for African American Children: Strategies for Teachers and School Managers.* San Francisco, CA: Caddo Gap Press.

Fiske, E.B. (1991). *Smart Schools, Smart Kids.* New York: Simon & Schuster.

Goodlad, J.I. (1984). *A Place Called School.* New York: McGraw-Hill.

Goodlad, J.I. (1994). *Educational Renewal: Better Teachers, Better Schools.* San Francisco: Jossey-Bass Publishers.

Levine, D.U. & Lezotte, L.W. (1992). *Unusually Effective Schools: A Review and Analysis of Research and Practice.* London, England; New York.

Mullis, I.V.S., Owen, E.H., & Owen, G.W. (1990). *Accelerating Academic Achievement: A Summary of Findings from 20 Years of NAEP.* Princeton, NJ: National Assessment of Educational Progress, Educational Testing Service.

Reynolds, D. & Cuttance, O. (Eds.), (1992). *School Effectiveness: Research, Policy, and Practice.* London: Cassell.

Taylor, B.O. (Ed.), (1990). *Case Studies in Effective Schools Research / Written by Practitioners in School Districts that Have Implemented Successfully School Improvement Programs Based on Effective Schools Research.* Dubuque, IA: Kendall/Hunt Publishing Co.

Teddlie, C. & Stringfield, S. (1993). *Schools Make a Difference: Lessons Learned From a 10-year Study of School Effects.* New York: Teachers College Press.

Wynne, E. & Kagan, S. (1993). *A Year in the Life of an Excellent Elementary School: Lessons Derived from Success.* Lancaster, PA: Technomic.

Professional Development

Teaching should be more than just a job. It is a profession and a career. It is a long-term commitment to doing your best to help young people blossom intellectually, emotionally, and behaviorally. It is a position of incredible importance; teachers with passion and compassion can profoundly influence the lives of their students. At the worst, teachers also have the power to discourage, humiliate, and crush the spirit of their students. Either way the lives we teachers touch become part of our heritage, our immortality.

Outstanding teachers are not born, but develop. True, some personality types are probably more attracted to education, but the art and craft of teaching is gradually honed through years of study, experimentation, reality-testing, and reflection. Development of the effective teacher does not end with the receipt of an undergraduate or even masters degree. A diploma is but a license to learn. The more that true professionals learn, the more they realize there is to learn.

Any teacher can become a better teacher, and with enough determination and hard work probably any teacher could become a successful teacher. However, teaching is hard work. Knowing your content is a necessary, though wholly insufficient, prerequisite to becoming an outstanding teacher. There are many in the teaching profession who are brilliant, possessing great knowledge and understanding of their chosen field of study, yet who will never be successful teachers. The skills of effective teaching are complex. It is not enough to be a scholar; a good teacher is also part salesperson, entertainer, psychologist, counselor, leader, mediator, conductor, guide, evaluator, advocate, and cheerleader. Different teachers develop different combinations of these talents, but all are helpful.

Believe it or not, there are many teachers who rarely read anything related to their teaching area. Their teaching repertoire is limited to what they knew when they walked into the classroom the first day. Imagine going to a physician, auto mechanic, or any other professional who had not continued to remain current with the latest techniques, research, and technology related to their profession. Indeed, an argument can be made that the person who fails to learn and use the most effective practices available to his or her profession is being both negligent and unethical.

Develop a purposeful plan of professional development. It is too important to be left to chance. Here are some ideas used by successful teachers to enhance their professional skills.

➤ Continued learning keeps you fresh. Experiment with new ways of doing old tasks. Include new content and skills in your courses or volunteer to develop new courses. It is impossible to maintain enthusiasm and peak performance while teaching the same things the same ways year after year. "Rust out" or "burnout" are inevitable if professional rejuvenation is not incorporated.

➤ Allow time, ideally each day, for reflection. Examine what works and what doesn't and how each lesson might be improved. Write it down in a journal or in the margins of your lesson plans. Keep an idea notebook to incubate and brainstorm teaching ideas.

➤ Peer coaching groups are now an integral part of many staff development programs. This is an effective, proven approach to improving instructional and classroom management skills. If your school does not yet have one, suggest it to your colleagues. Many will be threatened by the thought of being observed by another teacher. The truly professional teacher will welcome the opportunity.

➤ Develop or join a support group among fellow teachers. It may take the form of a study group where you read and discuss relevant educational materials. Or it might be a more unstructured gathering to offer mutual support and problem solving.

➤ Even if it is not required by your school, develop a professional development plan each year. It should target two or three areas for improvement. It might be in classroom management skills, developing specific teaching strategies, or in expanding your knowledge of some content area. Share your plan with your principal and seek suggestions. You are also more likely to later receive support (in either released time or money) if it is obvious your request is a part of a professional development plan and not a spur-of-the-moment whim.

➤ Create your own independent study. Each year identify a new topic you intend to study in depth. Attend workshops or classes, read books and journal articles, interview experts, or develop your own field trips. Within a year of concentrated effort you can develop a reasonable degree of expertise in most any subject.

➤ Don't overlook the benefits of acquiring a mentor, even if you are a veteran teacher. It may be a more experienced teacher, a supervisor or administrator, a professor, or perhaps an individual working in your subject area outside of a school setting. Working with a mentor should be a mutually rewarding experience. Show your appreciation of your mentor, through verbal acknowledgment, token gifts, and time spent helping him or her in special projects.

➤ Learn by observing good role models. In every building there are creative, successful teachers. Find them and study their style, techniques, and ideas. Seek their advice.

➤ If you ever have an opportunity to participate in a sabbatical, take it—even if it does entail some financial sacrifice. The trade off in mental health and renewed vigor are well worth the price.

➤ Each year try to attend at least one state or national conference related to your teaching field. Ask fellow teachers or local professors which ones are most worthwhile. These programs can provide refreshing and energizing experiences. Bring back samples and ideas to share with interested colleagues. If you are a regular at a conference, consider sharing your classroom experiences as a presenter. If you can't attend, most conferences provide tapes of many sessions. Borrow or buy these to listen to while commuting.

➤ Subscribe to at least one useful publication related to your teaching area. You need not feel obligated to read every issue cover to cover, but do scan it looking for new teaching ideas.

➤ Recognize that teaching as a profession cannot be limited to 40 hours per week for nine months per year. If education is really a passion, you will eagerly devote the time necessary to improve your lessons, develop new skills, and reflect on the daily challenges of the classroom.

➤ Attend inservice programs and workshops with an open mind. It is easy to develop a "red pencil mentality" and stubbornly refuse to rationally listen to new ideas. Of course, they have to be reality tested back in your classroom the next day, but give them a chance. Like developing any new skill—riding a bike, mastering a computer, or learning a new hobby—innovative teaching techniques will require a start-up learning curve. It may seem unnatural or awkward at first. Experiment and, after a fair trial, discard those things that clearly don't work for you and adapt those things that do. That is how we improve in any endeavor—whether golf, knitting, or painting; we keep those behaviors and ideas that work and eliminate those that do not. It is embedded in the concept of continuous improvement, constantly fine-tuning our performance.

➤ Develop options. If you have only one way to teach a concept or handle misbehavior, what do you do when your tactic does not work? However, if you have a smorgasbord of alternatives available, you can pragmatically experiment until you find one that succeeds.

➤ Use a student evaluation form appropriate to the age level of your students. Carefully and objectively read the results to see how your students rate your teaching effectiveness. While there are some limitations of student evaluations, they do provide one valuable source of information that should not be ignored.

➤ Examine your students' scores on standardized achievement tests related to your subject area. Are there any areas in which they seem to consistently score low? Is it important for your students to master these skills or concepts? How can these concepts be taught better in your class?

➤ Resist the temptation to rationalize poor student performance or behavior in your classes. Claims such as "I'd be a better teacher if I had better students," while perhaps true, don't excuse poor teaching. Imagine a physician lamenting that only sick people come to her office. Yes, kids are not the same today as when you went to school, and they probably never will be. Yet the fact remains that, for many kids, school represents the best hope they have. A true professional is committed to doing the very best possible with the skills, resources, and students available. There are noteworthy successes, such as Kay Tolliver featured in the PBS documentary, *Good Morning, Ms. Tolliver* or Jaime Escalante, the real-world East Los Angeles teacher depicted in the film, *Stand and Deliver*. The next time you become bogged down in negative self-talk and tempted to give up, rent one of these films. It will provide an uplifting and empowering experience.

➤ Don't automatically discount critical feedback you receive from others about your teaching performance. Supervisors' or principals' observations can be one, though not the only, valuable source of information. Listen objectively, not defensively. If you disagree with some aspect of an observer's conclusions, rationally present whatever documentation or evidence you might have to rebut the point. However, avoid arguing or quibbling to protect your ego.

➤ Develop relationships outside the field of education. One way of recharging your batteries is to cultivate interests beyond the school. Interacting only with other teachers invites too much shop talk and commiserating. While some colleagues are likely to be included in your circle of friends, seek a balance with others from diverse careers and experiences.

➤ Become a risk-taker. Don't repeat the same half-baked lessons year after year from habit. Experiment, try new things. Don't be afraid to make mistakes. Free yourself from the shackles of perfectionism. Strive for excellence, not perfection.

➤ Become an actor, not a reactor, on the stage of life. You possess a free will to choose how you will conduct your life, both in and out of the classroom. When we become a reactor we surrender control of our thoughts, actions, and feelings to those around us. When we worry about possible disapproval from our colleagues or not living up to the expectations of others, we yield control of our lives. When we defensively respond with revenge, gossiping, backbiting, sulking, and withdrawal, we have surrendered our autonomy. When we become creative problem solvers, we affirm our competence and efficacy. When we become tolerant of the foibles of others while admitting and occasionally laughing at our own, we reap dignity and the respect of our colleagues and students. True power arises from acceptance—of ourselves and those around us.

"Insanity is doing the same thing over and over again, but expecting different results."

—RITA MAE BROWN, SUDDEN DEATH, 1983

Professional Organizations

American Alliance for Health, Physical Education, Recreation and Dance
1900 Association Drive
Reston, VA 22091
(703) 476-3400

American Association of Physics Teachers
5112 Berwyn Road
College Park, MD 20740
(301) 345-4200

American Council of the Teaching of Foreign Languages
6 Executive Plaza
Yonkers, NY 10701-6801
(914) 963-8830

American Federation of Teachers
555 New Jersey Avenue, NW
Washington, D.C. 20001
(202) 879-4400

American Library Association
50 E. Huron Street
Chicago, IL 60611
(312) 944-6780

American School Counselor Association
5999 Stevenson Avenue
Alexandria, VA 22304-3300
(703) 823-9800

American Speech-Language-Hearing Association
10801 Rockville Pike
Rockville, MD 20852
(302) 897-5700

American Vocational Association
1410 King Street
Alexandria, VA 22314
(703) 683-3111

Association for Childhood Education International
11501 Georgia Avenue, Suite 315
Wheaton, MD 20902
(301) 942-2443

Association for Educational Communications and Technology
1025 Vermont Avenue, NW, Suite 820
Washington, D.C. 20005
(202) 347-7834

Association for Experiential Education
2885 Aurora Avenue, #28
Boulder, CO 80303-2252
(303) 440-8844

Association for Gifted and Talented Students
Northwestern State University
Natchitoches, LA 71497
(318) 357-4572

Association for Supervision and Curriculum Development
1250 N. Pitt Street
Alexandria, VA 22314-1403
(703) 549-9110

Comparative and International Education Society
Learning Systems Institute
205 Dodd Hall
Tallahassee, FL 32306-4041
(904) 644-5442

Council for Exceptional Children
1920 Association Drive
Reston, VA 22091-1589
(800) 845-6232

Council for Learning Disabilities
P.O. Box 40303
Overland Park, KS 66204
(913) 492-8755

International Reading Association
800 Barksdale Road
P.O. Box 8139
Newark, DE 19714-8139
(302) 731-1600

International Society for Technology in Education
1787 Agate Street
Eugene, OR 97403
(503) 346-4414

Kappa Delta Pi
P.O. Box A
West Lafayette, IN 47906
(317) 743-1705

Learning Disabilities Association of America
4156 Library Road
Pittsburgh, PA 15234
(412) 341-1515

Lutheran Education Association
7400 Augusta
River Forest, IL 60305
(708) 209-3343

Modern Language Association
10 Astor Place
New York, NY 10003
(212) 475-9500

Music Teachers National Association
The Carew Tower
441 Vine Street, Suite 505
Cincinnati, OH 45202-2814
(513) 421-1420

National Alliance of Black School Educators
2816 Georgia Avenue, NW
Washington, D.C. 20001
(202) 483-1549

National Art Educators Association
1916 Association Drive
Reston, VA 22091
(703) 860-8000

National Association for Bilingual Education
Union Center Plaza
1220 L Street, NW, Suite 605
Washington, D.C. 20005
(202) 898-1829

National Association for Gifted Children
1155 15th Street, NW, No. 1002
Washington, D.C. 20005
(202) 785-4268

National Association for Industry-Education Cooperation
235 Hendricks Boulevard
Buffalo, NY 14226-3304
(716) 834-7047

National Association for the Education of Young Children
1509 16th Street, NW
Washington, D.C. 20036-1426
(800) 424-2460

National Association of Biology Teachers
11250 Roger Bacon Drive, No. 19
Reston, VA 22090
(703) 471-1134

National Association of Elementary School Principals
1615 Duke Street
Alexandria, VA 22314
(703) 684-3345

National Association of School Psychologists
8455 Colesville Road, Suite 1000
Silver Spring, MD 20910
(301) 608-0500

National Association of Secondary School Principals
1904 Association Drive
Reston, VA 22091-1596
(703) 860-0200

National Business Education Association
1914 Association Drive
Reston, VA 22091-1596
(703) 860-8300

National Catholic Education Association
1077 30th Street, NW, Suite 100
Washington, D.C. 20007
(202) 337-6232

National Council for the Social Studies
3501 Newark Street, NW
Washington, D.C. 20016
(202) 966-7840

National Council of Teachers of English
1111 W. Kenyon Road
Urbana, IL 61801-1096
(217) 328-0977

National Council of Teachers of Mathematics
1906 Association Drive
Reston, VA 22091-1596
(703) 620-9840

National Education Association
1201 16th Street
Washington, D.C. 20036
(202) 833-4000

National Middle School Association
4807 Evanswood Drive
Columbus, OH 43229
(614) 848-8211

National Rural Education Association
Colorado State University
230 Education Building
Fort Collins, CO 80523-0002
(303) 491-7022

National Science Teachers Association
1840 Wilson Boulevard
Arlington, VA 22201-3000
(703) 243-7100

Phi Delta Kappa
P.O. Box 789
Bloomington, IN 47402-0789
(812) 339-1156

Teachers of English to Speakers of Other Languages
1600 Cameron Street, Suite 300
Alexandria, VA 22314
(703) 836-0774

Educational Journals

GENERAL EDUCATION PERIODICALS

American Education
American Educator
American Journal of Education
American School Board Journal
American Secondary Education
American Teacher
Changing Schools
Clearing House
Computers and Education
Computers in the Schools
Contemporary Education
Curriculum Inquiry
Curriculum Review
Education
Education, U.S.A.
Education and Urban Society
Education Digest
Educational Forum
Educational Horizons
Educational Leadership
Elementary School Guidance and Counseling
Elementary School Journal
Harvard Educational Review
High School Journal
History of Education
Instructional Science
Instructor
Interchance
International Education
Issues in Education
Journal of Classroom Interaction
Journal of Computer-Based Instruction
Journal of Curriculum and Supervision
Journal of Education
Journal of Education and Psychology
Journal of Educational Thought
Journal of Developmental Education

Journal of Humanistic Education and Development
Journal of Indian Education
Journal of Instructional Development
Journal of Modern Education
Journal of Moral Education
Journal of Negro Education
Journal of Philosophy of Education
Journal of Special Education
Kappa Delta Pi Record
Learning
Lifelong Learning
McGill Journal of Education
Merill-Palmer Quarterly
Middle School Journal
NASSP Bulletin
NEA Today
New Directions for Teaching & Learning
New Education
Notre Dame Journal of Education
Open Learning: Teaching and Training at a Distance
Peabody Journal of Education
Phi Delta Kappan
Pointer
Progressive Education
Scholastic Education
School Review
Teacher
Theory into Practice
Today's Education

RESEARCH JOURNALS

American Educational Research Journal
Educational Record
Educational Research
Elementary School Journal
Human Development
International Journal of Educational Development
International Journal of Educational Research
Journal of Counseling and Development
Journal of Educational Psychology

Journal of Educational Research
Journal of Experimental Education
Journal of Instructional Psychology
Journal of Nonverbal Behavior
Journal of Research and Development in Education
Journal of Research in Science Teaching
Journal of School Psychology
Journal of Teacher Education
Journal of Verbal Learning and Verbal Behavior
Journal of Vocational Education Research
Journal of Youth and Adolescence
Learning and Motivation
Learning Disability Quarterly
Review of Educational Research

SUBJECT SPECIALTY JOURNALS

American Biology Teacher
Arithmetic Teacher
Art Education
Athletic Journals
Business Education World
Childhood Education
Education and Training of the Mentally Retarded
Educational Theatre Journal
Electronic Learning
Elementary English
Elementary Teachers' Guide to Free Materials
English Education
English Journal
Exceptional Child
Exceptional Children
Focus on Exceptional Children
History and Social Science Teacher
History Teacher
Gifted Child Quarterly
Gifted Child Today
Journal of Business Education
Journal of Chemical Education
Journal of Drug Education

Journal of Economic Education
Journal of Environmental Education
Journal of Industrial Teacher Education
Journal of Nutrition Education
Journal of Physical Education, Recreation and Dance
Journal of Reading
Journal of Reading Behavior
Journal of School Health
Journal of Sex Education and Therapy
Journalism Educator
Language
Language Learning
Language Teaching
Mathematics in School
Mathematics Teacher
Mathematics Teaching
Modern Language Journal
Physical Educator
Physics Education
Psychology in the Schools
Reading
Reading Improvement
Reading Teacher
School Arts Magazine
School Health Review
Science and Children
Science Education
Science Teacher
Scholastic Coach
School Counselor
School Science and Mathematics
Social Education
Social Studies Professional
Social Studies Review
Speech Communication Teacher
Studies in Science Education
Teaching English
Teaching Exceptional Children
Technology Teacher
TESOL Quarterly

Stress and Burnout in the Classroom

Stress is an inescapable part of any teacher's job. Indeed, Hans Selye, pioneer stress researcher, suggested that the absence of stress is death. Stress is part of the price tag of living. The greater risk occurs when persons spend long periods of time under conditions of constant stress or tension. Researchers have identified some professions, including teaching, as particularly stress-prone. Over a period of time, teachers can begin to experience a condition commonly referred to as "burnout." Psychologist Christina Maslach has identified three phases of burnout. The first consists of emotional exhaustion, a loss of energy and enthusiasm, of being used up with nothing left to give. The second stage is characterized by insensitivity, cynicism, callousness. The language of this stage is depersonalized. Students might be referred to as "the animals" or "the beasts." Distrust and even dislike of one's students is evident. Of course this creates the spiral effect of making students behave in even more distrustful and unacceptable ways. The final phase embodies a feeling of despair that all one's efforts have been fruitless and the teacher is a failure. In short, burned-out teachers have lost their initial idealism, compassion, zeal, and energy. There is a discrepancy between one's efforts and the perceived rewards gained from that effort, accompanied by a sense of sadness, hopelessness, helplessness, and lower self-esteem.

Of course, most teachers don't burn out in the classroom. Researchers suggest that approximately three to four percent of the teachers still in the classroom exhibit chronic symptoms of burnout. Many others leave the profession at the onset of burnout. Some struggle, feeling trapped. Surveys have suggested that about thirty percent of American teachers would prefer to be doing something else. Various researchers have identified the following symptoms of burnout: physical exhaustion, absenteeism, abuse of alcohol or drugs (in some areas, teacher bars have arisen where teachers congregate after work), chronic fatigue, boredom, depression, cynicism, moodiness, impatience, ulcers, headaches, excessive eating, "blaming the victim" for their own problems, stubbornness, and resistance to change.

A first step in preventing burnout is to recognize its potential sources. It is the cumulative combination of many events over a period of time, not one event, that ultimately leads to burnout. Teacher burnout and stress have received a great deal of attention from educational researchers. The following items have been identified as particularly stressful for teachers:

- managing disruptive students
- being involuntarily transferred
- overcrowded classrooms
- unrealistic expectations or standards
- lack of planning time
- class interruptions
- curriculum changes
- faculty strikes
- being threatened
- lack of adequate supplies, materials, books
- incompetent administrators
- the first week of school

➤ receiving low evaluations

➤ angry parents

➤ verbal abuse from students

➤ school reorganization

➤ vandalism and destruction of personal property

Teaching will always entail some potentially stressful events. However, teachers can develop strategies to innoculate themselves to the tensions of school life. Listed below are suggestions for reducing stress and preventing the onset of burnout.

➤ Avoid the loneliness of teaching. Adult contact can become very rare for some teachers. It is tempting for beginning teachers to isolate themselves, avoiding contact with the more experienced teachers. You can gain much from interacting with your colleagues.

➤ One of the single best predictors of who will avoid burnout is interaction with a supportive group of colleagues—at least one or two people who understand your frustrations and can listen with empathy. Find one or two people you can eat lunch with each day. Many schools develop support groups that meet periodically to share problems and search for creative solutions.

➤ At the first sign of burnout do something different. Change grade levels, plan a new unit, or try teaching a different subject. Experiment with different curricular approaches: cooperative learning, independent study, learning centers, field trips, peer tutoring, teaming, or learning contracts. Continue to seek new challenges and break up old routines. Bring as much variety into your teaching as possible.

➤ Explore professional rejuvenation through continued education. Take a graduate course, subscribe to professional journals, attend professional workshops, or commit yourself to learning everything you can about a new topic. Learn something novel that you can incorporate into your teaching: some magic tricks, storytelling, drama, graphic design, or public speaking.

➤ Remember, you can't be all things to all people all the time. You are but a fallible human. The greatest baseball players in the world don't bat .1000. and you don't have to be perfect either. You won't win them all no matter how hard you try.

What counts is that you strive to do your best, to continually improve and to learn from your mistakes.

➤ Set priorities. One source of stress for many teachers is over-committing themselves. Feeling overwhelmed by all of one's time-demands is a cue that thought needs to be given to setting priorities. Establishing which things are truly both urgent and important helps allocate one's energies and time. The more thought you give to what you value and your professional and personal goals, the easier it is to set priorities.

➤ Learning to say "no" to unimportant, distracting activities is an essential stress-prevention technique. Learn to judiciously use the phrase "I have a previous commitment" when asked to commit yourself to unimportant activities. You need not elaborate on the exact nature of that commitment (well, you might want to give your spouse more detail!). You must save some reserve of private time to recharge your batteries and renew your enthusiasm. You do no one a favor if you say "yes" to so many requests that you have little energy left to fulfill those commitments. Learn what your limits are.

➤ Don't try to do everything yourself. Delegate some tasks to students, aides, volunteers, or colleagues.

➤ Take care of your body. Substantial research concludes that we are more susceptible to stress and burnout when our bodies are fatigued, out of shape, and deprived of proper nutrition. Make exercise and play a top priority. Get sufficient sleep and eat a healthy balanced diet. Remember, "if you take care of your body, your body will take care of you!"

➤ Many schools have incorporated sabbaticals as an option for their teachers. If available, take advantage of one to renew your professional commitment.

➤ Learn how and when to ask for help. Most people around you really do want you to succeed. Learn from the successes and failures of others. If symptoms of burnout persist for several weeks, consider getting professional help from a qualified counselor.

➤ Get away. Take advantage of your summers to travel. Take short weekend excursions.

➤ It is also essential to find some time to be alone every week, even if only for a few minutes. Some do it through quietly walking, playing a musical instrument, meditation, prayer, or simply "resting."

➤ Monitor your stress level. When you notice yourself becoming more tense, do something about it. Become proactive rather than reactive. Remember, "the time to relax is when you can least afford to." Take time for yourself.

➤ Seek a balance in your life. Develop interests beyond teaching. Save time for social activities, hobbies, and community service. Avoid talking only about school when you are with friends.

➤ Above all, strive to maintain a healthy sense of humor. It helps keep things in perspective. Remember Henry Ward Beecher's admonition that people without humor are like wagons without springs; they are jolted by every pebble in the road.

➤ Most important, always remember the adage that it is not events in our lives that cause stress, but rather what we say to ourselves about those events. Self-defeating, irrational assumptions about the things that happen to us invite feelings of despair, depression, and anger. Challenge that illogic thought pattern. Strive to change "I must..." to "I would prefer...."

The Shoelace

It's not the large things that
Send a man to the
Madhouse...
Not the death of his love
But a shoelace that snaps
With no time left...

—CHARLES BUKOWSKI

The only difference between a rut and a grave is the depth.

—ANONYMOUS

Laughter makes good blood.

—ITALIAN PROVERB

FOR MORE INFORMATION

Farber, B.A. (1991). *Crisis in Education: Stress and Burnout in the American Teacher.* San Francisco: Jossey-Bass.

Gmelch, W.H. (1993). *Coping with Faculty Stress.* Newbury Park, CA: Sage Publications.

Gold, Y. & Roth, R.A. (1993). *Teachers Managing Stress and Preventing Burnout: The Professional Health Solution.* London; Washington, D.C.: Falmer Press.

Maslach, C. (1982). *Burnout: The Cost of Caring.* Englewood Cliffs, NJ: Prentice-Hall.

Phillips, B.N. (1993). *Educational and Psychological Perspectives on Stress in Students, Teachers, and Parents.* Brandon, VT: CPPC.

Youngs, B.B. (1993). *Stress Management for Educators: A Guide to Manage Your Response to Stress.* Rolling Hills Estates, CA: Jalmar Press.

CHAPTER 6

Effective Use of School Time

The Erosion of School Time

In the past century schools have been charged with greater and greater responsibilities. Each time society faces a new problem, the schools are seen as part of the solution. We have added consumer education, drug education, sex education, moral education, values education, driver education, and career education. Schools are expected to turn out students who are "good citizens," have positive self-esteem, have mastered the "basics," have employable skills, and are mature, responsible adults. In short, we expect a lot of our schools.

Recent reports such as *A Nation at Risk*[1], *Educating Americans for the 21st Century*[2], and *Prisoners of Time*[3] suggest that even more must be demanded of our schools, urging a longer school day and extended school year. Proponents of the "Back to Basics" movement and educational accountability have focused attention upon the most precious of resources in the education of youth: *time*.

With the spectrum of objectives competing for time in the curriculum, the necessity of using it wisely is paramount. Because time is a finite resource, each wasted minute decreases the amount of time available for higher priority goals.

To increase learning time we are faced with two alternatives, or some combination of the two. We can increase the number of hours of schooling by lengthening the school day, yet, at a considerable expense—estimated in the billions. Beyond the financial restraints are the social and psychological impacts upon children and their families. Such a move is a policy decision that is being debated by legislators and educators. That debate is likely to continue for some time.

A more immediate alternative of increasing learning time is to use the presently scheduled school day more effectively. Research has found that as little as 50 percent of the scheduled school minutes are actually used for academic instruction.[4] Teachers vary greatly in their ability to manage classroom time. The ability to use time wisely in pursuing curricular goals is the most valuable teaching skill; time-management skills are essential for survival in the classroom. Where else in modern society do we place 30 people in one room with a single leader for six hours a day and expect constant, productive activity?

A SCHOOL DAY

There is no such thing as a typical school day. Although on paper, a teacher's schedule may look pretty routine day after day, the fact is that the unexpected will occur, as witnessed in the workday of a hypothetical teacher, Mr. Tom Dudley.

Tom has taught three years at Rollover Junior High. This year he has taken on the job of assistant track coach of the junior high team. With fewer younger teachers on the staff, he has been under increasing pressure to accept additional extracurricular activities. He can use the extra money, but it really doesn't pay that much considering all the extra time it consumes.

He meant to be at school early this Thursday to call the athletic director about ordering more tape and gauze. He mentally reminds himself that he must call during his free period.

Tom can hear the bell ring as he wheels into the parking lot. Of course, it's not his fault he is late. He left in plenty of time today. In fact, he was almost at school when he remembered he'd forgotten to bring the tests he was giving second period. He had taken them home to staple together last night. After returning home, he was caught 10 minutes by a train.

Rushing into his classroom, Tom finds most of the students lined along the windows watching two dogs fighting. As he begins to get them moving toward their desks, the school counselor pops in to remind Tom of the career interest inventory scheduled during his fourth-period class. They briefly exchange comments about last night's board of education meeting and make arrangements to play racquetball Saturday. It is now six minutes into the period.

Tom takes attendance, reads the morning announcements, and reminds the students that class dues will be collected tomorrow morning. He collects today's homework and returns those handed in Monday.

A girl asks permission to go to her locker to get her book; permission granted. Another girl wants to go to the restroom; permission denied. She had plenty of time before class!

The lesson begins. The bell rang nine minutes ago.

His lecture begins smoothly except for the momentary distraction of an ambulance roaring down the street. He reminds Steve to quit tilting his desk, and threatens to send Alice to the office if she doesn't stop chatting. Two girls are passing notes at the back of the room, but Tom doesn't notice.

Ten minutes before the end of the period he gives directions for tomorrow's homework and instructs the class to use the remaining time to begin working on it. After working for a couple of minutes, two students approach his desk for clarification of the instructions. Realizing that others may have the same problem, Tom again explains the assignment to the whole class. As they return to their work, Tom walks to the office to check on the film he needs to use right after lunch. Luckily the film arrived this morning. Between classes he must remember to request the projector from the teacher in charge of the A-V equipment.

By the time Tom leaves school at the end of practice, he is exhausted. He laments to himself that he didn't get everything done he had hoped to do. He carries his loaded briefcase home, promising to get caught up by Monday; just too much to do in too little time.

Tom's day isn't all that unusual. Interruptions, distractions, unanticipated problems, and decisions plague all teachers. Some may handle them more efficiently, but the challenges are there. Handling time demands is essential for classroom success!

THE SCHOOL CALENDAR

The upper limits of academic learning are set by the time school is in session. The average school year in America is 180 days or almost one-half of the days in a year.[5] (This compares with 243 days in Germany and 240 days in Japan.) The average school day is approximately six hours long, yielding an annual scheduled school calendar of 1080 hours.

No school is ever in session the total hours scheduled. Schools close for snow storms, fog, wind storms, ice, floods, and water shortages. Some buildings have been closed for fuel shortages, broken water lines, bomb threats, vandalism, funerals, or flu epidemics. Work stoppages by faculty or other school employees have caused some schools to close. A few school systems have a history of periodic strikes interrupting the school year. Schools have canceled sessions because their basketball team was competing in the state championship. In recent years many have shut the doors for weeks because they ran out of money.

On days schools are closed, teachers cannot teach and students do not receive supervised instruction. Most school closings are unavoidable, but yield vastly different amounts of exposure to instruction between schools.

More time is lost for delays of one or two hours because of inclement weather. In some areas frequent fog may force schools to delay opening more than 10 or 15 mornings per year. Impending storms occasionally force early dismissals. Some systems excuse students early for faculty meetings or parent conferences. Others have shortened the school day by moving to double shifts to alleviate overcrowding.

Even when school is in session, students are not always there. Absenteeism may severely limit the academic exposure of some students. Certainly, legitimate illnesses keep some students at home. Religious holidays or deaths in the family are also viewed as excused absences. Some parents keep their children home to baby-sit, go on early vacations, or help with work. Parents still schedule doctors' and dentists' appointments during school hours. In many rural schools it is not unusual for boys to miss school the first day of hunting season. Some students still "play hooky." Indeed for many schools, especially some inner-city buildings, it is not unusual for as many as one-half of the students to be absent.[6] That represents a serious loss of learning time.

INSTRUCTIONAL TIME

Even when school is in session, and the student attends, not all time is available for classroom instruction. Time is absorbed by class changes and recesses.

The time allocated to academic classes varies widely from school to school and even within the same building. The power to allocate school time among the various content areas is a most significant tool in determining school effectiveness; one that unfortunately has been abused in some instances. Differences as large as seven-fold have been observed in the amount of time spent on content areas such as math or reading, even within the same school system. In a large national study, John Goodlad reported that the hours of time allotted to instruction ranged from 19 to over 27 hours per week, with an average of 22-1/2 hours per week.[7] Wide discrepancies were also found at the secondary level.

The obvious explanation for such wide variation in time allocated to instructional areas is that the needs of students vary, demanding individualization. There is little evidence to suggest that this is the reason. The data to date suggest that students are exposed to large differences in content coverage merely because of the school they happen to attend or the teacher they are assigned. For example, one teacher reported that she spent very little time teaching fractions because she didn't like them![8] Her students will pay for such preferences later. Indeed, in the Beginning Teacher Evaluation Study, the amount of time allocated to reading and mathematics instruction and achievement test scores were significantly correlated.[9]

Scheduled events such as standardized testing, school pictures, assemblies, fire or tornado drills, or pep rallies cut into the time scheduled for instruction. Individual students are often absent from the room for school-sanctioned activities, such as visits to the counselor's office, special pull-out programs, in-school suspensions, or athletic events. In the spring many high school classrooms may have a third of the students excused early to travel to athletic contests. Teachers may be reluctant to introduce any new material to the remaining students, virtually eliminating the last period of the school day.

Teacher Time-on-Task

Not all regularly scheduled class time is devoted to academic instruction. Most teachers lose time for clerical tasks such as collecting milk money, taking attendance, collecting and distributing papers and materials, counting books, reading announcements, or writing passes; all tasks that do not require a college degree.[10]

Classroom research studies have recorded that as much as 18 percent of the class time may be consumed by discipline matters.[11] The simplest reprimand may further consume time by creating a break in the momentum in the lesson, causing the whole class to become off-task. The inertia of the lesson must be regained. Most time is used in managing student behavior; for example, giving students permission to go to the restroom or sharpen pencils eat away at class time.

Beginning the class a few minutes after the scheduled starting time or stopping the lesson a few minutes before dismissal robs more learning time, as much as 10 minutes of the class period.[12] By poor preparation and planning, a teacher can consume more time on non-instructional activities, such as hunting for misplaced papers and materials, clarifying directions, or setting up audio-visual equipment.

Additional class time is absorbed by a variety of interruptions: students arriving late, drop-in visitors, telephone calls, outside noises and distractions, equipment breakdowns, or ill students.

Transitions from one activity to another consume many minutes over the course of a year. Some teachers have been guilty of poorly using class time by reviewing last week's "big game," making the class wait while one student is helped, or excessive chatting about personal stories that are irrelevant to the lesson.

While the individual time robbers may vary from room to room, all schools lose a large proportion of time to non-instructional activities. Indeed, several research studies have found that less than 50 percent of the school day is actually spent in academic instruction![13] That is 540 hours of the 1080 allotted schools to "teach the basics," develop minimal competencies, and meet all the other assorted objectives imposed upon it by society.

THE PACE OF INSTRUCTION

The pace of instruction represents how fast a teacher covers the content during the time allotted to a content area. In the same span of time two teachers may cover different amounts of content.

Student achievement test results have been found to be higher for teachers who "push" their students through the material at a faster rate. In one study math teachers producing the greatest achievement gains covered 40 to 50 percent more pages during a time span than teachers of lower scoring students. This should not be interpreted as a maxim that faster is always better. Such research only reflects "average" gains for comparison groups. The faster pace may benefit middle and upper students, but harm the lower portion of the class.[14]

The guiding principle in pacing instruction is to aim for appropriateness. Too fast a pace and the student is left behind. The teacher is moving on to new material for which the prerequisite skills have not yet been mastered. Instruction paced too slowly becomes inefficient, producing boredom, repetition, and disinterest.

The reality of understanding individual differences among students is that not all require the same amount of time to master a concept. Research from mastery learning suggests that most concepts and skills taught in schools can be mastered by 80 to 95 percent of all students if they are given an appropriate amount of time.[15] The lockstep pacing of the traditional classroom moves everyone at the same pace, some before they are ready, others long after. Observational studies have found that teachers typically move on when approximately 80 percent of the class have grasped the concept or skill. Of course, conscientious teachers have always made attempts to provide remedial instruction to the lagging 20 percent through individual tutoring, small-group instruction, or homework assignments. Indeed, totally individualizing pacing of instruction remains a challenge to the most dedicated of teachers. With varying degrees of success, teachers have sought to individualize pacing through programmed instruction, peer tutoring, computer-assisted instruction, contract learning, enrichment activities, learning centers, and ability grouping. Matching the time provided with the time required for learning is the key to improving learning gains for all students but especially low achievers. We must continue to experiment with new techniques that provide the appropriate level of pacing. Part of the key is freeing teachers from the routine clerical and non-instructional tasks to provide the optimal instructional time for each student.

STUDENT TIME-ON-TASK

Just because teachers are teaching doesn't mean that students are learning. Educational efficiency is eroded further by student inattention and ineffective instruction. Two teachers may allocate the same amount of time to instruction, but their students may be engaged in that instruction at vastly different rates. The percentage of time-on-task or engagement rate has come under increasing scrutiny as a contributor to learning effectiveness. The percentage of time-on-task has been reported to range from 50 percent to 90 percent with an average engagement rate of 70 percent of the available instructional time.[16] But remember that 50 percent of the day may already be lost to non-instructional activity; therefore, the student time-on-task may be less than 70 percent of 50 percent or 350 hours out of the original 1080 hours per year!

Wide variations in student engagement rates have been observed.[17] Higher on-task rates are observed for girls, high-ability students, and good readers. The highest engagement rates are typically found in music, social studies, and foreign languages.[18] The lowest are in mathematics, language arts, and reading (ironically the subjects generally allocated the largest block of time). Students are also more attentive to those classes in which they are actively involved in activities, which likely contributes to higher on-task behavior in music and social studies.

The teaching format also influences time-on-task. Teacher-led discussions tend to elicit greater student involvement than lectures or audio-visual presentations or seatwork.[19] Croll and Moses found that the more time the teacher spends working with the whole class, the greater the percentage of time students spend on a task, even when they are working independently.[20] Small-group activities tend to provide the lowest amount of on-task behavior. This does not mean that instructional activities with lower engagement rates should not be used. The benefits gained from a seatwork assignment or small-group project may justify its use.

Student attention to lessons is also influenced by the weather, season, and time of the day.[21] Students experience the highest involvement at the beginning of the morning, but involvement decreases as the day passes.[22] Days right before or after a major holiday or special event usually suffer lower attentiveness.[23]

Not all engaged time is productive learning time. If students are attending to instruction that is ineffective, too easy or too difficult, they are gaining little. The goal must be to seek high engagement in appropriate learning tasks.

CONCLUSION

Before the school year is lengthened or the school day is extended, it is imperative to make every effort to assure that the current available time is being used as effectively as possible. Teachers must create an environment that demonstrates that school time is to be safeguarded. Setting the expectations and standards on the effective use of time must be done the first week of school. Well-prepared, organized lessons are more likely to maximize student time-on-task. Beginning the class on time and teaching until the end of the class period are two ways of gaining additional class time.

The educational community must work to assure that the learning time is protected. Every effort must be made to free teachers from non-instructional clerical tasks and to minimize interruptions and other time robbers. A humane and fun, yet business-like learning climate should be sought.

NOTES

1. National Commission on Excellence in Education, *A Nation At Risk: The Imperative for Educational Reform* (Washington, D.C.: U.S. Government Printing Office, 1983).

2. National Science Board Commission on Precollege Education in Mathematics, Science, and Technology, *Educating Americans for the 21st Century: A Plan of Action for Improving Mathematics, Science and Technology Education for All American Elementary and Secondary Students So That Their Achievement Is the Best in the World by 1995* (1983).

3. National Education Commission on Time and Learning, *Prisoners of Time* (Washington, D.C.: U.S. Government Printing Office, 1994).

4. J.I. Goodlad, *A Place Called School* (New York: McGraw-Hill, 1985); A. Harnischfeger, "School Time and Changing Curricular Goals" (Paper delivered at the American Educational Research Association, New Orleans, Louisiana, April 1984), 289-290; N.L. Karweit and R.E. Slavin, "Measurement and Modeling Choices in Studies of Time and Learning," *American Educational Research Journal* 18 (1981): 157-171); J. Murphy, "Instructional Leadership: Focus on Time to Learn," *NASSP Bulletin* 76: 542 (1992): 19-26.

5. Goodlad, *loc. cit.*

6. N.L. Karweit, *Time on Task: A Research Review* (Johns Hopkins University: Center for Social Organization of Schools, 1973).

7. Goodlad, *loc cit.*

8. Ibid.

9. C.W. Fisher, D.C. Berliner, N. Nikola, R. Marliave, L.S. Cahlen, and M.M. Dishaw, "Teaching Behaviors, Academic Learning Time, and Student Achievement: An Overview," *Time to Learn* (1980): 7-32.

10. J.L. Davidson and F.M. Holley, "Your Students Might Be Spending Only Half of the School Day Receiving Instruction," *The American School Board Journal* (1979): 40-41.

11. Hiatt, D.B. (1979). Time allocation in the classroom: Is instruction being short-changed? *Phi Delta Kappan, 61,* 289-290.

12. R. Lowe and R. Gervais, "Increasing Instructional Time in Today's Classroom," *NAASP Bulletin* 72 (1988): 19-22.

13. Goodlad, *loc. cit.*; Hiatt, *loc. cit.*; Karweit and Slavin, *loc. cit.*

14. Harnischfeger, *loc. cit.*

15. B.S. Bloom, *Human Characteristics and School Learning* (New York: McGraw-Hill, 1976).

16. Goodlad, *loc. cit.*; Karweit and Slavin, *loc. cit.*

17. Karweit and Slavin, *loc. cit.*

18. H.H. Ebmeir and R.L. Zoimek, "Engagement Rates as a Function of Subject Area, Grade Level and Time of Day" (Paper presented at the American Educational Research Association, New York, March 1982).

19. Karweit, *loc. cit.*

20. P. Croll and D. Moses, "Teaching Methods and Time on Task in Junior Classrooms," *Educational Research* 30 (1988): 90-97.

21. Karweit, *loc. cit.*

22. Ebmeir and Zoimek, *loc. cit.*

23. Karweit and Slavin, *loc. cit.*

An earlier version of this section appeared in *American Secondary Education*: "The Erosion of School Time," Ronald R. Partin. Reprinted with permission from *American Secondary Education*, vol. 17, #4, 1989, pp. 6-11.

Prisoners of Time

In April of 1994 the National Education Commission on Time and Learning issued its report, *Prisoners of Time*, which examined the relationship between time and learning in the nation's schools. The commission concluded that schools were very much controlled by the clock and that true school reform must reexamine the allocation and use of time in the schools. Its report labeled school time as the rudder of school reform. The commission issued eight recommendations:

1. Reinvent schools around learning, not time.
2. Fix the design flaw: use time in new and better ways.
3. Establish an academic day.
4. Keep schools open longer to meet the needs of children and communities.
5. Give teachers the time they need.
6. Invest in technology.
7. Develop local action plans to transform schools.
8. Share the responsibility: finger pointing and evasion must end.

Tips on Minimizing Classroom Interruptions

Interruptions are the bane of every classroom teacher. It is not merely the precious class time that is lost, but something even more essential: momentum. A class that is 100% on-task suddenly becomes 100% off-task as the interruption disrupts everyone's attention. You must then refocus everyone's attention back onto the topic at hand. While many interruptions are beyond your direct control (e.g., fire engines, P.A. announcements, or drop-in visitors), some interruptions are created by the teacher (stopping a lesson to hunt for materials or to verbally reprimand a student). While some interruptions are unavoidable, here are some suggestions for minimizing their impact.

➤ To assess the amount of time consumed by interruptions, carry a stop watch for a day or week. Each time you are interrupted, start the watch. When the interruption ends, stop the watch. At the end of the day, record how much time has elapsed. An alternative is to ask a student to do the timekeeping for you.

➤ Let the world know that intrusions are not welcome. Many interruptions occur simply because the offender is not aware that his or her behavior is disruptive. Open doors invite interruptions.

➤ Outside their doors, many teachers hang a sign such as "Important Learning in Progress" (or use the "Do Not Disturb: Learning in Progress" sign included in this book). Tape a note pad and hang a pencil beside the door for messages.

➤ Negotiate with the principal for custodians to schedule distracting work, such as mowing beside windows, before or after school. It may not always be possible, but let it be known that such activity detracts from learning.

➤ If doors or windows provide too many visual distractions to students, rearrange the furniture to face away from the distraction.

➤ Let other teachers know that sending students to borrow supplies during class is not welcome. Be tactful, but assertive. Conversely, you have a responsibility to respect the time of your fellow teachers. Do not send student messengers to their rooms during classes except in emergencies.

➤ The best prevention of interruptions is a well-planned, organized lesson. Have the necessary materials and equipment ready before class begins. Stopping a lesson to thread a movie projector or hunt for a book is usually an avoidable distraction. Not only does it use precious class time, but it invites student misbehavior.

➤ When an interruption does occur, your aims are to (1) keep it as brief as possible, (2) minimize the impact upon the learning activity, and (3) assure that the same interruption will not occur again. If you are interrupted by a telephone call, get to the point immediately. Be brief and assertive. If the call is going to take too long, give the caller a more convenient time when you can talk or volunteer to call back.

➤ Most principals have discovered the potential abuses of the intercom, restricting announcements to the first and last five minutes of the day. If your school has not implemented such a policy, suggest that they do so. Some have stopped using the public address system for routine morning announcements; instead, teachers read them to their classes.

➤ Many interruptions are caused by people who walk in unannounced. If someone comes to your door, stand in the doorway so you can talk with the visitor yet face the class. Try to avoid leaving the room unattended.

➤ At the beginning of the year when it is best to establish classroom routines, tell your students what they should do during such interruptions.

Teacher Time Robbers

The following list contains the activities most frequently cited by teachers as keeping them from doing their job better:

➤ filling out forms, paperwork
➤ repeating directions
➤ unplanned interruptions
➤ clerical tasks, photocopying
➤ handling classroom behavior
➤ grading student work
➤ attending meetings
➤ attending inservice programs
➤ cleaning their classroom
➤ playground supervision
➤ recordkeeping for money
➤ bus duty
➤ lunchroom supervision
➤ taking attendance

Classroom Routines

Effective teachers have learned the importance of establishing classroom routines the first week of school. There are many daily classroom events and tasks that must be accomplished with a minimum of direction and must flow smoothly using the least amount of time possible. Don't assume students know what you want; train them the first week of school. As each task arises the first time, explain carefully exactly how you would like it to be done. It helps to carefully explain why the routine is helpful in getting things done. Invite questions from students to clarify the procedure. For some you might want to put the directions in writing. If students later begin to deviate from the routines, reteach them. You are trying to create new habits. Research suggests it generally takes about a month to establish a new habit. Possible areas for which you might wish to establish routines include:

➤ Beginning the day
➤ Taking attendance
➤ What to do when the student arrives late
➤ Making up missed assignments when returning from an absence
➤ Making up missed tests
➤ Taking lunch count
➤ Seeking help
➤ Signaling when to stop talking
➤ Turning in homework papers
➤ Information to be included on their papers (location of their name, period, date, etc.)
➤ What to do when they finish a test or seatwork early
➤ Leaving the room (restroom privileges, library, office, etc.)
➤ What to do when a visitor comes to the door
➤ Distributing and collecting materials, assignments, etc.
➤ What to do if they don't bring pencils, paper, etc.

- ➤ Appropriate responses to emergencies (fire, tornado, earthquake)
- ➤ Beginning class
- ➤ Leaving and returning from recess
- ➤ Signing out materials, tools, books, equipment, etc.
- ➤ Seating arrangement
- ➤ Using learning centers
- ➤ Procedures for moving about the building as a grouup
- ➤ Attending assemblies
- ➤ Clean up
- ➤ Obtaining permission for field trips
- ➤ Leaving the room at the end of the day
- ➤ Transitions from one activity to another

Merely establishing a routine or procedure will not make it happen. You must clearly explain it to your students. If possible, demonstrate it or have a model for them to study. Then provide opportunities for your students to practice the routine. Walk them through it step by step if necessary. Reinforce them for complying with your routines. Show students you appreciate their cooperation.

Once routines are explained, consider posting them on the wall. When a new student is enrolled in your class, it is often helpful to appoint a partner who is responsible for teaching the various routines to the new student. Here are some specific routines some teachers find helpful in running the daily activities of their classrooms.

Taking Attendance or Lunch Count

Taking attendance is one of the necessary tasks of any teacher. There is no one way to take the roll. Your school policy, the number of students, grade level, and maturity of your students all influence the form of your attendance-taking routine. The important thing is to adopt a procedure which is least disruptive.

- ➤ Many teachers prefer to get their students to work immediately and then to unobtrusively take the roll. Generally, after the first week of school few teachers waste class time calling the roll aloud. Some have been ingenious in subtle ways to take attendance with little disruption and minimal time.

- ➤ Attach a library-book pocket for each student to posterboard that is attached to the wall near the door. Put the students' names on these pockets. Attach a separate one in which you insert brightly colored cards. As students enter the room, they pull out a blank card and insert it in the pocket with their name.

- ➤ To make an attendance or lunch count board, you need a board approximately 14″ × 18″, spring-type clothespins (one for each student), box or can to store clothespins, calendar, and attendance slips.

Decorate the board and box if desired. Print the first and last name of each student on the clothespins. Store the clothespins in the box or can on a small table or desk. Have the calendar and attendance slips handy. After students hang up their coats, they go to the table, get their clothespins, and place them on the board under the appropriate heading. When school actually starts, a volunteer student goes to the desk and fills out the date, teacher's name, counts those buying lunch, and records on the slip. Any clothespins left in the box are students who are absent. These the volunteer records on the slip and takes to the teacher for approval. The volunteer then takes the slip to the office or clips to the door, whatever is your school policy. When the student returns to the room, he or she is responsible for removing the clothespins from the board and putting them back in the box, ready for tomorrow. An alternative is to hang the pins around the rim of a bucket and have the students drop their names into the bucket.

➤ If not required, don't begin every class by taking attendance or reading the roll. Jump right into the subject matter. Students most remember the first and last things you do in the class. You can quietly take attendance while they are busy with independent work later in the period. Other teachers have an assignment written on the board. As soon as students enter the room, they are to go directly to their seats and begin work on the day's assignment. Once everyone has begun work, the teacher can quietly take attendance using the seating chart.

➤ Have each student record his or her name on 3 × 5 index cards. Different colors can be used for each class or grade level. They are kept in one small file box. When students are absent without being excused, their cards are turned sideways in the box and left there until the next day when a call or note is received. It is very easy to check who has not returned an approved absence slip.

➤ Keep a stack of brightly colored cards in a pocket attached to the wall near the door. Instead of having to take a lunch count, have the children be responsible for their own. Clip two folders (labeled "buy" and "pack") on the bulletin board, next to the folder containing the colored cards. Each day as students enter the room, they get a card and drop it in the "buy" pocket or "pack" pocket. A student volunteer can quickly count the number of cards in each folder, place the cards back in the original holding folder, and turn in the lunch count.

➤ For elementary school, record each student's name on a paper animal cutout. Hang these with a small string to a poster. As the students enter the classroom, they turn their tags over. Those students whose names still show are absent. At the end of the day, a student helper can turn them all back over to reveal the names again. (*Contributed by Janet Smith*)

➤ On the left side of an 8-1/2 × 11 inch sheet of paper, type your class roster in a column, listing your name, room number and the period at the top of the column. Copy or type the same information onto the right-hand side of the paper, giving you two identical lists of the class roster. Duplicate, cut, and staple into pads of attendance rosters for each class. At the beginning of the class, all you need do is circle the names of the absent students on the top sheet and tear it off. The pads can also be used for field trips, lunch counts, etc. This is especially appreciated by others if your hurried handwriting is illegible.

➤ Some teachers use a loose-leaf notebook to maintain attendance records. Create a section for each class, separating them by tabs. Within each section arrange sheets alphabetically by students' last names. At the top of each student's sheet have them enter basic information, such as locker number, home address, phone number, parents' names, student identification number, book number. A notation is made each day a student is absent, tardy, or fails to bring homework. If disruptive behavior occurs, it is noted on that student's sheet. Later problems will be handled much more smoothly with such documentation.

➤ Have students who are buying lunch stand up and count off. You have a quick head count. This also reinforces number skills for younger children.

DISTRIBUTING AND COLLECTING MATERIALS

Getting tools, books, papers, and other materials distributed to students can be a time-absorbing, chaotic, stressful event if a smooth routine is not developed.

➤ Don't distribute too many things at once and only distribute things in the order in which they will be needed.

➤ Assign a weekly monitor whose job is to assist the teacher in distributing any materials.

➤ Don't count papers when distributing them in class. Instruct the person at the end of the row to pass them to one corner where a student puts extras in a neat pile for you.

➤ If students are working in groups, you can unobtrusively place papers or supplies they will need beneath one person's seat in each group. At the appropriate time you can direct them to gather from beneath their seats the materials for their group.

➤ Delegate one student from each group to come pick up the materials needed for their group.

➤ When collecting papers, have students pass them across the rows to one side of the room rather than down the front. There is less poking people in the back and it is easier to monitor student behavior.

REGAINING STUDENTS' ATTENTION

Quieting a class to gain its attention is a challenge to many teachers. It is perhaps the first routine that should be taught the first day of school. Most successful teachers develop some form of signal or cue that tells students to stop what they are doing, be quiet, and focus their attention upon the teacher. Here are some strategies used by many teachers:

➤ Use a bell, chord on the piano, or chime to signal it is time to stop talking and give the teacher attention. Some teachers have collected an assortment of bells, whistles, and other novelty sound instruments that they use for this purpose.

➤ Hand signals might be employed to cue students to stop talking. Raising your hand palm up or holding up two or three fingers are commonly used signals. Don't say anything until you have everyone's attention. Some teachers have their students join the teacher in raising their hands.

➤ Another commonly used cue to quiet a group is to hold your index finger vertically across your lips.

➤ Others signal it is time to give the teacher attention by standing in a designated spot in the room.

➤ Slowly clap your hands together three times. When students hear the first clap, they are to join in on the second clap. This grabs the attention of everyone who didn't hear the first one. Typically the whole class has offered the third clap simultaneously. Now the room is silent and attention is focused upon the teacher.

➤ Another cue is to write a cue word (e.g., STOP or QUIET) on the chalkboard. Upon seeing the teacher writing that word on the board, all students are to comply immediately.

➤ Another signal can be used to cue the class that group activities are becoming too noisy and should be brought down to a lower level. It might be helpful to have everyone pause for 15 to 30 seconds before resuming their activities. Some teachers flick the light switch. This tends to work if used sparingly.

➤ Some teachers have constructed a flashing red light that is turned on when it is time to stop talking. One other option is to construct a replica traffic signal with green, amber, and red lights. The amber is used to signal students that one minute remains to finish a discussion or task.

➤ A useful way of indicating the time remaining without interrupting small-group discussion activities is to construct a picture of a traffic light, either on a poster or as an overhead transparency. When the discussion begins, show the light with a green light. When there is one minute left, reveal the yellow light. That is the cue for students to wind up their discussion. When time is up, reveal the red light. This serves as a signal for everyone to stop talking. (See the transparency master at the end of the chapter. You can create three overlaying transparencies and color the three lights appropriately.)

SEEKING PERMISSION TO LEAVE THE ROOM

➤ Restroom pass: Rather than have students raise their hands to ask to use the restroom, hang a sign from a string that has "GO" printed on one side and "STOP" printed on the other. If everyone is in the room, the sign is on "GO." If someone needs to use the restroom, he or she turns the sign to "STOP" (meaning all others can't leave the room because someone is out). When the person comes back, he or she must turn the sign back to "GO," and someone else may go out. Of course, if this privilege is abused, it is restricted.

➤ Nonverbal signals: At the beginning of the school year, teach your students the following signals: index finger raised (need to use the restroom) or pencil raised (it needs sharpening). Upon eye contact with the student, you can simply nod your head or raise your hand to indicate if the activity may be done. Using these signals avoids needless interruptions. Other nonverbal cues for signaling that students should be quiet and give you their attention might include: holding up an interesting object; pointing toward the clock; flipping the light switch once; gesturing across the throat with your index finger; using chimes, slide whistles or other noisemakers; holding your finger up to your lips; going to a specified spot in the room; or turning on a colored light.

➤ Laminate two pictures on cards—one for boys, one for girls. Add a string so it can hang on a hook or nail. The pictures are hung on a nail beside the teacher's desk. When a student needs to use the restroom, he or she takes the card from the nail and shows the teacher, but needs not talk. When the teacher sees the student, she nods her head for permission. The student places the picture on a hook by the door. When he returns, he puts the picture back on the hook beside the teacher's desk. Since neither student nor teacher talks aloud, there is no interruption of class.

➤ Save time when using written hall passes (such as those included at the end). Have the student fill out all the information except your signature.

➤ Instead of using written passes, many teachers have one made of wood. It is best to make it large enough not to fit into the students' pockets. Paint your name and room number on it. You might choose to decorate it in an interesting way (or delegate the task to a student). By having only one pass you assure that only one student at a time is out of the room.

SEEKING HELP

During seatwork students will occasionally need help from the teacher. It is important to let students know the procedure you expect them to follow to get help. If the teacher is not busy with other students, the simplest procedure is for the student to simply raise his or her hand until acknowledged by the teacher. (Teaching them to raise two fingers would help you differentiate seeking help from wanting to use the rest room which might be just the index finger.) The teacher either comes to the student's desk or nods permission for the student to approach the teacher. With reasonably well-behaved students, some teachers permit students needing help to come to the teacher's desk without first having to gain the teacher's consent. A greater problem occurs when the teacher is busy working with another student or group. A signal or cue needs to be established to let the teacher know that help is needed whenever the teacher has a chance to assist the student.

➤ Some teachers have a colored card taped to the front of each student's desk. When students need help, they flip the card down over the front of the desk. Another option is to have each student construct a stand-up placard by folding an 8-1/2 × 11 inch sheet of cardstock in half. They should print "I Need Help" on the face of the card. To signal the teacher that they need help, the student turns his or her card up so it is visible to the teacher.

➤ Teacher educator Harry Wong suggests using a toilet paper tube with one end covered with red construction paper and the other with green. A student needing help turns the tube with the red end up and continues to work until the teacher comes to help.

➤ To avoid being disturbed while working with a group, use a See-Me-Chair. If a student, who is working independently, has a question about his or her work and a classmate cannot answer it, the student must sit in the See-Me-Chair to ask for help. Check with the student when you have time.

➤ A signal used by many teachers is for students to turn their textbook up on edge when they need the teacher's help.

STUDENTS' TOOLS

For smooth operation of day-to-day instruction, students must know what supplies and tools they must provide, when they need them, and where to store them. The first week you should clearly specify all the materials they are required to provide. A written list works best.

It is important early in the year to clarify which items in the room are for student use and which are to be used only by the teacher. Also clarify which items students have free access to and those they must first have permission.

➤ Keep a store of pencils students can buy with cash or class points earned. Some teachers lend out pencils, but students must leave "collateral" (such as a dime or a shoe), which is redeemed when the pencils are returned.

➤ If they come without a pen or pencil, lend students a crayon. Some teachers scrounge vacated lockers the last day of school collecting all the left-over pencils. These are "loaners" next year. Some break them in half, sharpen both stubs and lend these. There is less willingness to depend on the teacher for writing instruments if they are not too attractive.

➤ Let students know when they may use the pencil sharpener. Some teachers only let students sharpen pencils before class and warn them to always bring two. Some teachers do not require students to seek permission to use the pencil sharpener as long as students do not abuse the privilege. Other teachers have students signal when they need to use the sharpener, usually by holding their pencil in the air. In either case, it is wise to only allow one student at a time at the pencil sharpener.

➤ Must assignments be completed in pencil or pen? Let students know your expectations. At first it might even be a good idea to note on the top of the assignment sheet "Complete in pen only." That minimizes debate later about whether a student knew he or she was to use a pen.

ASSIGNMENTS AND HOMEWORK

Procedures for completing assignments, turning them in, and returning them need to be established the first week of school. Here are some procedures that must be clarified.

➤ How will students be given each day's assignment? Will it be posted on the board each day when they enter the room? Will it be given at the beginning or end of class? Are they required to carry an assignment notepad? Will deadlines be announced?

➤ How do you want them to complete it? Where does their name go on the assignment?

➤ How should it be turned in? When are they to be turned in? As they enter the class? Do they pass them in? Or place them in a basket or box at a designated time? Should it be folded in any specific way?

➤ How should a student make up work after an absence? How do they find out the assignments? How long do they have to get caught up?

STORAGE SOLUTIONS

➤ It is easier to maintain an organized classroom if sufficient storage facilities are provided. This includes not only cabinets, shelves and furniture but also ample, accessible storage containers. Use an assortment of resealable, plastic sandwich and freezer storage bags to store game parts, bulletin board letters, crayons, art supplies, and any other small items that need to be kept together.

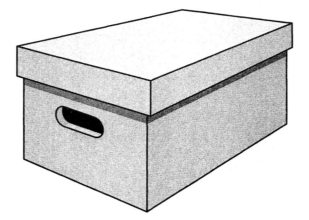

➤ Small hardware storage bins are ideal for storing many small items and supplies. Shoe boxes, especially the clear, plastic ones, are great storage containers for many items. Dish pans and coffee cans also are handy containers. Though harder to find today, cigar boxes are still one of the finest storage bins available. Parents or garage sales are inexpensive sources for many storage containers.

➤ Obtaining and organizing adequate storage solutions is only the first step. You must train your students to put materials back in their designated places. It is much easier to teach everyone to put things back where they belong than for you to spend time resorting and shelving misplaced items.

➤ As much as possible color-code items and storage compartments to facilitate returning things to where they belong.

➤ Clearly label all storage containers and cupboards. This task could be delegated to a student volunteer or aide.

➤ Assign a student to be the postal clerk, librarian, or stock supervisor. Their job is to see that everything is put back where it belongs that day. You might develop a checklist to facilitate their task. This can be especially helpful in laboratory or shop classes.

The Challenge of Paperwork

Two and a half trillion pages of paper are generated in America each year. According to a study by Partners for Environmental Progress, paper consumes 45% of the available landfill space. Another researcher found that of all the pieces of paper that go into filing cabinets in America today, 95% of it will never come out again. A good estimate of how long a person has been in education is to count the number of filing cabinets in his or her room and multiply by five. We seldom purge our cabinets. They simply fill up and about every five years we requisition another one! Author Tom Parker estimated that each day Americans buy 426 bushels of paper clips (approximately 35 million)!

Teachers consistently rate paperwork as their number one time-management problem. While some paperwork is inevitable in any profession, most teachers probably accumulate much more paper than they really need. Imagine how many pieces of paper you handle on a typical school day: magazines, quizzes, tests, attendance forms, grade records, requisitions, books, letters, forms, memos, mail, meeting notices and minutes. Then multiply that figure by 180 days. These reams and reams of paper we swap, hoard, file, and stack consume vast amounts of storage space, but also devour a significant proportion of our lives.

CAUSES OF THE PAPER DELUGE

Paper abounds for many reasons. Governmental, technological, and cultural forces interact to inundate us with paper. Our psychological weaknesses often make it difficult to rid ourselves of paper once it is in our possession. Here are some of the more pervasive causes of the paper deluge:

➤ Knowledge grows exponentially. The number of publications has exploded. In 1800 there were approximately 100 scientific journals; today there are close to 100,000. The numbers of non-scientific publications has increased as dramatically.

➤ In this "Age of Litigation" many people are concerned with documenting anything that might possibly be the subject of dispute in the future. Certain disciplinary decisions, personnel dismissals or sanctions, and financial transactions should be carefully recorded. Keep only what is absolutely necessary and file it so you can find it when you need it. Purge these files after a reasonable time. This environment creates an insecurity, prompting some—especially administrators—to hoard paper to "protect one's backside."

➤ Governmental red tape has proliferated. Additional mandates and standards by state and federal governments require massive documentation, consuming not only the mounds of paper it generates, but the valuable time of the school employees charged with tabulating, assembling, and submitting these documents. Every new educational program funded also creates a paper trail of accountability.

➤ The copy machine has abetted the paper explosion. It is just as easy to punch ten as to punch one, so we end up with nine more copies of everything, "just in case." Also the photocopier makes it easy for others to send us copies of their paper collection.

➤ The computer, while having the potential of saving time and paper, has thus far failed to create the paperless society. Indeed, many argue it actually makes it easier to generate more paperwork. With computers accessible to virtually everyone, the mass of form letters, targeted mailing lists, and databases abounds. Additionally, those of us who grew up before computers don't trust hard drives and floppy disks to hold our valuable information. We want papers we can touch, file, and carry.

TIPS FOR HANDLING PAPERWORK

➤ When in doubt, throw it out (or better yet, recycle it). Ask yourself, "What's the worst thing that would happen if I didn't have this piece of paper?" Few papers are totally impossible to replace if necessary.

➤ Never save papers simply because you "might" need it someday. Rather ask yourself, "If I need this at some time in the future, where will I be able to find it." Chances are there are nine other copies filed around the school system.

➤ Set aside one day a year (perhaps during the summer) to purge all your files of any piece of paper you don't need. A good measure is that if you haven't used it in the last three years, you probably don't need it.

➤ Time-management experts advise that we strive to handle each piece of paper only once. While not always possible, the less we shuffle papers back and forth from our briefcase to our desk and back, the more effective we are likely to be in controlling the paper plague.

➤ Label a basket or folder "To be filed." Set aside a few minutes every week to file papers. Don't let them accumulate longer.

➤ Label twelve file folders with the names of the months. Keep this in a convenient file drawer near your desk. As you receive pieces of paper that you will need at some time later during the year, file them under the month they will be needed. At the first of each new month, pull out the corresponding file.

➤ Tape or glue to your desk blotter important or frequently used lists, numbers, rosters, or schedules.

➤ Save only one copy of papers you need in the future. Be sure to save one clean master (or a computer file) of handouts and letters you use each year.

➤ In your desk or at the front of your file drawer, keep three folders labeled correspondence, schedules, and forms. Place master copies in these so the next time you won't have to redo them.

➤ Keep a colored manila folder in your briefcase or book bag labeled "To Do." Keep your "To Do" list in that folder as well as any memos, letters, forms, or other items you'll need to accomplish the tasks on your list. By keeping it in your briefcase it is always with you.

➤ Use colored folders or labels when you file papers. Use a different color for each subject you teach or for each period of the day. (If possible, match the color of your textbook. This minimizes the possibility of misfiling the folder in the wrong drawer.)

➤ When file folders get too fat, split them into smaller categories or move all the papers to a large three-ring binder. The same principle holds for accumulating files on your computer hard drive.

➤ Develop a test-question bank on note cards or computer. There are several excellent test-generation programs available from computer software suppliers. (See the list of addresses in Chapter 7.) This makes construction of tests and quizzes much easier.

➤ For each class you teach, keep a three-ring binder in which you file all lesson plans, handouts, assignments, sample problems, and other items you want to have available next year when you teach the class again. It is helpful to have a different colored notebook for each class.

➤ Plan to do your photocopying at times when there is no line. Right before school in the morning is probably the busiest time.

➤ Set aside a specific spot on your desk where you place items to go to the office. As you think of such items, always place them in that spot. Whenever you have to make a trip to the office, take those items with you. You should do the same thing with items you plan to take home each night. Strive to "make every trip count."

➤ Organize your work area at home with all the necessary supplies at hand (pens, paper, envelopes, stamps, paper clips, stapler, scissors, etc.).

➤ Probably the hardest things for teachers to discard are books, no matter how outdated, unused, or duplicative. This is doubly difficult for hardcover books. If it is not a much-used reference book, ask yourself, "Will I ever read this book?" If not a definite yes, then donate it to a book sale or library or give it to a student. Put a bunch of discarded books in a "Free" box for your students to pick the ones they want.

➤ If you have forms you must complete for many students, complete one form with all the basic information that is the same for all students (e.g., your name, date, school building, signature). Photocopy the necessary number of forms and only complete by hand the necessary individual information.

➤ If professional journals accumulate unread for more than three months, give them away or cut out the most promising articles and file for future reference. Do not feel guilty if you do not read every publication cover to cover. There might only be one or two articles really of interest to you.

➤ If it is your magazine, cut out the articles you want to read later. Save these in a file folder for free time. Some keep this file in their briefcase or take it with them when they are likely to be waiting, such as the doctor's office or the airport.

➤ You might put a blank label on the front cover of a magazine. As you read it jot down the page numbers you would like to copy. Another way is to keep small strips of scrap paper handy and mark the page numbers on these slips, which are then inserted as page markers.

➤ Cancel subscriptions to publications you don't have time to read or that really don't meet your needs. Avoid renewals simply out of habit. Set as a goal to reduce the volume of paper crossing your path.

➤ Set limits on how long you will save various types of papers (e.g., two years for professional magazines, six months for memos to parents, three years for grade books, two weeks for meeting minutes). Whenever you run across a piece of paper whose timeline has expired, discard it.

➤ Use looseleaf notebooks to preserve masters of tests and handouts for copying. Keep your masters sequential, easy to find. Use a separate notebook for each subject area.

➤ Keep a file box or drawer beside your desk. It is for all the worksheets and home-work sheets you use in all your classes. In the box place manila file folders labeled by subject and day (Example: Science—Mon.; Science—Tues.; Wed., etc.). Duplicate all materials you're going to use on Friday and fill up your box. (Obviously, not every subject has a ditto or handout for every day.) This makes it very easy for the rest of the week. If handouts are used for that day, they are easily found. If you are absent, you don't have to worry about a substitute finding the handouts to use.

➤ Always carry 3 × 5 note cards in your purse or pocket to record ideas and facts as you think of them to use in class and on tests. Also list home needs and class needs on these cards. An ideal time to use them is when you are waiting for an appointment or meeting to begin.

➤ In a manila folder keep reading material you would like to get to, but don't seem to find time to do. When you are traveling, or just find a few spare minutes, retrieve an item from the folder.

➤ Whenever possible, develop individualized form letters you can use for repeated correspondence. Also keep a file of letters you must send out every year so you do not have to redraft them each time. This is even easier if you maintain these as a computer file.

➤ Quickly sort your mail into four stacks: "Never," which you throw out unread; "Now," which receives top attention as it has some degree of urgency or impor-tance attached to it; "Later," which deserves attention, but is not urgent; "Maybe," which may get a cursory glance sometime, but probably isn't impor-tant or urgent (e.g., catalogs, general notices, and newsletters).

➤ For routine interoffice mail and school memos, jot your response on the same piece of paper and return to the sender immediately. Of course, don't do that with important pieces of correspondence, like job offers.

➤ As you read a piece of correspondence that will require a response, jot down a few notes in the margin to remind yourself of what you want to say. Use postcards rather then letters whenever possible.

➤ If you spend lots of time commuting to and from school, keep a microcassette tape recorder in your car. You can dictate into it as you drive. It is a great way to create letters, "To Do" lists, quiz questions, teaching ideas, etc.

➤ Eliminate junk mail by writing to Direct Mail Marketing Association, Mail Preference Service, P.O. Box 9008, Farmingdale, NY 11735-9099. Request their Mail Preference Form to be placed on their suppression list. Another option for help in stopping junk mail is to contact: Stop Junk Mail Association, 3020 Bridgeway #150, Sausalito, CA 94965; (800) 827-5549.

➤ A computer does have potential to help with all kinds of paperwork chores. You can get software to handle addresses, phone numbers, grade record-keeping, your "To Do" list, and your calendar. However, don't rush to put everything on a computer just because you can. Keeping your calendar on the computer may become an extra chore if you also have to carry a pocket calendar with you, duplicating the effort.

Most efforts to manage my time only succeed when I don't answer my mail.
                                        —ARTHUR MILLER

Never stack paper, to stack is to stay!
                                        —DON ASHLETT, AUTHOR
                                        <u>NOT FOR PACKRATS ONLY</u>

Communications

➤ Leave notes for teachers, administrators, or students—rather than taking the time to wait for someone. That person can write a short response and leave it in your mailbox or on your desk. It also saves time for the other person as there is little opportunity for idle conversation.

➤ Buy a Rolodex file which holds 3 × 5 size cards. Record not only names and addresses, but also FAX and electronic mail numbers if available. File any number you have to look up more than twice. You can also note special information about the individuals in your file, such as birthdates, spouses' and children's names, or interests. The file is also a useful place to record membership or subscription numbers, lock combinations, directions to places, and other miscellaneous bits of information that are easily misplaced.

➤ If you hate to write, try postcards. Or better, make your own. Cut 8-1/2 × 11 inch card stock in half, yielding two 5-1/2 × 8-1/2 inch cards. These can be folded in half to make inexpensive note cards. You could even type a master sheet with your name and address inserted in the upper left corner of each card when folded.

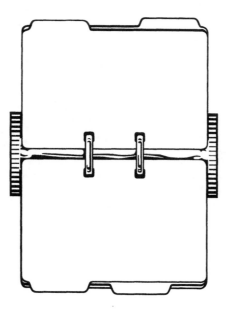

➤ Use a carbon-backed form for parent conferences. It gives a record of what was discussed, comments, etc. You can give the parent a copy and keep one for your class file. If necessary, you can send a copy to the guidance office or principal.

➤ Where available, transmit electronic text messages to colleagues and others having access to e-mail.

➤ Develop form letters to handle routine and repetitive correspondence. Storing your form letters as template computer files saves much time in written communications.

Teacher Time Log

One valuable technique for getting a more accurate picture of how your time is consumed is to keep a daily time log for three or four school days. Enter the data on the Time Log form from the time you get up until the time you go to bed. It is important to accurately record what you are really doing during these small segments to get an accurate reflection of where your time really goes. It does no good to enter what you *could* have done, *should* have done, or *would* have done. You must be honest for it to have any meaning.

Record the specific activity for each 15-minute block of time. You need not actually stop what you are doing every fifteen minutes to enter your information. A useful procedure is to carry a 3 × 5 card with you and take 15 to 20 seconds each hour to briefly note what you were doing in each of the previous 15-minute segments. At the end of the day, enter the information onto your Time Log form. At that time also enter comments reflecting upon specific activities. What were your most frequent interruptions? Were there any patterns? Which activities would you like to increase? Which would you like to decrease? In the priority column, assign a value to each activity: A = important activities that contribute to your essential life goals; B = activities that are urgent, but not particularly important to the fulfillment of your life goals; C = maintenance activities, routine chores, not especially important.

Analyze the log at the end of the week. The following questions may be helpful in analyzing your record:

➤ What percent of your total time did you spend on A, B, and C priority items?

➤ What were your major interruptions? Was there a pattern (time of day, in person, activity)? How can you decrease them in the future?

➤ What activities would you like to eliminate or decrease?

➤ Which would you like to increase?

➤ What strategies will help you spend more time doing higher priority items?

"To Do" List

As the cartoon character, Ziggy, claimed, "I made a mental note of it, but I lost it." That's exactly what happens to many of our mental notes—we lose them. A simple written reminder or "To Do" list can be an effective way of completing the many little tasks that comprise the profession of teaching.

➤ The trouble with keeping "To Do" lists is that it is too much fun crossing things off. At the end of the day we take delight in crossing off 12 of the 14 tasks. Unfortunately, the ones that get crossed off are too often the routine and petty tasks; the unpleasant or difficult ones get transferred to tomorrow's list. However, these are often the most important items on our list. If you are going to keep a daily "To Do" list, it is essential to indicate in some form the priorities of the items on the list. One way is to put an asterisk in front of the most important two or three items. Try to do the top-priority items first.

➤ Whenever you find yourself with a few minutes of free time, look at your list to see whether you can chip away any items. Many of the jobs, like returning a phone call or sending a note, can be done in as little time as a minute.

➤ Some find it more convenient to keep their "To Do" list on their calendar. This works well if you use the daily calendar that gives you one full page for each day. An alternative is to keep your list on Post-it™ notes that are stuck to the calendar each day. Rather than rewriting the list at the end of the day, scratch out those items accomplished, pull the list from today's page in your calendar, and stick it to tomorrow's page.

➤ Instead of keeping a daily "To Do" list, some people only keep a master list. The projects and tasks recorded on this list do not have to be done today, but do require attention within the next week or month. They need to be done, but are not urgent—yet. Of course, if they are procrastinated long enough, they could become urgent.

➤ Examine your list to see which ones someone else can do. Which are really not important to you? Ask yourself, "What is the worst thing that would happen if I don't do that?" Scratch out items that really don't have to be done. Some wise persons believe success is derived not so much from what we choose to do but rather in what we choose *not* to do. Effective time management is largely the ability to eliminate those activities that distract from the truly important ones.

"Everything I didn't do yesterday, added to everything I haven't done today, plus every-thing I won't do tomorrow completely exhausts me."
—ANONYMOUS

Assessing Student Time-on-task

The importance of attention and time spent on learning activities was touted by edu-cators at least as early as the nineteenth century, but has gained renewed attention during the past decade. A growing body of evidence shows that student time-on-task is a modest predictor of learning, but not a panacea. Research also emphasizes that increasing time-on-task is likely to have a greater effect for below-average students.

High engagement rates on ineffective or irrelevant instructional activities are of doubtful benefit. To result in learning gains, the instruction must be at the appropri-ate level for that individual student; too high, the student does not comprehend and is lost; too low and needless overlearning and perhaps boredom occur. Some educa-tors have been guilty of focusing solely upon time-on-task without attending to the other variables that contribute to instructional effectiveness. Time-on-task is best viewed as a necessary, but insufficient condition for academic success.

Past research has generally found time-on-task rates around 70 to 75 percent. But remember, that is 70 to 75 percent of 50 percent! The highest engaged rates do not exceed 90 percent. Rates as low as 30 percent for individual classrooms have been reported. If you experience engagement rates at the lower end of the range, it may be time to develop a plan of action. While striving for higher time-on-task, do not ignore the half of the teaching day that is lost to non-academic activities. It accounts for a greater proportion of time lost than does student off-task behavior. A complete school time-management plan must focus on decreasing non-instructional activity, as well as increasing student engagement rates. If the teacher isn't on-task, the stu-dent can't be.

How effectively do your students spend their in-class time? Are they engaged more or less than the 70 percent norm? What are they doing when they are off-task? These questions can best be answered by direct, systematic observation.

Your gut-level assessment may be a valid clue as to the on-task rate of your stu-dents, but it may be biased and inaccurate. It is difficult to observe the rest of the class when you are preoccupied with one student or with a small group.

Trade observations with a fellow teacher, giving each other feedback and support. Select someone who is reasonably objective and candid. A single observation may not be representative of your teaching. Try to have at least three separate observations on different days. Avoid special days, such as right before or after holidays, since the results are likely to differ from typical days. Devise an observation form that fits your classroom situation and provides the information you want. (You might use the form included in this book.)

At five-minute intervals the observer should scan the entire class in the same sequence. For each student a tally is placed on the chart. If, after a few seconds of watching a student, it is still unclear as to whether the behavior is on-task or off-task, record it as on-task. Students should be recorded as out of class if they leave to go to the rest rooms, principal's office, arrive late to class, or are told to leave.

After the observations are completed, divide the number of students scored as on-task by the total number of students included in each observation segment to arrive at your engagement rate.

The observer can also be instructed to note:

➤ How long does it take to get a class started?

➤ How much time is spent in clerical tasks, such as attendance and reading announcements?

➤ Which part of the class period suffers the most off-task behavior?

➤ How smooth are the transitions from one task to the next?

➤ What proportion of the class time is allocated to seatwork?

➤ How much class time is spent on discipline?

➤ How many interruptions are there? How much time do they consume?

➤ How much time do students spend waiting for help?

The answers to these questions may assist in setting goals for improvement. Later observations can help assess whether progress is being made in increasing time-on-task.

[The preceding material is adapted from "Time to Learn: Assessing Student Time on Task," Ronald L. Partin. Reprinted with permission from *Journal of Children and Youth*, 8 (1), Spring 1987, pp. 2-6.]

Conquer Procrastination Now!

Are you eligible for membership in the Procrastinator's Club, but haven't gotten around to sending your application? Its motto, "We're behind you all the way," has been accepted by some teachers. Are you one? Test your eligibility right now! Don't put it off another minute.

Educators' Procrastination Society

Eligibility Form

Answer each of the following now.

	YES	NO
Do you have a set of papers that has been waiting to be graded for a week or more?	____	____
Do you frequently finish jobs just before the deadline?	____	____
Are you regularly late handing in grades, reports, etc.?	____	____
Do your students usually have to wait a week or more to get their papers back?	____	____
Do weeks pass before you respond to your mail?	____	____
Does your principal regularly remind you that a deadline has passed?	____	____
Do you find it difficult to get started on the big projects?	____	____
Do you frequently tell people you work better under pressure?	____	____
Do you frequently feel guilty because you have not completed a task?	____	____
Do you have difficulty getting jobs completed because they may not be perfect?	____	____

Count the number of "yes" responses. Compare your score with the following scale:

0-3   **Early starter:** By doing things today you are free to do them again tomorrow if you choose.

4-7   **Amateur procrastinator:** Some potential problem areas may create stress for you and annoyance in those around you.

8-10 **Professional procrastinator:** Putting things off until the last minute is a way of life.

PROCRASTINATION PAYOFFS

Psychologists and motivational researchers have studied procrastination for decades in an attempt to uncover its causes and cures. As with most complex behaviors, people procrastinate because they expect to gain or avoid something.

It is likely that procrastination develops over a period of years, beginning in childhood. There is research evidence that many procrastinators tend to be perfectionists, immobilized by deadlines until they feel a masterpiece is achieved. They may feel that their work is of value only if it is perfect, and their self-worth is a reflection of their performance.

By doing jobs at the last minute, procrastinators may protect their egos, since their true ability is not judged, only their skill in doing jobs at the last minute under pressure. "Of course, I could have done a much better job if I had had more time!" may even elicit sympathy from some listeners. Another secondary gain is that if a person puts off a job long enough, someone else may do the job. Many adolescents are aware of this game. Their parents become impatient waiting for the garbage to be taken out or their bedrooms to be cleaned, so do the chores for them. What motivation do these children have to change? None; they have a good thing going. Unfortunately, that pattern may continue into adulthood.

Procrastination may also serve as a defense to avoid difficult or unpleasant tasks, although the habitual procrastinator may begin to delay even minor and enjoyable activities. Seldom is the procrastinated task totally avoided; it is only delayed.

Sometimes procrastination is the result of poor skills or insufficient knowledge. Being poorly organized, setting goals without deadlines, attempting to make decisions with insufficient information, and the inability to say "no" may all contribute to procrastination.

Which of the following are you most likely to procrastinate?

Grading papers

Completing report cards

Meeting with parents

Writing letters

Returning phone calls

Writing lesson plans

Making important decisions

Planning a speech

Meeting with your principal

Writing a grant request

Applying for a new position

Confronting a colleague

Cleaning off your desk

Buying presents

Making dentist appointments

If you confess to occasionally experiencing stress, guilt, and anxiety from procrastination, you may be ready for a change. If procrastination is a way of life for you, the following suggestions may help; but be patient. A lifetime of learning is not undone in a day, a week, or even a month. Not only new ways of behaving, but possibly new ways of viewing yourself may be needed.

Identify the task you would like to quit procrastinating and answer the following questions:

1. What do you gain from procrastinating this activity?

2. What do you fear might happen if you attempt this activity?

3. What do you lose by putting off this task? What price do you pay?

4. What are the positive consequences that would result from doing this particular activity?

5. What do you tell yourself to justify your procrastination?

ATTACKING PROCRASTINATION

The easiest thing to procrastinate is doing something about procrastination. You may be tempted to allow short-term avoidance to overpower the longer-term advantages. If you have become a slave to deadlines, immobilized by the big and small projects you face, it may be time to combat procrastination. In the previous activity you had an opportunity to analyze the motivation and costs of one problem area. Using those insights you can develop a plan of attack.

It is best to pick one area in which you find procrastination most annoying (e.g., grading exams, answering letters, filing papers). Begin small and progress as you experience success. Attempting to eliminate all procrastination from your life at once is much like dieting while trying to stop smoking. You are setting yourself up for frustration and failure. Be patient.

Adhere to the following guidelines to defeat procrastination:

1. Establish your own deadlines, and announce them to others involved. Be realistic in setting a timetable.

2. Break the project into smaller parts. Chip away at it in small bites. Don't wait for that "big chunk" of time.

3. Set a definite beginning point. You must break the inertia of inactivity. If getting started is especially troublesome, set a timer for 10 or 15 minutes. Commit yourself to doing something on the project until the timer rings. Then you can decide whether to stop or continue. Chances are you will gain momentum and continue after the timer stops. If not, try another 10 minutes later in the day.

4. Do the most important things first. Avoid the distractions of the trivial and routine tasks when a higher priority job needs to be done. Examining each task in light of your goals will help you set priorities.

5. Reward yourself for completing parts of a major task. It may be something as simple as a 10-minute walk, a soft drink, or a social phone call. Contract with yourself for a big reward for completion of important tasks. A night on the town, sleeping late on a weekend, or a purchase you have been wanting to make may help motivate you to complete the job. Be nice to yourself.

6. Avoid perfectionism. Excellence is a sufficient level of performance for most things in life, and for many tasks (doing the dishes, a new sport or hobby, dusting the lampshades), adequacy is all that is necessary. Give yourself permission to be less than perfect. You might double the amount of time spent typing a test, attempting to get the spacing and typing perfectly. Could that extra time be better spent in another activity that will better benefit your students or yourself? Probably so.

Procrastination is a learned habit, and can be supplanted with a more constructive habit, giving you greater control over your life. If procrastination has limited your achievements, do something about it *now!*

> *"Procrastination and worry are the twin thieves that will try to rob you of your brilliance—but even the smallest action will drive them from your camp."*
> —GIL ATKINSON

> *"Nothing is so fatiguing as the eternal hanging on of an uncompleted task."*
> —WILLIAM JAMES

Scrounging for Supplies

Are there activities you would like to try in your class but can't because there aren't funds for the necessary supplies? Cutbacks and tight budgets have led to rationing of paper and chalk in many schools with little money available for teaching materials. Yet, some teachers have a knack for gathering needed supplies at no cost. Since the earliest days of formal education, a core of teachers have mastered the delicate art of scrounging.

Those teachers who approach their supply shortage creatively realize that much is available for the mere asking and hauling. What may be seen as useless discards by a merchant may indeed be treasures in the hands of a teacher. Here are seven suggestions for improving your skills in scrounging for supplies.

➤ Be specific. Know exactly what you need and the quantity. This helps you identify potential donors. Emphasize the specific instructional purpose of the desired item.

➤ Time your request appropriately. Avoid the rush hours when merchants will be most preoccupied with their customers. Also try to time your inquiries to miss peak holiday business. Submit your request directly to the owner or manager when possible. A direct request made in person is more likely to be taken seriously.

➤ Emphasize the educational purpose. Most citizens are aware of the strained finances of schools. Your invitation permits them to help in a small and usually painless way. Mentioning the potential tax deduction for donated items also helps.

➤ Make moderate requests. Certainly don't ask a donor to deliver merchandise. Any special labor expenses are likely to deter much generosity.

➤ Use your contacts. Parents of present or past students, previous donors, vocal supporters of schools, relatives, and personal friends are prime prospects. A cousin of the school custodian has a connection with your school that may encourage generosity. A note sent to parents or a brief notice in the local newspaper describing your need may be successful. Make your needs known!

➤ Don't fear rejection. There are many legitimate reasons why a request cannot be filled. Usually, it is because the source does not have what you are requesting. For example, if a newspaper office has just discarded all of their old newsprint, you might ask that they hold future waste newsprint for you. Try to pinpoint a specific date to check back.

➤ Show appreciation. Future donations are more likely if a gift is acknowledged. A special note of thanks from the teacher is a minimum. For a large gift, a note from the principal or letters from the class or even an acknowledgment in the school or local newspaper is warranted.

By looking at the Yellow Pages of your local phone directory, you can quickly identify a great many potential donors for needed supplies. To stimulate your thinking, the following suggestions should be considered.

POTENTIAL SOURCES FOR TEACHING SUPPLIES

Airline: magazines, courtesy kits

Appliance store: large cartons, cardboard

Bank: coin wrappers, free maps

Business: computers, computer software, storage bins, boxes, cabinets

Carpet store: carpet remnants, cardboard tubes

Caterer: leftover crepe paper, party supplies

Computer store: software, demo disks (to be reused), used computers

Contractor: scrap lumber, boards, plastic pipe, bricks

Dentist: toothbrushes, posters, pamphlets, old magazines

Department store: holiday decorations (after season), damaged merchandise

Discotheque: albums, records

Dry cleaner: hangers, plastic bags

Electrician: electrical wire, small pieces of conduit

Farmer: burlap bags, grains, biological specimens, twine

Florist: floral wrapping paper, ribbon, plants

Garage sale: books, magazines, toys, window shades, storage bins, dish pans, books, etc.

Greenhouse: pots, starter plants, flowers

Hairdresser: wigs, cosmetics

Hospital: pill bottles, various containers, boxes, health literature, tongue depressors

Insurance company: note pads, calendars, actuarial tables

Liquor store: boxes, cartons

Lumber yard: scrap boards, nail aprons, yard sticks, rulers, metal bands

Motel/Hotel: linen, soap, matches, cups

Newspaper office: newsprint from roll ends, photos, film canisters

Nursing home: pill bottles, boxes

Paint store: wallpaper samplers, paint, paint mixer sticks, yard sticks, buckets

Parent: furniture, carpeting, books, cloth material, containers, clothing, greeting card fronts, old shirts for smocks, margarine containers, wallpaper remnants, yarn, etc.

Photography store: film canisters, outdated film

Pizza parlor: round cardboard plates, pizza boxes for storage

Plasterer: five-gallon buckets

Plumber: scrap plastic pipe

Post office: outdated FBI wanted circulars, stamp posters

Printer: paper, card stock, ink, cardboard boxes with lids

Professor: books, journals, used computer cards, computer printouts

Radio/TV repair shop: magnets, wires, electrical parts, knobs

Radio/TV station: records, albums, discarded film, used audiotape, slides

Real estate company: note pads, calendars, local maps

Restaurant: bottle corks, party supplies, straws, paper cups, coupons, containers, posters, napkins, bottles, ice cream cartons, ice cream vats

Supermarket: Styrofoam trays, egg crates, berry baskets, shelving, paper bags

Tailor: cloth, empty thread spools

Theater: tickets to be used as prizes, movie posters, promotion photos

Travel agency: travel posters, maps

Upholsterer: scrap remnants, thread

Student Help

Allowing students to help with many classroom tasks not only saves valuable class time, but also gives them an opportunity to assume responsibility and may help them feel needed and included. It may, in some instances, also give students a chance to learn new skills. The best time to introduce the idea of student assistance is the first week of school when you are establishing your classroom routines. Some tasks that teachers have delegated to students include:

- ➤ collecting papers, books, materials
- ➤ distributing papers, materials, etc.
- ➤ tutoring other students
- ➤ constructing bulletin boards
- ➤ collecting lunch money
- ➤ taking attendance
- ➤ running errands
- ➤ filing papers
- ➤ tending classroom plants
- ➤ running audio-visual equipment
- ➤ taking inventory of books, supplies, etc.
- ➤ checking completed assignments
- ➤ picking up litter in the room
- ➤ constructing or arranging holiday decorations
- ➤ rearranging desks and furniture
- ➤ dusting erasers
- ➤ erasing or cleaning chalkboards
- ➤ recording brainstormed ideas on the board or newsprint
- ➤ videotaping class presentations
- ➤ keeping time for class activities
- ➤ putting away lab equipment
- ➤ setting up experiments, demonstrations
- ➤ greeting classroom visitors
- ➤ answering the telephone
- ➤ tending pets, fish, etc.
- ➤ keeping the class calendar
- ➤ straightening the bookcase
- ➤ making in-school deliveries
- ➤ collating papers
- ➤ posting assignments and special events on the board

Some teachers ask for volunteers for each task as the need arises. Others allow students to sign up for a job for a period of a week or month. Some draw names (or assigned numbers) whenever a role needs to be filled. Occasionally, particularly attractive jobs are awarded as rewards for outstanding performance. Some teachers assign teams of students to different responsibilities. In some classrooms, every student is assigned a job on a rotating basis.

Sometimes assigning groups of students to complete specific tasks can be successful. One elementary teacher assigned pairs to each task, trained each pair in their job, and then rotated the assignments on a staggered schedule every week, so that one person moved on to a new job. The "experienced" partner trained the new partner in the job.

It is helpful to arrange a couple of brief after-school training sessions for some of the more demanding jobs, such as running audio-visual equipment. Demonstrate what needs to be done and then give the helpers a chance to practice. It is important in delegating responsibilities that you be specific in communicating your expectations. Consider the capabilities and interests of your students in assigning the more difficult jobs. Another possibility is to construct a job chart listing the various functions and who is responsible. You might color code it for easier reading.

Some creative teachers draw up official looking contracts with official sounding names, like Director of Distribution or Multimedia Technician. The students sign the contracts, which detail their responsibilities and the duration of the agreement.

Construct a board with the list of duties printed on the left side. On the right side attach clips (or you could use wooden slots) into which you insert cards with the names of the students assigned each task. To change duties each week, just rotate the name plates. (This works well in shop and art classes for clean-up assignments.)

With some particularly hostile classes, you'll probably have a difficult time getting students to volunteer as "teacher helpers." They would be put down by their peers. It's probably best to privately ask individual students to do particular tasks as the need arises. The less official their role, the more likely they will comply with your request.

Always remember to thank students for completing their tasks. For students who are particularly helpful, a note to them or even their parents, a certificate, or some small privilege is a thoughtful way to express your appreciation.

Teacher Time Survey

DIRECTIONS: After reading each question, indicate whether it is generally true for you.

Do you frequently . . .

	Yes	No
1. Have to rise early to prepare that day's classes?	___	___
2. Set deadlines for yourself?	___	___
3. Get up late?	___	___
4. Stop in the lounge to socialize before classes begin?	___	___
5. Fret and agonize when interruptions outside of your control occur?	___	___
6. Begin classes on time?	___	___
7. Visit the lounge between classes?	___	___
8. Allow sufficient time at the end of the period (or day) for assignments, clean up, summary activities, etc.?	___	___
9. Disrupt your own classroom momentum?	___	___
10. Begin the day without interest in what you are teaching?	___	___
11. Teach lessons for which you are unsure of what you want the students to learn?	___	___
12. Schedule tests, movies, seatwork primarily to occupy students while you get caught up?	___	___
13. Relate the amount of instructional time spent on a particular objective to its importance?	___	___
14. Procrastinate grading papers and tests?	___	___
15. Wait more than five minutes for staff meetings to begin?	___	___
16. Write down ideas as they occur rather than relying upon memory?	___	___
17. Anticipate problems and alternative solutions to them?	___	___
18. Handle extracurricular activities during the academic hours?	___	___
19. Make decisions systematically rather than "muddling through?"	___	___
20. Spend time complaining to peers?	___	___
21. Run out of prepared lesson material before the period or day is over?	___	___
22. Find yourself going to the office to duplicate materials more than once per day?	___	___
23. Bring up unscheduled business at faculty meetings?	___	___
24. Set reasonable limits on parent conferences?	___	___
25. Use student volunteers to help with routine tasks of which they are capable?	___	___
26. Copy information from one form to another?	___	___

Teacher Time Survey, continued

	Yes	No
27. Use parent volunteers whenever possible to assist in instructional activities?	_____	_____
28. Spend instructional time dealing with disruptive behavior?	_____	_____
29. Prevent duplicated effort by systematically filing and saving curricular materials, lesson plans, tests, etc.?	_____	_____
30. Arrive late for meetings?	_____	_____
31. Participate in a regular schedule of physical fitness?	_____	_____
32. Get a sufficient amount of rest each night to begin each day fresh?	_____	_____
33. Think of a creative idea, only to forget it later?	_____	_____
34. Do work for which others are paid?	_____	_____
35. Have a balance of interests including leisure activities apart from your teaching?	_____	_____
36. Choose to do menial tasks, like stapling papers, as opposed to creative, productive tasks like designing new instructional strategies?	_____	_____
37. Strive to handle each piece of paper only once?	_____	_____
38. Set priorities each day for the things you have to do?	_____	_____
39. Have to repeat directions to students?	_____	_____
40. Lose material because of a poorly organized, cluttered desk?	_____	_____
41. Fail to make assignments clear and specific?	_____	_____
42. Attend classes or workshops to develop new teaching ideas?	_____	_____
43. Maintain contingency lesson plans in case of emergencies, sickness, etc.?	_____	_____
44. Share ideas with colleagues?	_____	_____
45. Review your long-term professional goals?	_____	_____
46. Have difficulty saying "no" to requests for your time?	_____	_____
47. Fall prey to perfectionism?	_____	_____
48. Use vacation days and weekends to catch up?	_____	_____
49. Begin class late?	_____	_____
50. Make planning time a top priority?	_____	_____

Scoring instructions: Give yourself one point for each of the following items to which you responded "yes": 2, 6, 8, 16, 17, 19, 24, 25, 27, 29, 31, 32, 35, 37, 38, 42, 43, 44, 45, 50. Give yourself one point for each of the following items to which you responded "no": 1, 3, 4, 5, 7, 9, 10, 11, 12, 13, 14, 15, 18, 20, 21, 22, 23, 26, 28, 30, 33, 34, 36, 39, 40, 41, 46, 47, 48, 49.

Total the number of points and find your score on the scale below.

40-50	*Peak Performer:*	You are getting a high return on your investment of time and energy.
30-39	*Striver:*	You are probably pretty effective, but still have a few inefficiencies.
20-29	*Plodder:*	You're making your job tougher than it needs to be.
0-19	*Struggler:*	How do you get anything done? Serious time management problems impede your effectiveness.

School Interruption Survey

Directions: Using the scales under the subheadings, indicate when, how frequently, and how disruptive each of these interruptions is for you.

When	How	How Disruptive
BS = Before school	0 = Never	0 = Not at all
AS = After school	1 = Seldom	1 = A little
P = During planning period	2 = Occasionally	2 = Somewhat
C = During class time	3 = Quite frequently	3 = Quite
		4 = Constantly

Interruptions	When	How Frequently	How Disruptive
Messengers from:			
Principal's office	_____	_____	_____
Guidance office	_____	_____	_____
Other teachers	_____	_____	_____
The principal	_____	_____	_____
Former students	_____	_____	_____
Custodian	_____	_____	_____
Parents	_____	_____	_____
Other teachers	_____	_____	_____
Outside observers, visitors	_____	_____	_____
Aide or volunteer helper	_____	_____	_____
Classroom behavior disturbance	_____	_____	_____
Student(s) leaving class	_____	_____	_____
Student(s) arriving late	_____	_____	_____
Assemblies	_____	_____	_____
Standardized tests	_____	_____	_____
P.A. announcements	_____	_____	_____
Audio-visual breakdowns	_____	_____	_____
Telephone calls	_____	_____	_____
Hallway traffic	_____	_____	_____
Noise from other classrooms	_____	_____	_____
Outdoor distractions:			
Weather events	_____	_____	_____
Animals	_____	_____	_____
People	_____	_____	_____
Street traffic	_____	_____	_____
Airplanes	_____	_____	_____
Sirens	_____	_____	_____
Other noise	_____	_____	_____
Your actions:			
Hunting lost items	_____	_____	_____
Changing topics	_____	_____	_____
Going back to previous topic	_____	_____	_____
Publicly reprimanding student	_____	_____	_____

Place asterisks (*) in front of the three interruptions you would most like to eliminate.

Please do not disturb. Learning in progress!

Please do not disturb!
Testing in progress

NOISE (crossed out / prohibited)

Attendance Record

Teacher _____

Date _____

Preiod _____

Name	Absent	Excused	Comments

Restroom Pass

Good for one three-minute visit to the restroom.

For emergency use only.

Restroom Pass

Good for one three-minute visit to the restroom.

For emergency use only.

Restroom Pass

Good for one three-minute visit to the restroom.

For emergency use only.

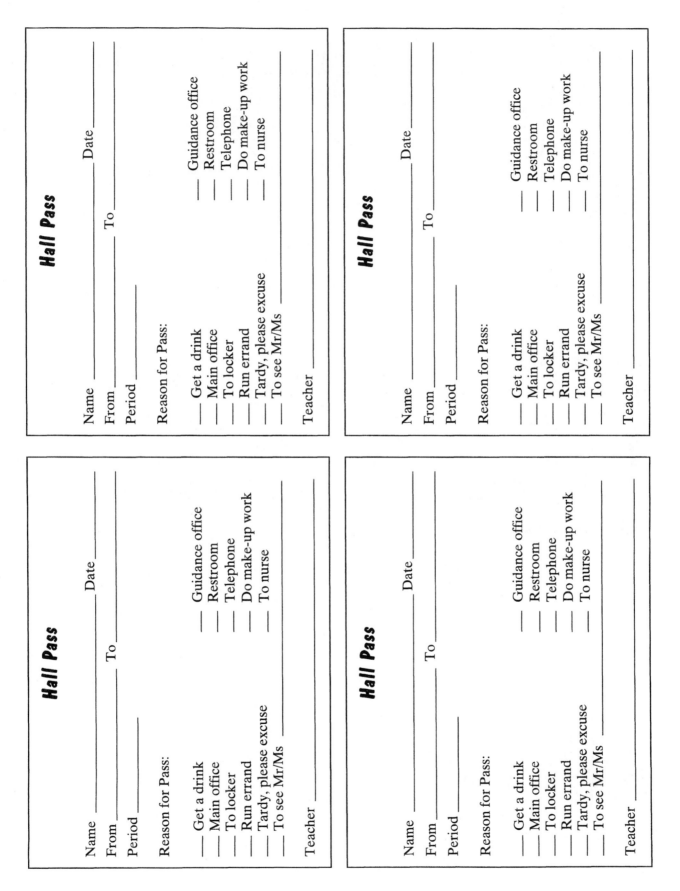

Hall Pass

Name _____ Date _____

From _____ To _____

Period _____

Reason for Pass:

____ Get a drink   ____ Guidance office
____ Main office   ____ Restroom
____ To locker   ____ Telephone
____ Run errand   ____ Do make-up work
____ Tardy, please excuse   ____ To nurse
____ To see Mr/Ms _____

Teacher _____

Hall Pass

Name _____ Date _____

From _____ To _____

Period _____

Reason for Pass:

____ Get a drink   ____ Guidance office
____ Main office   ____ Restroom
____ To locker   ____ Telephone
____ Run errand   ____ Do make-up work
____ Tardy, please excuse   ____ To nurse
____ To see Mr/Ms _____

Teacher _____

Hall Pass

Name _____ Date _____

From _____ To _____

Period _____

Reason for Pass:

____ Get a drink   ____ Guidance office
____ Main office   ____ Restroom
____ To locker   ____ Telephone
____ Run errand   ____ Do make-up work
____ Tardy, please excuse   ____ To nurse
____ To see Mr/Ms _____

Teacher _____

Hall Pass

Name _____ Date _____

From _____ To _____

Period _____

Reason for Pass:

____ Get a drink   ____ Guidance office
____ Main office   ____ Restroom
____ To locker   ____ Telephone
____ Run errand   ____ Do make-up work
____ Tardy, please excuse   ____ To nurse
____ To see Mr/Ms _____

Teacher _____

Hall Pass

Student: _____

From: _____ To: _____

Period: _____ Time: _____

Date: _____ Time Returned: _____

Teacher: _____

Hall Pass

Student: _____

From: _____ To: _____

Period: _____ Time: _____

Date: _____ Time Returned: _____

Teacher: _____

Hall Pass

Student: _____

From: _____ To: _____

Period: _____ Time: _____

Date: _____ Time Returned: _____

Teacher: _____

Hall Pass

Student: _____

From: _____ To: _____

Period: _____ Time: _____

Date: _____ Time Returned: _____

Teacher: _____

Hall Pass

Student: _____

From: _____ To: _____

Period: _____ Time: _____

Date: _____ Time Returned: _____

Teacher: _____

Hall Pass

Student: _____

From: _____ To: _____

Period: _____ Time: _____

Date: _____ Time Returned: _____

Teacher: _____

Hall Pass

Student: _____

From: _____ To: _____

Period: _____ Time: _____

Date: _____ Time Returned: _____

Teacher: _____

Hall Pass

Student: _____

From: _____ To: _____

Period: _____ Time: _____

Date: _____ Time Returned: _____

Teacher: _____

Teacher Time Log

Teacher _____ **Date** _____

Time	Activity	Importance	Comments

Things to Do

Date _____

Today's Schedule		Activity	Priority	Done
7:00				
7:30				
8:00				
8:30				
9:00				
9:30				
10:00				
10:30				
11:00				
11:30				
12:00				
12:30				
1:00				
1:30				
2:00				
2:30				
3:00				
3:30				
4:00				
4:30				
5:00				

Evening:

Memo

Telephone Log

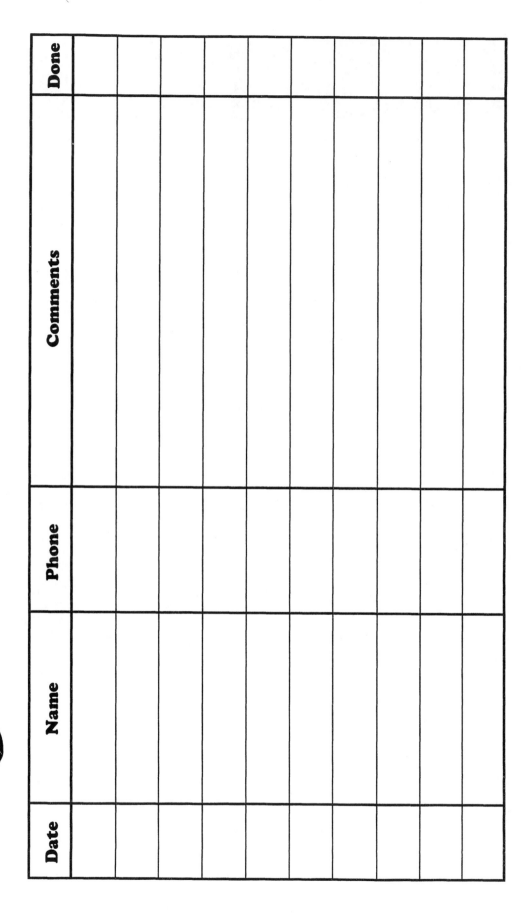

Date	Name	Phone	Comments	Done

© 1995 by The Center for Applied Research in Education

256

Weekly Schedule

Dates _____

Time	Monday	Tuesday	Wednesday	Thursday	Friday

Book Sign-out Record

Teacher: _____

Name	Book Title	Date Out	Date In

CHAPTER 7

Helpful
Teaching Resources

ERIC Clearinghouses

ERIC obtains copies of virtually all significant documents related to any aspect of education. The ERIC Clearinghouses synthesize information on specific issues and publish information analyses. Each clearinghouse also provides educators with services such as searches, workshops, and responses to inquiries. ACCESS ERIC publishes brochures, a magazine, and numerous other documents and products.

ERIC Clearinghouse on Assessment and Evaluation
Catholic University of America
210 O'Boyle Hall
Washington, D.C. 20064-4035
Telephone: 202-319-5120
Internet: eric_ae@cua.edu

ERIC Clearinghouse on Counseling and Student Services
University of North Carolina at Greensboro
School of Education
Greensboro, NC 27412-5001
Telephone: 800-414-9769
Internet: ericcass.uncg.ed

ERIC Clearinghouse on Disabilities and Gifted Education
Council for Exceptional Children (CEC)
1920 Association Drive
Reston, VA 22091-1589
Telephone: 800-328-0272
Internet: ericec@inet.ed.gov

ERIC Clearinghouse on Educational Management
University of Oregon
1787 Agate Street
Eugene, OR 97403-5207
Telephone: 800-438-8841
Internet: ppiele@oregon.uoregon.edu

ERIC Clearinghouse on Elementary and Early Childhood Education
University of Illinois
805 West Pennsylvania Avenue
Urbana, IL 61801-4897
Telephone: 800-583-4135
Internet: ericeece@ux1.cso.uiuc.edu

ERIC Clearinghouse on Languages and Linguistics
Center for Applied Linguistics (CAL)
1118 22nd Street, NW
Washington, D.C. 20037-0037
Telephone: 800-276-9834
Internet: jeannie@cal.org

ERIC Clearinghouse on Reading, English, and Communication
Indiana University
Smith Research Center, Suite 150

2805 E. 10th Street
Bloomington, IN 47408-2698
Telephone: 800-759-4723
Internet: ericcs@ucs.indiana.edu

ERIC Clearinghouse on Rural Education and Small Schools
Appalachia Educational Laboratory (AEL)
1031 Quarrier Street
P.O. Box 1348
Charleston, WV 25325-1348
Telephone: 800-624-9120
Internet: u56d9@wvnvm.wvnet.edu

ERIC Clearinghouse on Science, Mathematics, and Environmental Education
Ohio State University
1929 Kenny Road
Columbus, OH 43210-1080
Telephone: 614-292-6717
Internet: ericse@osu.edu

ERIC Clearinghouse for Social Studies/Social Science Education
Indiana University
Social Studies Development Center
2805 East 10th Street, Suite 120
Bloomington, IN 47408-2698
Telephone: 800-266-3815
Internet: ericso@ucs.indiana.edu

ERIC Clearinghouse on Teaching and Teacher Education
American Association of Colleges for Teacher Education (AACTE)
One Dupont Circle, NW, Suite 610
Washington, D.C. 20036-1186
Telephone: 202-293-2450
Internet: jbeck@inet.ed.gov

ERIC Clearinghouse on Urban Education
Teachers College, Columbia University
Institute for Urban and Minority Education
Main Hall, Room 303, Box 40
525 West 120th Street
New York, NY 10027-9998
Telephone: 800-601-4868
Internet: cue-eric@columbia.edu

Educational Resources Information Center (ERIC) Digests Archives are available
through several computer channels:
TELNET: telnet bbs.oit.unc.edu
login: launch
Directions for registration will appear on screen.
FTP: ftp ericir.syr.edu
login: anonymous

password: your e-mail address

cd pub

e-mail: mail askeric@ericir.syr.edu

Submit your question in the message area. Someone will respond within 48 hours.

Gopher: ericir.syr.edu (port 70)

The Internet as a Learning Resource

Over the past decade approximately two billion dollars have been spent to put an additional two million computers in America's schools. The advent of cyberspace and explosive expansion of the information highway have the potential to profoundly influence American education. Though they will never replace effective teachers, computers will play an increasingly dramatic role in reshaping teaching in the coming decades.

Schools throughout the nation, indeed the world, are plugging into the Internet. The global classroom is fast becoming a reality. Thousands of classrooms already have access to the Internet and many more are joining each month. A number of states have already made a commitment to connecting every school to the Internet.

The Internet is a world-wide collection of over 40,000 computer networks connecting millions of computers to one another. People using different kinds of computers can be linked together. The Internet is an enormous learning resource of almost unimaginable potential for enhancing education.

Many teachers and students have already discovered exciting, creative, and productive applications of this technological revolution. Those who do not obtain access to the Internet will surely be at a disadvantage. The Internet holds tremendous promise for use in all aspects of education: administration, instruction, professional development, and community involvement. Students in the most remote schools in the nation can soon have the world at their fingertips.

The services and resources available on the Internet are rapidly expanding. Access to the Internet lets teachers and students send and receive messages (e-mail), join thousands of on-going discussion groups on virtually every topic imaginable, and access the latest information on any topic and download millions of files through file transfer. The advent of user-friendly search and retrieval tools, such as Gopher and the WorldWideWeb, has accelerated school use of the Internet. As an emerging technology, some of the most exciting uses of Internet probably are yet to come.

Professional development opportunities abound with the Internet. Every day teachers can interact with others teaching the same subjects and facing the same problems. Collaboration with teachers halfway around the world can be facilitated. Discussion groups already exist for virtually every topic being taught in school. Via e-mail, teachers have direct access to top experts in virtually every field. The potential for using Internet as a tool to enrich global and cultural awareness is unlimited.

Millions of files are open to your use as teaching resources, including guides and images for use in the classroom. Students can directly communicate with students from other countries and states.

Here is just a sampling of what may be found on the Internet:

➤ The Library of Congress offers photographic and sound collections from the American Memory Project, the African-American Culture and History online exhibit, and access to LOCIS (the Library of Congress Information System). Access to the Library of Congress catalog is also available (locis.loc.gov).

Internet provides access to the EdWeb Project, an on-line tutorial for K-12 educators concerned with the use of telecommunications in teaching. (For information, contact: acarvin@k12.cnidr.org).

➤ KIDSLINK is an electronic forum where students can communicate with one another via Internet. More than just electronic pen pals, discussions focus upon specific topics, such as the environment or peace. Over 46 countries are already linked through this project. Within KIDSLINK are many individual forums, such as KIDSCAFE (open discussion of kids' interests), KIDLEADER (for teachers, parents, leaders), KIDPROJ (for planning projects for kids on KIDLINK network), or KIDS-93 (facilitates dialog on the desired future of the Earth). (Internet address for more information: kidlink-info@vml.nodak.edu).

➤ Opportunities exist for students to engage in cross-cultural language exchanges with French, Russian, Spanish, Japanese, or German students.

➤ Global Laboratory Project permits students around the world to share ecological data over the Internet.

➤ An assortment of electronic publications—journals, books, newsletters, newspapers, and digests—are available through Internet. The full text of these publications is available for on-line reading or retrieval through FTP (File Transfer Protocol).

➤ The daily CNN (Cable News Network) Newsroom curriculum guide is a valuable source of teaching ideas. CNN Newsroom Daily Lesson Plans (gopher://ericir.syr.edu:70/00/Lesson/CNN/Current) is a treasure chest of lesson plans on current events.

➤ Educational Resources Information Center (ERIC) provides a wide assortment of information to educators. AskERIC (http://ericir.syr.edu/) features a question-answering service for teachers. Submit any question related to K-12 education and within 48 hours an answer is returned via e-mail. The service is free.

➤ "Thomas," the Internet link to documents from the House of Representatives (http:/thomas.loc.gov), provides full texts of the *Congressional Record* and pending legislation.

➤ "Live From Antarctica" is an electronic project that allows teachers and students to experience what life is like in Antarctica. The project provides instructional support through interactive television, computer networks, and classroom activities. Teachers and students can ask questions of the scientists in Antarctica and also answer challenge questions posted by the scientists. The project also provides links to international research centers where users can access full-color pictures of penguins and view computer images of the current ozone hole. A teacher's guide can be downloaded free or ordered free in a printed format from the Prentice Hall School Division. A variety of learning projects are also available. (http://quest.arc.nasa.gov/livefrom/ livefrom.html)

➤ Log into NASA's SpaceLink database (Telnet address: spacelink.msfc.nasa.gov) to check on progress of space shuttle flights.

➤ Images can be downloaded from the National Oceanic and Atmospheric Administration, National Climate Research Center, or the National Weather Service to study weather patterns. Global weather changes can be observed almost as they are occurring.

➤ WWIInet is an Internet archive maintained by Jim Dethlefsen (Internet: dethle-jd@galt.osd.mil). It provides facts on events and personalities related to World War II.

➤ The Perry-Castañeda Library Map Collection (lib.utexas.edu) at the University of Texas at Austin holds an extensive collection of maps from every area of the world. Many items in the collection are available on-line via the Internet.

➤ Daily White House press releases and briefings are available on-line on the World WideWeb (http://www1.ai.mit.edu/search/whitehousepublications).

➤ A computerized cadaver is available through the National Library of Medicine. Magnetic resonance imaging and computerized tomography were used to scan 1,900 slices of the corpse of a 205-pound man. Portions of this database may be viewed. (ftp site nlmpubs.nlm.nih.gov.)

ELECTRONIC MAIL

E-mail is the most frequent use of computer networks. Any Internet user can send text messages to any other computer users if you know their Internet addresses. A variety of directories can help locate the Internet address of another user (one directory is NETFIND at the University of Colorado. Telnet: bruno.cs.colorado.edu). Software such as Eudora or Pine have made the sending and receiving of e-mail messages much easier. You can also append files to your messages. Messages are stored in a "mail box" or holding file until you log in and read your messages.

➤ Some students practice their new foreign language skills communicating with native students speaking that language.

➤ Anyone can send messages to the President or Vice President through e-mail (president@whitehouse.gov or vpresident@whitehouse.gov).

➤ Often the top experts in any field of study can be contacted via e-mail.

➤ Many schools use electronic pen-pal connections to learn more about other cultures.

DISCUSSION GROUPS

Thousands of discussion groups exist on the Internet, covering virtually every conceivable interest. They are often referred to as LISTSERVs, newsgroups, electronic conferences, discussion groups, or discussion lists.

LISTSERVs or discussion groups provide opportunities for participants to interact with a group of persons with a common interest. Some LISTSERVs are moderated, meaning someone screens the messages to assure they are related to the group's focus. You can post messages for all other subscribers to that discussion group or you may choose to reply via e-mail directly to another group member.

To join a discussion group, you subscribe by sending an e-mail message to the LISTSERV. Most are free. Subscribers automatically receive any new message posted to the discussion group. You'll need to check your mailbox regularly. Some of the more active groups will post several dozen messages each day.

Another way of accessing newsgroups is to use a newsreader. This is a piece of software that permits you to screen which newsgroups you want to monitor and to select which articles you want to read. You can also use the newsreader to post articles.

Discussion groups and newsgroups can facilitate the professional development of teachers.

Ednet is a free mailing-list interest group devoted to exploring educational uses of the Internet. To subscribe to the list, send an e-mail message to:

Listserv@nic.umass.edu

Skip the Subject blank, but on the first line, type:

Subscribe Ednet (Your name)

SELECTED EDUCATION-RELATED DISCUSSION GROUPS

ACSOFT-L.	Educational Software	listserv@wuvmd.wustl.edu
AERA-A	Educational Administration	listserv@asu.edu
AERA-B	Curriculum Studies	listserv@asu.edu
AERA-C	Learning and Instruction	listserv@asu.edu
AERA-D	Measurement and Research	listserv@asu.edu
AERA-E	Counseling and Development	listserv@asu.edu
AERA-F	Educational History	listserv@asu.edu
AERA-G	Social Context of Education	listserv@asu.edu
AERA-H	School Evaluation	listserv@asu.edu
AERA-I	Education in the Professions	listserv@asu.edu
AERA-J	Postsecondary Education	listserv@asu.edu
AERA-K	Teaching and Teacher Education	listserv@asu.edu
ASAT-EVA	Distance Learning Discussion	listserv@unlvm.unl.edu
ASCD-SCI	Teaching of Science	listserv@psuvm.psu.cdu
ALTLEARN	Alternative Education	listserv@sjuvm.stjohns.edu
BGEDU-L	School Reform	bgedu-l@ukcc.uky.edu
BIOPI-L	Teaching Biology	listserv@ksuvm.ksu.edu
CESNEWS	Coalition of Essential Schools News	listserv@BROWNVM.brown.edu
CHATBACK	Special Education Discussion	listserv@sjuvm.stjohns.edu
CREWRT-L	Creative Writing in Education	listserv@mizzou1.missouri.edu
CURRICUL	Curriculum Issues	listserv@saturn.rowan.edu
ECEOL-L	Early Childhood Education	listserv@maine.maine.edu
ECID-L	Educational Computing	listserv@vm.cc.purdue.edu
EDAD-L	Educational Administration	listserv@wvnvm.wvnet.edu
EDLAW	Legal Issues in Education	listserv@ukcc.uky.edu
EDNET	School Uses of Internet	listserv@nic.umass.edu
EDSTYLE	Learning Styles	listserv@sjuvm.st.johns.edu
ERIC-L	Teaching Literature	eric-l@iubvm.ucs.indiana.edu
EDTECH	Educational Technology	listserv@msu.edu
ELEMUG	Elementary School Users' Group	listserv@uicvm.uic.edu

GEOGED	Geography Education	listserv@ukcc.uky.edu
HSJOURN	High School Scholastic Journalism	listserv@vm.cc.latech.edu
KIDCAFE	Kid's Discussion Group	listserv@vm1.nodak.edu
KIDINTRO	Pen Pal Group for Kids	listserv@sjuvm.stjohns.edu
KIDS-ACT	Activity Projects for Kids	listserv@vm1.nodak.edu.
KIDSNET	Student Discussions	listserv@unmvma.unm.edu
K12ADMIN	School Administration	listserv@suvm.syr.edu
LEARNING	Child-Centered Learning	learning@sea.east.sun.com
MIDDLE-L	Middle School-Aged Children	listserv@vmd.cso.uiuc.edu
MUSIC-ED	Music Education	listserv@vm1.spcs.umn.edu
NCTM-L	National Council of Teachers of Mathematics	listproc@sci-ed.fit.edu
NEWEDU-L	Educational Innovations	listserv@uscvm.bitnet
OUTDOOR-ED	Outdoor Education	listserv@latrobe.edu.au
PHYSHARE	High School Physics Resources	listserv@psuvm.psu.edu
SIGTEL-L	Telecommunications in Education	listserv@unmvma.unm.edu
SUPERK12	Computers/Internet in K-12 Schools	listserv@suvm.syr.edu.
T321-L	Teaching Elementary School Science	listserv@mizzou1.missouri.edu
TAG-L	Talented and Gifted Education	listserv@vm1.nodak.edu
TEACHEFT	Teacher Effectiveness	listserv@wcupa.edu
TIPS	Teaching Psychology	listserv@fre.fsu.umd.edu
UAARTED	Art Education	listserv@arizvm1.bitnet
VOCNET	Vocational Education	listserv@cmsa.berkeley.edu
WWWEDU	WorldWideWeb in Education	listserv@k12.cnidr.org

FILE TRANSFER PROTOCOL (FTP)

A broad spectrum of freely accessible archives exist on the Internet. Files (e.g., books, software, images, sounds, guides, documents) from these can be downloaded onto your own computer. FTP (or File Transfer Protocol) is the procedure that transfers files from one computer to another over Internet. Sometimes FTP is used as a verb meaning to transfer a file via Internet. Most FTP sites allow you to log on as an "anonymous" user. When prompted for the password, enter your Internet address. A tremendous assortment of software, graphics, text files, movies, and sounds are available for transfer to your computer. You will probably need special software (e.g., Kermit or ProComto) to download files.

Files are often sent in a compressed format to save time. If a file arrives in a compressed form, you will need a decompression program to expand the file before you can use it. Several inexpensive decompression programs are available.

Gopher (or TurboGopher on the Macintosh) is a software browsing tool that facilitates navigating the Internet. It is menu-driven, so you don't have to have the computer address to locate a file. Such master software index files are available on the Internet and provide a gateway for locating and retrieving these resources. WAIS (Wide Area Information Servers), WorldWideWeb, Hytelnet, and Archie are similar search-and-retrieval systems.

➤ The Smithsonian Institution provides an assortment of information and pictures via the Internet. The Smithsonian Institution Photo Server stores many images in a variety of formats from the various museum collections. These can be downloaded with FTP (photo1.si.edu).

➤ Through the Internet protocol "telnet" teachers and students can access on-line library catalogues and databases at virtually every major library in the United States, including the Library of Congress and many in other nations. Databases such as ERIC, the world's largest collection of information about education, can be accessed.

➤ The Lyric and Discography Archive (cs.uwp.edu) houses many song lyrics, biographies, and discographies.

➤ The Digital Tradition is an Internet archive containing the lyrics and music to thousands of folk songs (http://pubweb.parc.xerox.com/digitrad).

➤ Workshops and courses are already being offered over Internet. Thousands of learners can participate simultaneously in a broad and rapidly expanding array of tutorial programs. Its use as a virtual classroom is likely to increase in the coming decade. The paperless classroom is not beyond imagination. The electronic town hall meeting is fast becoming a reality.

➤ Project Gutenberg (ftp mrcnext.cso.uiuc.edu) is a master depository of "etexts," full textbooks available over the Internet. Dartmouth College's Shakespeare has on-line the full text of all Shakespeare's sonnets and at least 33 of his plays.

➤ NASA Archive (ames.arc.nasa.gov) has available a vast selection of pictures and other space-related information.

➤ The Science Education Archive (ftp.bio.indiana.edu) has many files of interest to science teachers.

➤ ERIC's lesson archives provide a wide assortment of lesson plans for virtually all academic areas (gopher://ericir.syr.edu/11/Lesson).

➤ Janice's K12 Cyberspace OUTPOST provides an impressive listing of how schools are already using the Internet (http://edweb.cnidr.org/janice_k12/k12menu.html).

➤ The Telescopes In Education (TIE) program demonstrates desktop astronomy and astrophysics to students. Two remote automatic telescope systems are available on-line. TIE provides an archive of images from the Mt. Wilson Observatory (http://www.mtwilson.edu/tie/sampler.html).

➤ The HPCC (High Performance Computing and Communications) K-12 education program developed at NASA Langley focuses on strengthening the mathematics and science curriculum. The program provides Internet access for K-12 teachers and students. Materials related to the program may be accessed via FTP at k12mac.larc.nasa.gov.

➤ A summary of the 1990 census data for each state is available through Project Gutenberg (spinaltap.micro.umn.edu).

➤ Virtual Frog Dissection Kit sponsored by Lawrence Berkeley Laboratory is one of the most exciting examples of the educational potential of the Internet and computer applications for education (http://george.lbl.gov/ITG.hm.pg.docs/dissect/info.html). Users can select the body systems or organs to be revealed.

➤ The CIA World Factbook is available on-line (http://www.ic.gov/94fact/fb94toc/fb94toc.html). It provides current information on the nations of the world.

➤ CELIA (Computer Enhanced Language Instruction Archives) maintains a collection of public domain, shareware and freeware computer resources helpful in teaching languages. It can be accessed via an Internet Gopher client. Some files can be downloaded by FTP. (*Gopher Access*: gopher gopher.archive.merit.edu and look in Merit Software Archives. *FTP Access*: archive.umich.edu in the directory celia-ftp).

➤ FTC Consumer Brochures (http://www.webcom.com/~lewrose/brochures.html) provides on-line the full text of 100+ consumer brochures issued by the Federal Trade Commission's Office of Consumer and Business Education.

➤ EE-Link is a project of the National Consortium for Environmental Education and Training (eelink@nceet.snre.umich.edu). Access to a spectrum of activities and projects related to environmental education is maintained through EE-Link.

➤ The DeweyWeb (http://ics.soe.umich.edu/) is a "global education" experiment in using the WorldWideWeb to facilitate communication between students from around the world. A fascinating variety of interactive computer simulations bring students together worldwide. "The World Forum: Viewing the World Through the Eyes of Others" is an adventure learning activity that enables students to participate in a simulated dramatic adventure to an exotic locale. "The Arab-Israeli Conflict Simulation: Political Reality in the Classroom" is a role-playing simulation exercise designed to encourage students to delve into the Middle East drama. Students assume the roles of key leaders in the Arab-Israeli conflict. All communications are conveyed by computer, as country teams of student role-players are drawn from schools around the world.

➤ A collection of curriculum materials related to teaching about the Holocaust are available on-line (gopher://info.asu.edu:70/11/asu-cwis/education/other/k12 resources/holocaust).

➤ The Grand Canyon National Park Home Page (http://www.kbt.com/gc/gc_home) provides WorldWideWeb users with historical, geological, and recreational information about the Grand Canyon.

➤ The INSPIRE gopher (INnovative SPI Resources for Educators) provides access to and an extensive archive of curriculum materials related to all K-12 subjects.

➤ Answers to commonly asked "Primary and Secondary School Internet User Questions" are available through the Internet School Networking group (chs.cusd.claremont.edu). The archive addresses questions related to benefits and sample uses of the Internet for K-12 schools, technical requirements, costs, and security.

TIPS ON GETTING STARTED ON THE INTERNET

Joining the Internet pathfinders is not yet a easy task. Two challenges face the teacher wanting to capitalize on the opportunities of cyberspace: (1) Getting access to the Internet, and (2) Finding your way around the massive network of networks. Fortunately, both tasks are getting easier by the week. With perseverance, "leading-edge" teachers excited at the prospects of "surfing the Internet" can find many treasures awaiting them.

➤ An Internet account is required for access. Most universities and colleges already are connected to the Internet and many states have statewide networks exit. Access can also be gained through independent vendors such as Prodigy or CompuServe. Seek a local resource person who can help you discover the options available in your area.

➤ Finding a mentor to help you learn the intricacies of Internet access and navigation will save you a lot of time and frustration. Most schools have at least one person who is already experimenting with the Internet. Seek their help only after you have made a reasonable attempt to discover the answer yourself.

➤ Local universities or colleges are also good sources for help. Many offer workshops on getting started on the Internet. Some state departments of education are also providing training opportunities.

➤ A variety of books and guides are available to help you through the maze of the Internet. Some are available free and can be accessed on-line. Several helpful resources are listed below; read at least one.

➤ A variety of free tutorials designed for teachers learning to use the Internet are available on-line through NCSA's Education Group (http://www.ncsa.uiuc.edu/ Edu/Tutorials/TutorialHome.html). They can be downloaded to your own computer.

➤ Don't worry about trying to learn every aspect of the Internet at once. Work on developing some comfort with one function, such as e-mail. There is a learning curve to work through. You will gradually develop additional expertise.

➤ Don't be afraid to experiment. Explore files and connections to see what is available. It is wise to limit exploration to late evening hours when work-related use of the networks will be lightest.

➤ Be patient. Access to the Internet is becoming faster, simpler, and cheaper. In some form, Internet will have a profound effect upon education. The early users or pathfinders will stay on the cutting edge of this exciting new technology and will play a role in defining how it is used.

➤ Set time limits on how much you will stay on the Internet. Fascination with the masses of opportunities can consume hours of your time. It is best to save such experimenting for expendable, leisure time. One of the newest discussion groups is titled "Internet Addiction!"

➤ Most of the excellent resources listed below discuss "netiquette," the etiquette of the Internet. Over a million users use the Internet each day. For many it is an integral part of their jobs. Only courtesy and sensible use of the Internet will keep the system flowing smoothly.

CATALOGS AND DIRECTORIES

Numerous catalogs describing Internet services and resources are available. Many of these catalogs can be downloaded from the Internet.

Some of the more helpful ones include:

➤ John December maintains an extensive listing of Internet resources. It can be downloaded via FTP (decemj@rpi.edu) or accessed on the WorldWideWeb (http://www.rpi.edu/Internet/Guides/decemj/icmc/toc2.html).

➤ An extensive listing of Black/African related resources to be found on the Internet is available via anonymous FTP from ftp.netcom.com.

➤ *Yahoo—A Guide to WWW* (http://akebono.stanford.edu/yahoo/Education/) is an outstanding master index to much of what is available on the WorldWideWeb.

➤ *Alex: A Catalogue of Electronic Texts on the Internet* (gopher: rsl.ox.ac.uk, select "Librarian's Corner", and then "Alex") provides access to full text electronic versions of over 700 books covering a wide range of topics. Also available on the WorldWideWeb (http://www.cs.cmu.edu:8001/Web/books.html).

➤ *Ednet Guide to Usenet Newsgroups* is available to subscribers of the EDNET. To subscribe send an e-mail message to:

listserv@nic.umass.edu

Leave the subject blank, but on the first line, type:

Subscribe Ednet (Your first and last name)

To resign from the list, send e-mail again to the same address with the message:
Unsubscribe Ednet

HELPFUL RESOURCES

Fraase, M. (1993). *The Mac Internet Tour Guide: Cruising the Internet the Easy Way.* Chapel Hill, NC: Ventura Press.

Gilster, P.A. (1993). *The Internet Navigator: A New User's Guide to Network Exploration.* New York: Wiley.

Hahn, H. & Stout, R. (1994). *The Internet Complete Reference.* Berkeley, CA: Osbourne/McGraw Hill.

Kehoe, B. (1994). *Zen and the Art of the Internet: A Beginner's Guide.* Englewood Cliffs, NJ: Prentice-Hall.

Krol, E. (1993). *The Whole Internet: User's Guide & Catalog.* Sebastopol, VA: O'Reilly and Associates.

LaQuey, T. (1993). *The Internet Companion: A Beginner's Guide to Global Networking.* Reading, MA: Addison-Wesley.

Marine, A., Kirkpatrick, S., Neou, V., and Ward, C. (1993). *Internet: Getting Started.* Englewood Cliffs, NJ: Prentice-Hall.

Newby, G. (1994). *Directory of Directories on the Internet: A Guide to Information Services.* Westport, CT: Meckler.

Parker, T.L. (April, 1994). The Internet–K12 Connection: How Students and Teachers Are Using the Internet, *ConneXions: The Interoperability Report.* Foster City, CA: Interop, Inc.

ORGANIZATIONS

AskERIC
ERIC Clearinghouse on Information Resources
030 Huntington Hall
Syracuse University
Syracuse, NY 13244-2340
Internet: askeric@ericir.syr.edu

Consortium for School Networking (CoSN)
1112 Sixteenth Street, NW, Suite 600
Washington, D.C. 20036
Internet: info@cosn.org.
Email: cosn@bitnic.bitnct
Gopher: gopher.cosn.org

The Global SchoolNet Foundation (GSN)
7040 Avenida Encinas 104-281
Carlsbad, CA 92009
Email: andresyv@cerf.net

Internet Society (ISOC)
12020 Sunrise Valley Drive, Suite 270
Reston, VA 22091
Email: isoc@nri.reston.va.us
Gopher: gopher.isoc.org

The National Science Foundation
4201 Wilson Boulevard
Arlington, VA 22230
ftp://stis.nsf.gov/nsf907

DICTIONARY OF INTERNET-RELATED TERMS

Archie: An on-line catalog of millions of publicly accessible files through over 1200 FTP archive sites. TurboGopher is a user-friendly tool for searching Archie's indexes.

BBS (Bulletin Board System): Computerized bulletin boards where computer users can leave messages for each other.

Database: A collection of organized information that can be searched to retrieve data of interest.

Download: To transfer information or files from one computer to another.

e-mail (electronic mail): The computer function that allows individuals to exchange personal messages via a computer network. Through e-mail any person on the Internet can communicate directly with any other person also on the Internet.

Freeware: Software of computer files that are available without charge, but the creator holds the copyright. Usually you may give it to others but may not sell it.

FTP (File Transfer Protocol): As a noun FTP refers to the procedure by which files can be transferred from one computer to another over Internet. Sometimes FTP is used as a verb, meaning to transfer a file via Internet. Most FTP sites allow you to log on as an "anonymous" user. When prompted for the password, enter your Internet address.

Gopher (or TurboGopher): Menu-based Internet exploration software.

Hytelnet: Software that identifies the log-in address and passwords of all known FTP sites on Internet. It facilitates locating and connecting to these resources.

LISTSERVs: Software that allows an Internet user to subscribe to particular discussion groups.

Login: To sign on to a computer allowing you to access its software. A password may also be required.

Newsreader: Software that permits selection of newsgroups to monitor and select specific articles to read.

Public Domain: Refers to computer software that is not copyrighted. There is no restriction on its use, distribution, or modification. Many computer user clubs maintain large depositories of public domain software. Many can also be downloaded from archives through the Internet. Washington University Public Domain Archive (wuarchive.wustl.edu) has an extensive depository of freeware and public domain software.

Shareware: Software that you may use before you decide whether to buy it. If you decide to keep it after the trial period, you are honor-bound to send a small fee to the creator. You may make copies to give others to try out, but may not sell it.

Telnet: A protocol that allows a computer user to login on a remote computer and to access its files (e.g., to search a university's library catalog). Sometimes you'll need a password.

USENET: A network of discussion groups accessible through an Internet connection's newsreader.

WAIS (Wide-Area Information Service): Public domain software that aids the search for information Internet databases.

WorldWideWeb (WWW): A menu-driven search system that creates direct links between related resources. A most useful and time-saving tool for browsing the Internet.

> *"And I said, with my net*
> *I can get them I bet.*
> *I bet, with my net,*
> *I can get those Things yet!"*
> —THE CAT IN THE HAT

Sources of Educational Computer Software

Academic Hallmarks
P.O. Box 998
Durango, CO 81302
(800) 321-9218

Academic Software
141 Ayers Court
Teaneck, NJ 07666
(800) 227-5816

B5's Educational Software
1024 Bainbridge Place
Columbus, OH 43228
(614) 276-2752

Barnum Software
2201 Broadway, Suite 201
Oakland, CA 94612
(800) 553-9155

Benjamin Cummings Publishing Co.
390 Bridge Parkway
Redwood, CA 94065
(800) 322-1377

Broderbund Software-Direct
P.O. Box 6125
Novato, CA 94948-6125
(800) 521-6263

CAE Software
P.O. Box 6227
Washington, D.C. 20015
(800) 354-3462

Chariot Software Group
3659 India Street, Suite 100C
San Diego, CA 92103-9722
(800) 242-7468

Compu-Teach
16541 Redmond Way, Suite 137-C
Redmond, WA 98052
(800) 448-3224

Computer-Using Educators, Inc.
1210 Marina Village Parkway, Suite 100
Alameda, CA 94501
(510) 814-6630

CONDUIT
The University of Iowa
100 Oakdale Campus M306
Iowa City, IA 52242-5000

Continental Press
520 E. Bainbridge Street
Elizabethtown, PA 17022-2299
(800) 233-0759

Data Command, Inc.
P.O. Box 548
Kanakee, IL 60901
(800) 528-7390

Davidson & Associates, Inc.
P.O. Box 2961
Torrance, CA 90509
(800) 545-7677

Decision Development Corporation
2680 Bishop Drive, Suite122
San Ramon, CA 94583
(800) 835-4332

Edmark
P.O. Box 3218
Redmond, WA 98073-3218
(800) 362-2890

Education Express
123 Skokie Valley Road, Suite 200
Highland Park, IL 60035
(800) 733-3396

Educational Activities
P.O. Box 392
Freeport, NY 11520
(800) 645-3739

Educational Publishing Concepts
61 E. Main Street
P.O. Box 2075
Walla Walla, WA 99362
(800) 323-9459

Educorp
7434 Trade Street
San Diego, CA 92121-2410
(800) 843-9497

Electronic Bookshelf Inc.
Route 9, Box 64
Frankfort, IN 46041
(317) 324-2182

EMR
41 Kanosia Avenue
P.O. Box 2805
Danbury, CT 06813-2805

Fas-Track Computer Products
7030C Huntley Road
Columbus, OH 43229-1053
(800) 927-3936

Gamco Educational Materials
P.O. Box 1862H5
Big Spring, TX 79721-1862
(800) 351-1404

Hartley Courseware
3001Coolidge Road
East Lansing, MI 48823
(800) 247-1380

Humanities Software, Inc.
408 Columbia Street, Suite 222
P.O. Box 950
Hood River, OR 97031
(800) 245-6737

Intellimation Library for the Macintosh
Dept. 4SCH
130 Cremona Drive
P.O. Box 1922
Santa Barbara, CA 93116-1922
(800) 346-8355

J. Weston Walch
321 Valley Street
P.O. Box 658
Portland, ME 04104-0658
(800) 341-6094

Jay Klein Productions, Inc.
1695 Summit Point Court
Colorado Springs, CO 80919
(719) 591-9815

Lawrence Productions, Inc.
1800 South 35th Street
Galesburg, MI 49053
(800) 421-4157

Lexia Learning Systems, Inc.
P.O. Box 466
Lincoln, MA 01773
(800) 435-3942

Logo Computer Systems, Inc.
P.O. Box 162
Highgate Springs, VT 05460
(800) 321-5646

Micrograms
1404 N. Main Street
Rockford, IL 61103
(800) 338-4726

Micro Learningware
Route 1, Box 162
Amboy, MN 56010
(507) 674-3705

Mindplay
P.O. Box 36491
Tucson, AZ 85740
(800) 221-7911

Morning Star
222 N. Midvale Boulevard, Suite 23
Madison, WI 53705
(608) 233-5056

Mountain Lake Software, Inc.
298 Fourth Avenue, Suite 401
San Francisco, CA 94118-2468
(800) 669-6574

Phillip Roy
P.O. Box 130
Indian Rocks Beach, FL 34635
(800) 255-9085

Queue, Inc.
338 Commerce Drive
Fairfield, CT 06430
(800) 232-2224

Research Design Associates
35 Crooked Hill Road, Suite 200
Commack, NY 11725
(800) 654-8715

Right on Programs
755 New York Avenue
Huntington, NY 11743
(516) 424-7777

Roger Wagner Publishing, Inc.
P.O. Box 710582
Santee, CA 92072

Skills Bank
15 Governor's Court
Baltimore, MD 21244
(800) 847-5455

Society for Visual Education, Inc.
55 E. Monroe Street, 34th Floor
Chicago, IL 60603-5803
(800) 829-1900

SRA
Macmillan/McGraw-Hill
P.O. Box 543
Blacklick, OH 43004-0543

Stone and Associates
7910 Ivanhoe Avenue, Suite 319
LaJolla, CA 92037
(619) 693-6337

Substance Abuse Education, Inc.
670 S. 4th Street
Edwardsville, KS 66113
(800) 530-5607

Sunburst
101 Castleton Street
P.O. Box 100
Pleasantville, NY 10570-0100
(800) 321-7511

Teacher Support Software
1035 N.W. 57th Street
Gainesville, FL 32605
(800) 228-2871

Techbyte International
908 Niagra Falls Boulevard
North Tonawanda, NY 14120
(800) 535-3487

Tom Snyder Productions
80 Coolidge Hill Road
Watertown, MA 02172-2817
(800) 342-0236

Tutorsystems
Woodmill Corporate Center
5153 West Woodmill Drive
Wilmington, DE 19808
(800) 545-7766

Ventura Educational Systems
910 Ramona Avenue, Suite E
Grover Beach, CA 93433-2154
(800) 336-1022

Computer Software for Improving Teacher Productivity

Classmaster
$59.00 (Macintosh, DOS)
Grade weighting, attendance, individual progress reports, graphs, and reports for parents
Techbyte International
908 Niagra Falls Boulevard
North Tonawanda, NY 14120

Electronic Bookshelf, The
Program disk: $399.95 (Macintosh, DOS)
Book titles (over 500 available): $54.95–$60 each
A reading motivation and record-keeping management system; administer quizzes and keep track of books read

Electronic Bookshelf Inc.
Route 9, Box 64
Frankfort, IN 46041
(317) 324-2182

Electronic Gradebook
$29.95 (Apple II)
Hold grade information for up to ten classes with up to 40 students in each; calculate statistics and a variety of reports
Continental Press
520 East Bainbridge Sreet
Elizabethtown, PA 17022
(800) 233-0759

Excelsior Grade2
$195 (Macintosh, Windows, DOS)
Keep grades and attendance records, individual student mastery of objectives

Gradebook Plus
$69 (Macintosh, DOS)
Calculate student grades, class performance, summary reports
Research Design Associates
35 Crooked Hill Road, Suite 200
Commack, NY 11725
(800) 654-8715

Grade Busters
$99.95 (Macintosh, Apple II, DOS)
Grade keeping, attendance records
Jay Klein Productions
1695 Summit Point Court
Colorado Springs, CO 80919
(719) 591-9815

Grade Machine
$59.00 (Apple II), $79.00 (Macintosh, DOS)
Grade keeping and reports
Misty City Software
11866 Slater Avenue, N.E.
Kirkland, WA 98034
(800) 795-0049

Grade Quick!
$79.95 (Macintosh, DOS)
Automated gradebook, attendance, progress reports
Compu-Teach
16541 Redmond Way, Suite 137-C
Redmond, WA 98052
(800) 448-3224

Learning Styles Inventory
$98.00 (Macintosh, DOS)
Identify student's preferred mode of learning

Educational Activities
1937 Grand Avenue
Baldwin, NY 11510

MakeTest
$89 (Macintosh)
Organize and print tests and answer keys
Mountain Lake Software, Inc.
298 Fourth Avenue, Suite 401
San Francisco, CA 94118-2468
(800) 669-6574

MicroTest III
$139.00 (Macintosh, Windows)
Test bank, customize tests

Micrograde
$95.00 (Macintosh, Windows)
Grade record-keeping system
Chariot Software Group
3659 India Street
San Diego, CA 92103
(800) 242-7468

Name Tag Kit
$69.95 (DOS)
Design and create a variety of name tags
Power Up Software Corp.
2929 Campus Dr.
San Mateo, CA 94403

Quiz2
Test bank management system
$155 (single user) (Macintosh, DOS)
Excelsior Software Inc.
P.O. Box 3416
Greeley, CO 80633
(800) 473-4572

Scholastic Hyperscreen 2.0
$99.95 (Macintosh, DOS)
Create interactive computer presentations; includes clip art, fonts, sound effects, and music

The Teacher Tool Kit
$81.95 (Macintosh, Windows)
Generate tests, worksheets, puzzles
Learning Lab Software
1-800-899-3475

Test Quick!
$59.95 (DOS)
Automated testing tool; give and grade tests automatically

Compu-Teach
16541 Redmond Way, Suite 137-C
Redmond, WA 98052
(800) 448-3224

Sources of Rubber Stamps

Educational Insights
19560 South Rancho Way
Dominguez Hills, CA 90220
(800) 933-3277

Kidstamps
P.O. Box 18699
Cleveland Heights, OH 44118
(800) 727-5437

The Learning Works
P.O. Box 1370
Goleta, CA 93116
(800) 235-5767

Mari, Inc.
1025 25th Street
Santa Monica, CA 90403
(800) 955-9494

Personal Stamp Exchange
345 S. McDowell Boulevard, Suite 324
Petaluma, CA 94954
(707) 763-8058

Stamp Sedona
301 N. Highway, 89A #D
Sedona, AZ 86336
(602) 282-0008

Suppliers of Instructional Materials

American Guidance Service (AGS)
4201 Woodland Road
P.O. Box 99
Circle Pines, MN 55014-1796
(800) 328-2560
Instructional and guidance-related materials for all levels; tests, videotapes, books, teaching aids, professional development materials

Argus
(800) 527-4748
Banners, posters, expanded Spanish products, pre-K to 3 catalog of award certificates, etc., visuals to inspire

Biosphere Press
(800) 992-4603
Educational activity modules (adult and children's titles), videos, posters, Spanish publications

Blip Productions
P.O. Box 33146
Minneapolis, MN 55433
Kids-of-the-world alphabet lines, school year timeline, numbers, punctuation, color, dinosaur and phonic lines plus reference books that correlate; tracing art kits, file folder games, math detective flip strips

Carson-Dellosa
P.O. Box 35665
Greensboro, NC 27425
(800) 321-0943
Math: overhead manipulatives, reinforcements, games, floor puzzles, early childhood manipulatives, pocket charts; *books:* social studies, geography, jumbo books, language arts, whole language; teacher resources, notes and gift sets, stickers and dots, charts, bulletin board and door decor, calendars, workshops

Center for Applied Research in Education
Order Processing Dept., P.O. Box 11071
Des Moines, IA 50380-1071
Practical pre-K–12 hands-on guides, resourcebooks, series, and multimedia programs to help teachers, specialists, and administrators of reading/language arts, math, early childhood, ESL/multiculturalism, discipline, library skills, guidance & counseling, science, social studies, special needs, health

Century Select Educational Media
1979 Palomar Oaks Way
Carlsbad, CA 92009
(800) 523-0988
An assortment of educational videotapes on parenting, building self-esteem, substance abuse, life values

Chelsea Curriculum Publications
Dept. NA94
Attn: School Division, P.O. Box 5186
Yeadon, PA 19050
(800) 362-9786
Hard and softcover curriculum sets for comprehensive Native American studies programs grades 4–secondary

Continental Press
520 E. Bainbridge Street
Elizabethtown, PA 17022-2299
(800) 233-0759
Instructional materials for pre-K through grade 12; instructional booklets and computer software for reading, literature, language, social studies, and early childhood

Creative Publications
5040 West 111th Street
Oak Lawn, IL 60453
(800) 624-0822
K–12 math and language arts. *Mathland curriculum*: manipulatives, overheads, time, counters, money, number concepts, base 10 blocks, decimals, fractions, pattern blocks, cooperative problem solving, tangrams, pentominoes; *geometry:* geometry boards, jobcards, geometric concepts, tools; *algebra:* concepts, problem solving, logical thinking, teacher resources; calculators; *language arts*: themes, literature, story telling and writing; posters

Creative Teaching Press
P. O. Box 6017
Cypress, CA 90630-0017
(800) 444-4CTP
K–6. Jack Grunsky music on tape, CD, record; multicultural art activities; *books:* literature, resources, writing and poetry; theme series; pocket charts, calendars, charts, bulletin board materials, stickers, rewards, organizers; Youngheart music

Crestwood Company
6625 N. Sidney Place
Milwaukee, WI 53209-3259
(414) 352-5678
Communication aids for children and adults; talking pictures and holders, communication boards, attention getters, portable communication aids and adaptations, language skill aids, adapted toys for children with special needs.

Crystal Springs Books
(800) 321-0401
Resources for K–6. Whole language, multi-age classrooms, developmental education, cooperative learning, inclusion, assessment and evaluation, math and science, discipline and self-esteem.

Cuisenaire Co. of America
P.O. Box 5026
White Plains, NY 10602-5026
(800) 237-0338
Materials for teaching mathematics. Wide assortment of manipulatives. Teaching resources, models, transparencies

Curriculum Associates, Inc.
5 Esquire Road
N. Billerica, MA 01862-0901
(800) 225-0248 (U.S. and Canada)
Pre-K–8. *Language arts/reading*: multicultural titles, spelling, writing, phonics, literature, software, plays public speaking, language arts, vocabulary; *early childhood*: screens, assessments, big books, poetry, music; *parent resources*: videos, activities, books (Spanish translations); *study skills/test-taking*: test prep, note-taking, outlining, memory expansion, portfolios, organization and time-management skills; *problem-solving math*: nonroutine problem-solving, math computation, assessment, software; *social studies/geography/science*: world and U.S. geography, map reading, citizenship, history, health, environment; *self-esteem/drug education*: self-esteem series, drug prevention

game and glossary; *ESL/bilingual*: language learning technology, Spanish language and ESL materials

Adult—Vocational—Secondary: Life skills, employability, basic skills, test-taking, parenting, reading/language arts, problem-solving math

Dale Seymour Publications
P.O. Box 10999
Palo Alto, CA 94303-0879
(800) 872-1100

K–8 educational materials. *Math:* replacement units, classroom management, problem-solving, data analysis and statistics, reference, alternative programs, manipulatives, pre-algebra and algebra, geometry, measurement, calculators and computers; *science:* explorations, earth and environment, nature study, gardening, animal study, experiments, science fairs, inventions, teaching resources, projects; *language arts*: literature, family involvement, reading, real-world problems, references, writing and editing, spelling and vocabulary, supplementary reading; *visual and performing arts*: creative dramatics, drawing, art history, art education, multicultural art, African American art, Native American art, references, paper folding posters, art projects; *thinking skills*: critical and creative thinking, logic, simulations, visual thinking, games and puzzles; *teacher resources*: teaching strategies, self esteem, cooperative learning, multicultural education, teaching the gifted, study skills, across the curriculum, reference

Education Center, The
1607 Battleground Avenue
Greensboro, NC 27429-0753
(800) 334-0298

Teacher's Helper magazine, *The Primary Mailbox* magazine, Storybook clubs, learning center clubs, displays and bulletin board materials, seasonal activity books, shape books and activities, jumbo patterns, door decor, classroom helpers, 3-D awards, cold laminating film

Educational Insights
19560 South Rancho Way
Dominguez Hills, CA 90220
(800) 933-3277

Electronic teaching aids; games; materials for reading, language/writing, phonics; big books, beginning language arts; *aids for*: early learning, art, science, math, time and money, critical thinking, social studies, geography; stamps and ink pads

Evan-Moor
18 Lower Ragsdale Drive
Monterey, CA 93940-5746
(800) 777-4362

Books: math, science, geography, writing, art, rhymes and chants, animal units, thematic units, "Around the World"; *early learning*: arts and crafts, dramatic play, readiness, whole language; Spanish activity books; bulletin board materials, clip art; *multicultural:* ecology and geography aids

Fearon Teacher Aids
1204 Buchanan Street
P.O. Box 299

Carthage, IL 62321-0299
(800) 435-7234; (217) 357-3981
Teacher resources, seasonal activities; *books and aids*: reading, language arts, creative writing, literature, music, thematic units, creative/gifted, thinking skills, science, math, social studies, responsibility education, self-concepts, arts and crafts; early childhood; bulletin board materials; notepads, games and activities; teacher's holiday helpers; seasonal series

Filette Keez
3204 Channing Lane
Bedford, TX 76021
(817) 283-5428
Markets a variety of file care paper supplies for organizing educational computer software

Frank Schaffer Publications, Inc.
23740 Hawthorne Boulevard
P.O. Box 2853, Dept. 477
Torrance, CA 90509-2853
(800) 421-5565
Literature: notes, multicultural literature notes, theme books; *bulletin board sets*: alphabet, numbers, colors, shapes, calendars, birthday, reading, writing, literature, math, science, nature, ecology, health, history, geography, African-American; *charts and activities*: language arts, reading, writing, work skills, critical thinking, math, science, social studies; teacher resources; photo charts; giant floor puzzles (shaped and extra-long), games, stickers, seals, badges, name tags; early childhood activity books, workbooks

Gamco Educational Materials
P.O. Box 1862H5
Big Spring, TX 79721-1862
(800) 351-1404
Instructional games, transparencies, manipulatives, videos, filmstrips/cassettes, books, transparencies, microcomputer software

Good Apple
1204 Buchanan Street
Box 299
Carthage, IL 62321-0299
(800) 435-7234; (217) 357-3981
Teacher resources; seasonal books and activities; *books*: reading, language arts, creative writing, literature based, creative/gifted, thinking skills, thematic units, creative drama, science, math, social studies, responsibility, self-concept; arts and crafts, bulletin board materials, posters, software

Great Kids Company, The
P.O. Box 609
Lewisville, NC 27023-0609
(800) 533-2166
Early childlhood toys and parent helpers: outdoor toys, sand and water toys, puppets, arts and crafts, construction toys, puzzles, games

Gryphon House
(800) 638-0928

Teacher/parent resources for early childhood

Hubbard Scientific
P.O. Box 760X
Chippewa Falls, WI 54729-0760
(800) 323-8368
Broad assortment of instructional materials for teaching science; models, video-tapes, videodiscs, laboratory equipment, manipulatives, activity sets

Incentive Publications, Inc.
3835 Cleghorn Avenue
Nashville, TN 37215-2532
(800) 421-2830
Books; *language arts*: literature/whole language, reading/language arts, varying exceptionalities, writing, thinking and life skills, multicultural language arts, drama, library; *social studies*: America, multicultural, self-awareness; science; math; arts and crafts; teacher resources; early learning

Kagan Cooperative Learning
27134 Paseo Espada, Suite 303
San Juan Capistrano, CA 92675
(800) 933-2667
A wide assortment of books and materials related to cooperative learning and cooperative discipline

Lakeshore Learning Materials
2695 E. Dominguez Street
P.O. Box 90749
Carson, CA 90749
(800) 421-5354
Arts and crafts supplies, puppets, role-playing supplies and props, classroom fur-niture, storage and organizer equipment, play equipment, manipulatives, teaching resources, children's books, science experiments, rewards and motivators

Learning Company, The
6493 Kaiser Drive
Fremont, CA 94555-9985
(800) 852-2255
K–12 educational software. *Writing and publishing*: clip art libraries, bilingual (Spanish), writing centers; math/problem solving; reading/language arts; *home/school connection*: ready for letters, music, super solvers, ancient empires, American history, etc.

Learning Well
P.O. Box 3759, Dept. 4
New Hyde Park, NY 11040-1042
(800) 645-6564; (516) 326-2101
Pre-K–8. Reading comprehension skills; books and software; *language arts*: games, activities; *literature:* books; *whole language*: books, cassettes; *writing skills*: books; early learning materials; *spelling, grammar, vocabulary, and thinking skills*: software, books and games; *math skills*: videos, software, games, books

Learning Works, The
P.O. Box 1370

Goleta, CA 93116

Innovative books K–12: reading, creative writing, values, and feelings, creative thinking skills (gifted and talented), listening and following directions, handwriting, environment, science, health, math, language arts, holidays, doodles, art, puppetry; rubber stamps

MAR*CO
1443 Old York Road, Dept. E
Warminster, PA 18974-1096
(800) 448-2197; (215) 956-0313
Materials for teachers, counselors, and parents: self-esteem, friendship, affective topics, social skills, behavior, divorce and step families, dysfunctional families, abuse, high risk, grief and loss, drugs, decision making, special education, study skills, test-taking skills, career education, counseling materials, parenting; inservice programs; stickers

Mari, Inc.
1025 25th Street
Santa Monica, CA 90403
(800) 955-9494
K–5. Study units, mini-units; reference books, whole language library, resource books; literature notes, file folder games, math workbooks, "Quick Starts" software guides; sticker books, puzzle pads, erasers, rubber stamps

Marsh Media
P.O. Box 8082
Shawnee Mission, KS 66208
(800) 821-3303
Videos, filmstrips, software on health wellness, guidance, drug education, and consumer education

Nes Arnold
899H Airport Road
Glen Burnie, MD 21061
Materials for the early years: multicultural, math, science, arts and crafts; multicultural dolls; books; math kits; design and make

NIMCO
117 Highway 815
P.O. Box 9
Calhoun, KY 42327-0009
(800) 962-6662
Drug education and sex materials, videos, books, and supplies

Optical Data Catalog
30 Technology Drive
Warren, NJ 07059
(800) 524-2481
K–12 materials and implementation products; multisensory kindergarten and elementary science programs with interdisciplinary connections; barcoded editions; science, reading and writing activities on CD-ROM; inquiry-based elementary science modules; *secondary*: interactive videodisc programs for earth, life, and physical sciences; videodisc field trips, space exploration, health subjects, government, major

issues; *National Geographic* on videodisc and CD-ROM; training programs, funding sources, hardware and accessories

Parker Publishing
Order Processing Dept., P.O. Box 11071
Des Moines, IA 50380-1071
Practical pre-K–12 hands-on guides, resourcebooks, series and multimedia programs for art education, music education, science, P.E. and coaching, and school administration

Perfection Learning Corporation
1000 N. Second Avenue
Logan, IA 51546-1099
(800) 831-4190 (U.S. and Canada)
Books for a literature-based classroom including audio books, big books, software, videotapes and African-American, multiethnic/Asian, or Spanish and Native American fiction K–6

Phillip Roy
P.O. Box 130
Indian Rocks Beach, FL 34635
(800) 255-9085
Multimedia materials for use with adult basic education, alternative education, Chapter 1, dropout prevention, ESOL, Even Start, family literacy, functional literacy, JTPA/PIC, special needs students, students at-risk, workplace literacy, transition from school to work; *focus:* initial GED, pre-GED/GED, vocational education, social-basic-functional skills, literacy skills, critical thinking skills, communication skills; duplicable materials; Aquarius instructional software

Positive Promotions
222 Ashland Place
Brooklyn, NY 11217
(800) 635-2666
Safety and health-related promotional materials, calendars, health guides, monthly planners, coloring books, pens, mugs, buttons

Prentice-Hall
Order Processing Dept., P.O. Bos 11071
Des Moines, IA 50380-1071
Practical pre-K–12 guides and resourcebooks for school administrators, reading/language arts, math, social studies, science

Quartet
5700 Old Orchard Road
Skokie, IL 60077
(800) 541-0094
Office and visual communication products: boards of all kinds, easels, instructional posters; early learning; maps, tempera, chalk, pastels; teacher aids

Scholastic Professional Books
555 Broadway
New York, NY 10012-3999
(800) 325-6149

Instructor books: integrated language arts, science, social studies, math, art; transition books for new educational strategies; reference library books; teaching strategies books

School Matters
P.O. Box 35444
Colorado Springs, CO 80935-3544
(800) 533-4939
Large-format books, motivational posters, geography resources, science books, room decorations, room organizers, certificates, rubber stamps, teaching supplies

Sunburst
39 Washington Avenue
P.O. Box 40
Pleasantville, NY 10570-0040
(800) 431-1934
Videos for K–12: learning with the Muppets, numbers, math, probability and problem solving, spatial visualization, geometry, algebra, trigonometry and matrices, calculus, life science, earth science, biology, physics, chemistry, memory and discrimination, reading and writing; games, posters, curriculum modules 2–12; staff development; guidance/health, building self-esteem, drug education, AIDS education, first aid/nutrition, health and family life (some open caption and Spanish), sex education, career education

Sundance Publishers and Distributors
P.O. Box 1326, Newton Road, Room #100
Littleton, MA 01460
(800) 343-8204
Pre-K–6. Paperbacks and instructional materials; literature programs; multicultural big book calendar program; classroom libraries; videos, audios and book/audio packets; annotated titles (Spanish version editions)

Teaching Resource Center
P.O. Box 1509
San Leandro, CA 94577
(800) 833-3389
K–8. Math manipulatives, language arts materials, *Math Their Way* support materials; *A Treasury of Themes*; pocket charts, big books, big book easels, *The Pocket Book*

Tom Snyder Productions
80 Coolidge Hill Road
Watertown, MA 02172-2817
(800) 342-0236
K–12 educational technology. Software, videodiscs, videos, CD-ROM, books, inservice; science, math, timeline tools, U.S. and world geography, history, reading and writing, language arts, music; *decision series*: urbanization, environment, prejudice, immigration, AIDS, substance abuse, colonization, revolutionary wars, balancing the budget, foreign policy, media ethics, campaign trail; *teacher tools*: exam in a can for math and science, grade busters, test designer and more; Spanish products

Trend Enterprises
P.O. Box 64073
St. Paul, MN 55164
(800) 328-0818
Wipe-off manipulatives; awards, classroom decorations; early childhood helpers; Earth Watch™ products; motivators, teacher helpers; *topics:* health, safety, and self-esteem; language arts; math, money and time; multicultural and social studies; science; whole language helpers; posters, stickers, bulletin board sets, letters and trimmers

T.S. Denison
9601 Newton Avenue South
Minneapolis, MN 55431-2590
(800) 328-3831
Librarian and teacher resources: multicultural, library, preschool and elementary; Series: library skills, time travelers, discovery themes; books and activities for language arts, art education, science, poetry and storytelling; awards, notes, incentives, bookmarks, multicultural clip art; Spanish editions

United Art and Education Supply Co.
P. O. Box 9219
Fort Wayne, IN 46899
(800) 322-3247; (219) 478-1121; Canada (800) 858-3247
Paints, brushes, crayons, markers, drawing supplies, office supplies, crafts, puzzles, block printing supplies, papermaking, scratchboard, papers, clay, yarn; classroom management resources, holiday helpers, signing helpers; religious education; flannel boards; musical instruments and rhythm bands; floor puzzles; early learning materials; bulletin board materials; handwriting; thematic units; math skill builders; globes, maps, posters, displays; seals, stickers, rewards, pencils, notelets; flags.

Zaner-Bloser
2200 W. Fifth Avenue
Columbus, OH 43272-4176
(800) 421-3018
K–8. Integrated language arts, science, critical thinking, self-esteem/decision making/substance abuse prevention, handwriting, spelling, research papers and expository writing, children's literature, supplementary reading, handwriting paper and supplies, alphabet models, journals, big books